# IF MEN WANT PEACE

THE MACMILLAN COMPANY
NEW YORK · BOSTON · CHICAGO · DALLAS
ATLANTA · SAN FRANCISCO

MACMILLAN AND CO., Limited
LONDON · BOMBAY · CALCUTTA · MADRAS
MELBOURNE

THE MACMILLAN COMPANY
OF CANADA, Limited
TORONTO

# IF MEN WANT PEACE

## The Mandates of World Order

*By*

MEMBERS OF THE FACULTY OF THE
UNIVERSITY OF WASHINGTON

*Editors:*

JOSEPH B. HARRISON
Professor of English

LINDEN A. MANDER
Professor of Political Science

NATHANAEL H. ENGLE
Professor of Economics and Business

THE MACMILLAN COMPANY · *NEW YORK*

1947

# *Preface*

THE cooperative effort which has produced this book began with the organization of the University of Washington branch of the Universities Committee on Post-War International Problems which latter was initiated at Harvard early in 1943 under the chairmanship of Professor Ralph Barton Perry. The Washington committee was organized by Professor Everett Nelson and carried on, after Professor Nelson had joined the Navy, under the vigorous leadership of Professor Melvin Rader. As the activities of the committee drew toward a close a group of its members conceived the project of concluding its work with a book which should grow out of some of the ideas and findings of the committee supplemented by additional chapters from contributors most of whom were members of the faculty though not of the committee.

Among the latter special acknowledgment is due to Professors Thomas I. Cook, Charles E. Martin, Howard H. Preston, and C. Eden Quainton, and, outside the faculty, to the Reverend Josiah R. Bartlett and Rabbi Arthur Zuckerman.

Other participants whose names do not appear in the Table of Contents but whose cooperation was invaluable include Professors Carlos Garcia-Prada, Charles M. Gates, Angelo Pellegrini, Ivar Spector, and Curtis C. D. Vail.

In addition we must express our appreciation of the general advice and promotional enthusiasm of Professor George M. Savage which did much to make the book possible; and of the patience and efficiency of Mrs. Oleen Weeth, Mrs. Marjory Grunder, and Miss Dorothy Greenhut in preparing the manuscript.

The departments of instruction in the University of Washington, or other institutional connections of the contributors, are as follows:

Sverre Arestad, Scandinavian
Josiah R. Bartlett, University Unitarian Church

v

Thomas I. Cook, Political Science
Edith Dobie, History
Nathanael H. Engle, Economics and Business
Gilbert L. Gifford, Economics and Business
Edwin R. Guthrie, Psychology
Joseph B. Harrison, English
Melville H. Hatch, Zoology
Lesley M. Heathcote, Library
Melville Jacobs, Anthropology
Donald H. Mackenzie, Economics and Business
Linden A. Mander, Political Science
Arthur W. Martin, Physiology
Charles E. Martin, Political Science
Franz H. Michael, Far East
Howard L. Nostrand, Romance Languages
Howard H. Preston, Economics and Business
C. Eden Quainton, History
Melvin Rader, Philosophy
Kline R. Swygard, Political Science
Richard G. Tyler, Civil Engineering
Frank G. Williston, Far East
Arthur Zuckerman, Hillel Foundation

THE EDITORS

# Contents

## PART ONE: THE MAINTENANCE OF PEACE

## PART TWO: POLITICAL AND HUMAN RIGHTS

## PART THREE: Economic and Social Welfare

## PART FOUR: The Cultural Basis of World Order

# PART ONE: The Maintenance of Peace

# CHAPTER I

# *The Collapse of World Order*

LIKE everything else the world after the war will grow out of its antecedents and in fact can neither be foreseen nor planned without due regard to the influence and impulse of historical forces. This is not to say that the future is always the slave of the past: rather it is conditioned by the past, yet susceptible of molding in particular forms. We cannot create a future immaculate and perfect but we can take a by no means spotless heritage and in some degree shape it to our will. To do this involves reflection on the past and realization of the needs of the present.

The lessons of history are not self-evident, yet few would disagree with the proposition that the historic experience of the human race has now brought us to the point where man must recognize and give expression to his oneness with man or perish. But unity is many-sided, and western civilization in the course of its development has produced certain kinds of unity at certain times and in certain places. For example, ancient Rome gave to Western Europe and the Mediterranean basin a political unity that has not been seen there since the Caesars. It was an extraordinary achievement, unparalleled in historic times. We may well stand in awe as we contemplate an empire stretching from Scotland in the north to the Sahara in the south and from Portugal in the west to Armenia in the east—an empire in which there was peace. Unity under the sway of Rome made possible the rule of law and the pursuit of daily occupations without fear of war. No man today can call that achievement negligible.

This unity, however, did not last. Gradually disintegration took place; the political unity of the Roman Empire broke up and in its stead emerged a new kind of unity based not on a common allegiance to a temporal head but on a common faith—Christianity. The Roman

2

Empire became Christendom. Politically a process of fragmentation had taken place, and that has been characteristic of Europe ever since. Thus on the social, economic, and political ruins of ancient Rome were built the feudal societies of Western Europe. The bond of unity that held them together, the framework within which men lived and died, was their common Christianity. A Charlemagne in the ninth century might revive the secular imperial tradition of political unity, and later Holy Roman Emperors might revive the traditions of Charlemagne, but it is truer to say that the Roman tradition of unity had come to rest more on the shoulders of the Roman Pontiff than on any individual Emperor. Unity was now religious.

Nevertheless, the imperial tradition lived on. Nothing is more characteristic of medieval thinking than that since Christendom was one under a single head, the Pope, so also politically the faithful should be under one temporal head, the Holy Roman Emperor. But where religious unity was a reality and a going concern in its original form, the Catholic Church, political unity throughout the Middle Ages was a theory and nothing more. Pope and Emperor were in theory the twin heads of a united Christendom. In practice they fought each other for supremacy, and when Gregory VII could force Henry IV to come to Canossa in 1077, to sue for peace, it was clear that imperial pretensions would henceforth be vain and insubstantial.

Similarly, kings and princes resisted the claims of empire to lordship over them. They had successfully challenged the jurisdictions of local feudal dynasties and power had become centralized and concentrated. The rise of the national state not only meant the appearance of a new political organization but carried with it the development of that most fateful political idea—national sovereignty. Power always seeks justification. Possessors of power commonly strive to augment it and when challenged or opposed seek to justify it. National monarchs were challenged by forces at home and found also, as Holy Roman Emperors had done, that they had to meet what they regarded as encroachments by the papacy upon the political sphere. Out of such conflicts grew the doctrine of sovereignty and the claim of rulers to absolute authority over their subjects. When the sixteenth century opened it was clear that the idea of the sovereign national state had come to stay. In strife and battle it had proved itself stronger than medieval political ideals whether feudal or papal. Soon Machiavelli could eulogize power and the possessors thereof and set up the criterion of success as the acid test of policy. The spirit of secularism, which is the inner essence of the Renaissance spirit, was now triumphant in politics. A sovereign prince, as a possessor of political power, could acknowledge no earthly authority or sanction superior to himself.

Contemporary society owes much, for good or ill, to the sixteenth century. To it belongs the Reformation which destroyed the organized unity of Christendom and in so doing reinforced the political development of absolutism and sovereignty by bringing under princely domi-. nation the consciences of men as well as their bodies and purses. Religious liberty does not belong to that age. On the contrary the power of kings and princes was increased and sanctified as never before in the Christian era. Yet the struggle of religious minorities to establish themselves in the face of hostile authority planted the seeds of liberty. Resistance against the sovereign state for reasons of religion had to be justified in public, and in the long run it followed that if such resistance were justified it must be justified for political reasons as well. In this conception lies the right to revolution, the right to resist oppression which later became an American tradition and was incorporated by the French into the Declaration of the Rights of Man. Today this idea is as alive as it ever was, nor will it die as long as men are not, and do not feel, free.

With the rise of the national state and the concept of sovereignty went the development of the Balance of Power. The restraint of anarchical tendencies in international relations was as much a problem in 1600 as, *mutatis mutandis,* it is in 1945. The balance of power was the historic attempt to find the answer. Abstract theory had nothing to do with it. Grim facts and realities produced an answer which in the course of time hardened into a theory. The essence of the theory is that power should be distributed so that equilibrium or balance is created. No single state or dynasty—in the sixteenth century the Hapsburgs, in the seventeenth Louis XIV, in the eighteenth Napoleon, in the twentieth Germany—should be allowed to dominate the continent of Europe, for that would mean undistributed power and the certain extinction of the small and weak states. It is often forgotten that the balance of power has on numerous occasions operated in the interests of small states as in the examples just cited. But it is too mechanical a method for keeping the peace and fundamentally misses the point.

The real problem for the past three or four hundred years has been to find some way of substituting effectively in international relations the rule of law for anarchy. The balance of power does not touch this problem at all.

It is something of a paradox that the national state which turned the mind of man away from the idea of a larger unity should in the economic order have served to expand his horizons and enlarge his vision. The state took over and exercised the minute details of economic regulation that medieval townsmen had developed. In addition, the great voyages of discovery that began with Columbus (1492) and Vasco da Gama (1497) revolutionized knowledge of geography and opened the way to enormous extension of overseas trade. Other continents soon felt the impact of European civilization partly through trade and partly through settlement, as in the Americas. Already the world had begun to shrink and the foundations were being laid for that global economic interdependence which later on the Industrial Revolution was so powerfully to reinforce.

In spite of the great achievements of medieval and early modern times society in Europe continued to be dominated by aristocratic privilege until the French made the first successful onslaught on that system in 1789. The French Revolution was indeed the work of the nation but it was the bourgeoisie who supplied leadership and direction. Profoundly dissatisfied with the *status quo,* they had fed their spirits on the rationalism of the eighteenth-century philosophers and were deeply imbued with the new doctrine of progress which has been the occident's great affirmation of faith ever since. Here lay the realization that conscious effort of the reason and will, for man was "rational man" to them, can bring about desirable change and improvement. No longer was it plausible to urge, as the defenders of ancient privileges always tend to do, that duration of time or the will of God are justification enough.

Historically the French Revolution was the successful attempt of the middle class to destroy a society of privilege and build in its place a social order that conformed to their own ideas and interests. In spite of their class limitations they both said and did things that far transcended the narrow interests of their own group. In the Declaration of the Rights of Man they asserted principles which were universal in scope. This declaration was supremely important, for it implied in the last analysis that an exclusive nationalism is not enough. A principle of unity, therefore, had again been asserted, though its implications were lost to sight in the din and uproar of the revolution. Permeating the Declaration of the Rights of Man is the idea of liberty under law and the supplementary idea of popular sovereignty which would assure that law would be the expression of the people's will. This is the tradition that became the essence of middle-class liberalism generally during the nineteenth century, but the period of Jacobin ascendancy in 1793–94 introduced also a tradition of equality, not in the sense in which you find the idea of equality in the Declaration of the Rights of Man but in a social and economic sense which contemplates a society in which there will be no extremes of wealth and poverty. As one looks at the world today that tradition of equality may turn out to be the strongest of all.

The French, however, could not complete their own revolution, and when it had reached a hopeless impasse by 1799 turned to the military dictator, Napoleon Bonaparte, who came nearer than anyone so far since Roman times to uniting Europe politically. The Napoleonic Empire was a flat defiance of the balance of power and fundamentally a denial of the revolutionary principle of liberty. When the victorious powers met at Vienna in 1815 to reconstruct Europe they restored the balance of power which their common victory over France seemed to have vindicated so triumphantly. After twenty years of war they were concerned with the problem of keeping the peace and endeavored to keep it by continuing the alliance which bound them together and thus forming a concert. They soon discovered how difficult it is to maintain such a union when profound differences of opinion, purpose and principle emerge. Fundamentally the Vienna settlement which above all else aimed at restraining the principles of the French Revolution illustrates that sheer compulsion may succeed for a time but that in the long run any settlement that fails to conform to what men conceive to be their basic interests and desires is bound to fall. In a word the men at Vienna built on a groundwork of ideas that society generally was coming to regard as obsolete.

In the first hundred years that lie between the Congress of Vienna and the outbreak of the First World War there are two forces of paramount importance. For convenience sake one may separate these two forces—nationalism and the Industrial Revolution—though in reality they come more and more to overlap and intertwine. Nationalism was no longer a matter of royal policy but was linked in the minds of people with the doctrine of popular sovereignty, which placed the concept squarely on the tradition of the French Revolution. But though in varying degrees all the peoples of Europe were imbued with the spirit of nationalism, after 1871 they had to face the fact that in the center of Europe there had been created a new national state, Germany, that began its life in the debt of Prussian militarism.

Broadly interpreted the second force means much more than technological change in the process of manufacture. In fact the whole social and economic fabric has been and is still profoundly affected by the Industrial Revolution. It is worth noting that industrial development came not only gradually but unevenly. Thus during most of the nineteenth century Great Britain was industrially far ahead of every other great power. Industrialization amounted to little in France before 1850, and in Germany before 1870. The late flowering of industrialization was however not necessarily a serious handicap. In Germany, for example, it was possible to start with industrial techniques as they were in 1870 without having to go through the generations of earlier development. Japan in the nineteenth century and Soviet Russia in the twentieth have demonstrated the same thing.

However, in the fact that the Industrial Revolution developed in a world of national states lies the great contradiction of modern times. On the one hand, the Industrial Revolution necessitated expanding markets, brought new and more rapid means of communication, and vastly accelerated the pace at which the world was getting smaller. In a word it means economic interdependence. On the other hand, economic policies were the policies of national states and were framed with a view to serving national interests rather than the interests of the world community. Economic nationalism like political nationalism is a principle of exclusion that sets the well-being of the part above that of the whole. The desire to keep a market as an exclusive preserve or to acquire exclusive control over material resources, all of which led to imperialism and a scramble for material advantage, was an inescapable accompaniment of economic nationalism. This type of policy impinged upon every part of the globe. Sometimes trade followed the flag and sometimes the flag followed trade, but all the time European ideas and values, good and bad, were affecting or beginning to affect the outlook of the peoples of Africa and Asia.

Great reserves of capital created by industrial expansion also impinged upon all parts of the world. This capital sought investment and found it partly in further expansion at home but even more in imperialist ventures, especially in Africa and in the Orient and in backward areas like the Balkans. Consequently, powerful states were made more powerful and rivalries became sharper and more dangerous, for these were rivalries between national states some with empires attached and some without but all with enlarged interests to serve and defend. For this purpose increased armaments seemed necessary. Thus while the world was still a world of international anarchy, national states were finding it necessary to enlarge the burden of armaments, trusting in their own strength first to defend themselves. Though all the facts indicated that there must be world order or none at all, the policies of national states flagrantly contradicted this truth.

Not only were tensions increasing in the international sphere but they were also mounting within national states themselves, particularly in those that were highly industrialized. The role of the state as an agency of welfare was looming even larger. Antagonism was rising between those who shared most in the wealth of the nation and those who felt that at best they received only the crumbs from the capitalists' table. Working-class pressure was strong enough to force the beginnings of social security in which the state played a crucial role, but when technology and economics proclaimed the fact of growing interdependence it became anomalous to base welfare on the national state rather than on the well-being of the world as a whole. This anomaly became still more glaring as developments in war, and therefore in preparedness for possible war, began to absorb a nation's total technological, economic, and psychological resources. In the long run total war and total preparedness are incompatible with the welfare state and doom freedom to extinction.

There were, however, those who realized that the developments of modern times required some kind of world order. The idea of collective security, expressed in the League of Nations, had immense popular appeal. But such an attitude was largely a by-product of war weariness and indicated acceptance by the heart rather than by the head. The great mass of people welcomed the League in a sort of orgy of hope but the past twenty years have shown that they either could not or would not understand what collective security involves. World order was a high-sounding phrase which could be insubstantial at best as long as men thought basically and primarily in national terms. Nationalism was not curbed by the League and the doctrine of national interests in an exclusive sense was still paramount. Though the need for it was growing all the time world order was not achieved. The world rushed headlong toward World War II and the problem of world order remains as yet unsolved.

In part this catastrophe can be traced to the failure of the victorious nations of the last war to translate their professed ideals into action. Beginning almost immediately to revert to the old pattern of conduct which had led to the last war, they indulged in disputes over bound-aries and territories and quarreled over secret treaties made during the war. They ignored the basic law that sovereign states were entering into a new period wherein science was so to revolutionize warfare that more and more time and money must be devoted to defense, with the consequence that the demands of economic welfare and of military power were becoming increasingly incompatible at the very time that Hitler's Germany was subordinating all ideas of general economic wel-fare to that of military power. Thus the very effort of the democracies to secure a greater degree of economic justice for their people rendered them peculiarly vulnerable. They had committed the fatal error of assuming that national social welfare is possible within an anarchical world. They did not see that unless economic factors are to be sub-ordinated to military considerations an international order must be created and that economic welfare can be safely promoted only under conditions of international security.

And the blunders of the Allies did not end there. In endeavoring both to maintain their separate national defenses and to cater to selfish group interests the nations ignored the stern warnings of economists by erecting tariff barriers and by demanding impossible reparations from Germany. The victorious Allies, who had urged the Germans to throw off their military masters and had talked in terms of the fourteen points (modified it is true by subsequent statements), pursued a policy that did not appear to discriminate between the Imperial Germany which had declared war and the Weimar Republic which came into being as a result of revolution against it. Had the Allies held the old regime to account, had they occupied Berlin and made the defeat of German militarism clear to the German people, the Hitlerian legend that Germany had been stabbed in the back by socialists, Jews, and democrats would not have been possible. Seldom, if ever, did the Allied Powers give any encouragement to the new democratic regimes in Austria and Germany. In vain did Chancellor Bruning as late as 1932 beg the Allies to give him something to take back to a Germany now growing restless under the influence of the growing Nazi propaganda. In July, 1932, Bruning went home empty-handed, having been unable to obtain even the concession of theoretical equality for Germany in the Disarmament Conference. More unfortunately still the Allied Powers did not stand logically even upon this ground. What they would not concede as a matter of principle to Bruning they later conceded under threat of force to Hitler. By that time they had forfeited all claims to gratitude, for the Germans interpreted the belated surrender as an acknowledgment of Hitler's masterly skill.

Meanwhile those who had won the war were forfeiting the confidence of another large section of the world by thus failing to make their actions conform to their professions. As the hopes of the smaller nations spread through the world the peoples of Africa and Asia took with great seriousness the doctrine of self-determination and the promise of freedom. But the white nations, which had enjoyed a brief three centuries supremacy in the Orient, although it had become continent-wide only in the nineteenth century, seemed unwilling to transform their imperialisms into political and social partnerships. And not for nothing had Oriental students studied western political and economic systems and doctrines. They had read John Milton and John Stuart Mill on liberty, and had studied western science; now they asked that the principles recognized within western society be allowed to operate in the relations between European rulers and Asiatic peoples. The victorious Allies, however, refused to do more than make a few timid concessions. Indeed, one of the Allies, Japan, was unable to obtain recognition of the principle of racial equality at the Paris Peace Conference. China, which had been lured into the war against Germany, found that the so-called unequal treaties imposed by the Western Powers several decades previously were to remain substantially in force, and she obtained control of her tariffs only by unilaterally announcing to the world that she was throwing off the restrictions. And this was scarcely twenty months before Japan invaded Manchuria.

Great Britain, which also had fought a war for the rights of small nations, was sending her troops into Ireland in 1920 and 1921 to put down nationalist revolts, as she was also doing in Egypt. (Is it a coincidence that both Eire and Egypt maintained neutrality in the recent war?) Moreover, Great Britain in undertaking her mandates over Palestine and Iraq had to intervene by military force in those areas, as she had to take forceful action in India. France, a champion of liberty, crushed a Syrian revolt in 1920 and for the next twenty years was at loggerheads with Syrian nationalists. Negroes in both the United States and Africa began to demand in clearer and more uncompromising tones the human rights which the white man had denied them under slavery and which he was now including among specious professions of liberty for all. And while these movements were going on a profound psychological change was taking place. The subject peoples of the world were beginning to learn the white man's techniques and were planning to use them to overthrow the white man's power. By 1941–42 Japan, a nation with but seventy million people on a few small islands, a nation which three-quarters of a century earlier had a civilization based upon wood, had transformed itself into such a military power as to be able within the space of a few months to wipe out the Western empires in southeastern Asia. The profound effects of this conquest and of the indignities to which the former proud and superior white people were subjected will not be erased by the military defeat of Japan. Some seven or eight hundred million Orientals are determined to have the respect and position to which they feel entitled as human beings. William B. Ziff has put the matter well:

If the yellow and brown peoples must gain everything by threat and force, they will have learned the technique at an efficient and able school. They will not stop when they have achieved the equivalent of those modest demands which might satisfy them now. When once the successful application of force has been learned, its use does not cease until the end. (William B. Ziff, *The Gentlemen Talk of Peace,* Ziff Publishing Company, 1944, pp. 234–35).

The United States which a quarter of a century ago battled against German militarism also had put itself in a curiously embarrassing moral position. In 1915 it intervened in Haiti, in 1916 in San Domingo; earlier it prevented a liberal government from assuming control in Nicaragua and under the Platt Amendment was exercising increased control over Cuba. Although American intervention lessened after the middle twenties the nations of Central and South America had already written and spoken much against Yankee imperialism. The Pan-American conferences did little to reconcile the opposing viewpoints of the United States and the other American Republics until President Roosevelt and Secretary Hull in 1933, by announcing the good neighbor policy, explicitly recognized the policy that President Hoover had begun to develop in the late twenties. But the recent developments of Pan-Americanism, while they have strengthened hemisphere solidarity, have not erased memories of the dollar-diplomacy period of the first twenty-five years of this century and the Manifest Destiny doctrines of the mid-nineteenth century.

The nations victorious in the last war also had to face unanswered questions as to the meaning of democracy within their own borders. Minority groups claimed freedoms in political, social, and economic realms, and the working classes became more vocal in their demands for economic justice. Poland and Jugoslavia treated their national minorities with scant consideration in the 1920's; they were typical of many nations which did not see the importance, if only from an expedient point of view quite apart from loftier claims of justice, of attaching dependent minorities to themselves by bonds of affection. For the Nazis were to make devastatingly effective use of disaffected minorities in the psychological offensive with which they preceded their military conquests. Within such democracies as Great Britain and France and even in the United States no general philosophy of national welfare sufficed to overcome the divergent and often conflicting economic interests of various classes and sectional groups. Many British and French conservatives seemed more determined to maintain their class position by appeasing Nazi Germany, Fascist Italy, and even Franco's Spain than by joining the League of Nations to prevent fascist aggression. Though national unity could still be rallied when the enemy was at the gates the grim truth now stood revealed that those who had won the last war had developed neither a comprehensive enough philosophy to include divergent minorities nor a comprehensive enough economic policy to unite their nations in a serious attack upon poverty and unemployment.

The victorious powers were likewise unable to ward off economic depression. Since the economic factors are treated elsewhere in this volume, it suffices here to point out that during peace time millions of citizens of all countries, in the words of Herbert Agar, "never felt that they were wanted, that it made any difference to society whether they were alive or dead, employed or unemployed, fed or hungry." What the democracies could not or would not do for peace—namely, provide employment—Nazi Germany did in preparations for war. Germans gave up their freedom, especially the freedom to go hungry, in order to obtain a measure of economic security, however apparent it should have been that the price of their surrender was ultimate German ruin. With a similar blindness the democratic countries laid men off work because of seasonal slumps or technological unemployment.

Especially did the Allies gravely miscalculate the problem of security. As the next chapter will show in more detail they continued in practice the principles of power politics even though they gave lip service to the League of Nations and the ideal of collective security. Thus scarcely had the war ended when they found themselves unable to agree upon more than a limited naval disarmament at Washington in 1921–22 and at London in 1930. The important point to note is that none of the defeated powers was involved; it was the victorious powers who after having fought the war of 1914–18 to defeat militarism failed to arrest the growth of armaments except in a halting fashion. The result was that when one of them, Japan, denounced the agreements no effective international organization existed to take adequate counter-steps. And at the general disarmament conference held between 1932 and 1934 after seven years of preparation the one-time Allies again failed to agree on even the most limited objectives. They must bear a heavy responsibility for permitting conditions to develop which allowed the Axis powers to strike when they were ready to do so.

Finally, the decline of vitality in the ideals of freedom and democracy, which had lost some of their inner driving power within the course of the hundred years preceding World War II, became especially noticeable between the years 1920 and 1940. The new governments of

Europe which set up democratic constitutions after 1918 failed to make democracy work, and dictatorships appeared in Poland, Austria, Jugoslavia, and elsewhere. In part, the failure was due to inexperience and to the undue complexity of their constitutional systems; in part, it must be sought in the unfavorable international and economic situation. But when every allowance is made we must candidly admit that everywhere the tendency was for freedom to run shallow, for people to interpret liberty in a selfish and irresponsible manner. Even in the United States and Great Britain they were not responding to the deeper principles of life which alone could save free peoples from becoming indifferent to the larger truth. Pseudo-philosophies setting forth the racial basis of truth, the class basis of truth, the national basis of truth, obscured the vision, the really basic truth which should be obvious to all—that man is primarily a creature of the universe, that his essential nature cannot be limited to nation, race, class, or creed. Popular prejudice was blazoned in the headlines of the press and skillfully transmitted over the radio. In the dictator countries books were burned and shackles were imposed upon men's minds. All the while international conferences to promote intellectual and cultural cooperation were being held in a race between education and catastrophe which catastrophe won in the second round with the outbreak of the Second World War.

This comment on the period between the wars has emphasized the blunders of the powers victorious in the earlier war not for the purpose of singling them out for blame or of accusing them of starting another war. Rather it has sought to point out how the failure to make creative use of victory enabled aggressor countries to let loose another cataclysm, and to suggest the urgency of insuring that we shall not permit a similar defaulting of intelligence, moral standards, and civic energy again to pave the way to disaster. Our blundering last time is no reason for pessimism this time. Rather should we make certain that we will profit by our mistakes. In subsequent chapters the way is charted for a practical realization of a peaceful world.

C. EDEN QUAINTON

# CHAPTER II

# *The Problem of Security*

FOR centuries men have dreamed of the day when they would beat swords into ploughshares and would learn war no more. From the fear and heartbreak of the masses of men who have fought the wars that man's cunning or goodwill could not prevent have come great denunciatory warnings. Time and again the people have reaffirmed the fear and faith of the prophets that unless men could somehow conquer this destroyer they were doomed. The Universe would ultimately weary of their suicidal strife.

The grim irony of our day is that the world had never been so persistent and eloquent in its appeals for peace as on the very eve of the two great wars which have been fought within the span of this one generation. Peace societies by the score which had come into being before 1914 carried on energetic campaigns, and official plans proliferated. As long as men contented themselves with declaring their desire for peace, agreement was possible, but when the time came to discuss the methods by which it could be obtained and made secure general ideas no longer sufficed. Practical decisions involving hard thinking were required. The mere recognition that we must find a way to eliminate war if we are to survive will no more achieve that end than the discovery that bacteria cause diseases will eliminate the latter. Equally important is the constant reminder that alternatives by which we would win our security are often poles apart. Before the American public can pass judgment on the latest of a bewildering number of plans there must be some understanding of the previous attempts and failures of men to build a general international organization that would bring the security we have the right to expect and demand.

Men have sought to eliminate or diminish the age-long threat and terror of war in two principal ways. In the first place, they have tried to set up certain limits beyond which belligerents must not go. The Greeks worked out an elaborate code by which the Greek states were bound to fight their internecine wars. As new techniques of fighting developed and new weapons were evolved similar attempts were made to restrict their use so as to cause a minimum of mutilation and suffering. This approach to the problem presupposes the continuance of war and seeks only to modify its worst features. The nature of modern war in its total aspects, however, has virtually cancelled out even this little; the inability to distinguish between civilian and military objectives means that all attempts to make war a more gentlemanly pursuit will henceforth come to naught.

The other line of development was to diminish the occasions for war, to discover possible alternatives, or to eliminate in advance causes of friction which might develop into full fledged war. It is chiefly along this line that mankind has latterly been working and thinking and out of it has evolved the small amount of international machinery so far constructed.

Generally speaking, there have been two approaches to the problem of war itself; one has been protection through power and the other protection through a complete repudiation of the use of force. Proponents of the former have argued that only as man has armed himself adequately has he been able to protect his own, and that for nations to trust themselves to international agreements in place of armies, navies, and air forces is little short of suicidal. We have had wars and will continue to have them. Our only hope is to be so thoroughly prepared for them that we shall cause our prospective enemies to hesitate in attacking us, or if war is joined shall assure our own victory in the speediest time and with minimum expenditure in men and material. In the late war this group has expressed its concern that the United States shall maintain its war forces intact and have none of the proposed disarmament; and that even if we join an international organization we shall at all costs maintain our own military equipment ready for instant and overwhelming use. Men have argued seriously for the retention of all the Pacific islands which our forces have conquered. They have likewise argued that these islands should be strongly fortified and amply defended by land, air, and sea contingents, and that the United States, which now has a navy as large as the rest of the world combined, must retain its preponderance of power.

Former President Coolidge, who was certainly no pacifist, bluntly warned the American public that there was no hope that we could arm ourselves adequately against a hostile world. The struggle we have just undergone, aided as we were by the strong and mighty military power of our allies, ought to bring us the sober realization that a unilateral attempt to gain security by such means is hopelessly inadequate. Any American who assumes that the rest of the world will be content to sit quietly by while we build for ourselves and maintain an actual predominance of military or naval power is naively ignoring the history of modern states.

And if unilateral armament is inadequate, still more unwise and unusable is the old balance of power. Its defects are fundamental. If, for example, in a balance of power system, the United States should become stronger than Great Britain or the Soviet Union, the latter powers would feel insecure and would increase their armaments in order not, be it noted, to restore the balance but rather to gain a new preponderance of power. The new security of Great Britain or the Soviet Union in turn would become the insecurity of the United States, and the seesaw would go on with mounting armaments and increasing tension proceeding without limit. In an age of total war, all aspects of life become increasingly subordinated to the military. Economics become economics in uniform, and psychological weapons are added to the arsenal. Rumors play a disproportionate role. Suspicions mount, and every nation engages in measures which it believes to be defensive but which appear to other nations as potentially directed against themselves.

The balance of power system is also based upon another unsound principle; namely, that nations insist upon being judges in their own cause. Unless we can devise a system by which third-party judgments can be given and enforced, unless therefore more power is at the disposal of the community as a whole than is at the disposal of the disputants, there can be no basis of order. This truth applies to local communities, to nations, and to the world as a whole. Unless international society possesses force superior to that of the nations which comprise it, the basis of peace remains extremely fragile.

At the other extreme from the balance of power position is that of the pacifist who has argued persuasively that since war is so wholly undesirable the only reasonable position to take is that of complete repudiation by the individual of the whole system. The pacifist's position has seldom been firmly understood nor his essential strength recognized. The pacifist has not sought simply to escape some of the grim reality of war but in conjunction with his denial of the use of war has honestly and passionately sought substitutes for it. But the hope of the pacifist—the hope that if a sufficiently large number of determined individuals should make clear in advance to their respective states that a sizable minority would have no part in a war they would compel their states to seek more satisfactory alternatives—has not materialized. Albert Einstein, once an avowed pacifist, insisted that if but two per cent of the population of any country would go on record as refusing to participate in war it would be sufficient to paralyze any modern state's war activity; but the scientist abandoned his position after the tragic experience of Hitler's assumption of power in 1933.

Nonetheless, the pacifist's contribution to this problem has been too long and too often ignored. The way in which our own sensitivity has been deadened by the frightful progress of this war is a moral warning. Less than a decade and a half ago the civilized world thrilled with horror at the story of the bombing of Chinchow. Though this city could not have been identified by one in a million the Japanese raid aroused the moral conscience of the world. We have gone so long a way since then that we now accept with little more than a shrug of the shoulders military actions which would have horrified us but a few short years ago.

In the course of years man has tried various devices to eliminate the occasions for war or to make alternatives more attractive than the recourse to arms, but not until the League of Nations was born out of the First World War were these desires expressed in the form of a potentially effective organization. The six principles underlying the organization were: (1) War was a matter of concern to every state; (2) disputes, likely to lead to war, must be settled by peaceful means; (3) all states must join in the prevention of war; (4) to assure peace, there must be a general reduction of world armaments; (5) provision must be made for the peaceful change of the status quo; (6) machinery must be devised and used to create social and economic conditions which will obviate the causes of war. The machinery of the League comprised a Council consisting of permanent and non-permanent members, an Assembly which included all member states, a Secretariat to serve as a fact-finding agency and a coordinating body. Closely associated with the League were the Permanent Court of International Justice and the International Labor Organization.

Unfortunately, neither the League itself nor its Council and Assembly was strongly enough implemented to lay the foundations for peace in a world society. Whatever may have been the hope of those who brought the League into existence, it was no more than an association of states which had given but reluctant and limited powers to the League. Article V of the League Covenant laid down the principle that unanimity in both the Council and the Assembly should be required for the transaction of the bulk of the business of the League. Nations were not yet ready to surrender sovereignty.

If a League member went to war in disregard of the Covenant it was deemed to have committed an act of war against the other League members who then were "immediately" to break off trade and financial relations. The Council was to "recommend" to the League members "what effective military, naval or air force" each should contribute to restrain the aggressor. Thus was provision made for international force to be directed against a nation which had broken the peace.

The question naturally arises why the League should have failed to prevent war and aggression. Was the failure due to fundamental defects or to faulty use of a sound instrument? The main weaknesses of the League were several. (1) Because no clear cut definition of "war" existed it was no easy matter to decide when a nation had resorted to war. (2) Under international law nations could adopt forcible measures short of war in protecting their citizens abroad. But there seemed to be no limit to what might be regarded as legitimate protection of national citizens and no methods existed of deciding if and when such actions were merely war in disguise. Japan, indeed, utilized this situation to engage in the conquest of Manchuria after September, 1931, all the time denying that she was making war on China and asserting that she was merely protecting Japanese interests against Chinese bandits. (3) The League Council or Assembly had to make exhaustive inquiries to ascertain the rights or wrongs of a given dispute but had no power under the Covenant to require a disputant to refrain from aggravating the dispute by making movements of troops and extending the area of military operations. Consequently, the aggressor-minded countries like Japan after 1931 and Italy during 1935 kept debating the question before the League while at the same time each was taking possession of the territory of another disputant. (4) The League Council could only *recommend* to the member states that they join in military sanctions but had no power to *compel*. France, especially, was alive to the danger that, in the absence of completely binding commitments by the members to supply an adequate force against the Covenant breaker, the latter would be able to finish its conquests before the League machinery could come into effective operation. The Ethiopian crisis of 1935–36 showed that these fears were not groundless and that the League's power should (in this age of total preparations and sudden attack) have been much more certain, swift, and overwhelming than it was. (5) In the transition from the pre-1920 system of power politics to what many people hoped would be the post-war system of collective security the French doubted whether in the early years of the League it would be possible to get unanimity on the League Council even under Article 15, which provided that if all members of the Council *except the disputants* were unanimous both parties to a dispute must agree to accept the decision. They thought it likely that the survival of the alliance psychology would be sufficiently strong to make it improbable that Council members would reach a unanimous decision. Hence, it would not be safe to trust national security to the operation of the League with the gaps which we have just mentioned rendering it a highly precarious instrument. Moreover, the large membership of the League did not necessarily mean a strong international force capable of mobilizing quickly. "Many of the nations were scattered and far distant, and their guarantee to uphold collective security promised to be of little practical value." (6) The refusal of the United States in 1920 to join the League and of the United States and Great Britain to guarantee aid to France in case she were attacked convinced Frenchmen more than ever of the uncertain nature of the new international society.

In order to provide the security which she so desperately needed in the light of the German invasions of 1870 and 1914 France sought to strengthen her position by two contrasting methods. First, she made alliances with Poland and the Little Entente, hoping to render Germany helpless by means of a ring of steel. Second, she attempted to strengthen the League of Nations so that the system of collective security might become really effective. It is obvious that sooner or later a definite choice had to be made between these two methods, power politics and collective security. For a time, however, it seemed possible to pursue the two policies simultaneously; and those who favored building increased armaments could appeal to their nationals on the ground that these armaments could be used both to defend their own nation and to help strengthen the League of Nations security system—an appeal which the British conservative government skillfully used during the 1935 elections to gain votes both from empire enthusiasts and from those devoted to the League of Nations. It is important to note that at the present time similar appeals are being made in Great Britain, the United States, China, and the Soviet Union; their governments are saying that their respective countries must be strong in order to be effective members of the United Nations. The history of the last twenty years shows the dangerous character of this line of argument, for in the period between the two wars the mounting national armaments came to be the servant not of a collective system but of intensified international power politics.

Between the years 1920 and 1924 two important attempts were made to strengthen the League of Nations. The first, the Draft Treaty of Mutual Assistance prepared during 1922 and 1923, provided for special regional defensive agreements by which two or more states could plan to give immediate aid to each other if a third state attacked either one, with the League Council approving such agreements. Unfortunately, in trying to give effect to the principle of regionalism the Draft merely gave grounds for suspicion that the special defensive arrangements "might easily degenerate into little more than a military alliance of the old type." Two states with a precautionary agreement might attack a third state, alleging the urgency of self-defense. Later inquiry might show the attack to have been without justification, but the damage would have been done—conflict would not have been prevented and justice not necessarily done. For this and other reasons the British government opposed the scheme.

The second great attempt to strengthen the League came in 1924 when the Powers discussed the Geneva Protocol. The Protocol closed the gap in the Covenant by providing an absolutely water-tight system of arbitration. Under no circumstances whatever could a nation go to war; it must continue the arbitral process even though the first

arbitral agencies could not render a verdict; the matter must be transferred to another and another body until a decision was reached.
The far-reaching Protocol was unanimously adopted by the League
Assembly on October 1, 1924. Unfortunately, the British government
rejected the Protocol, alleging that the scheme was too ambitious; it
imposed too many obligations upon the member states which would,
when the time came to live up to their commitments, find some excuse
for evasion. The British distrust of large general commitments won a
temporary but Pyrrhic victory.

In 1925 the British approach found expression in the Locarno Agreements. Germany, Belgium, France, Britain and Italy guaranteed the
finality of the boundary between France and Germany and thus
appeared to make a substantial contribution to the cause of world peace
by overcoming the French fears that some day Germany would again
attempt to take Alsace-Lorraine and no stability in Europe could be
hoped for. For a time this particularist approach seemed justified by
events. Germany was admitted into the League in 1926, the reparations problem apparently was ceasing to be a storm center, and the
Rhineland was evacuated by Allied troops before the dates agreed
upon in the Versailles Treaty. By 1928 when through the Kellogg-
Briand Pact the nations of the world renounced war as an instrument
of national policy, international crises had become less frequent and
an era of good feeling appeared to have been ushered in.

To many students of international affairs, however, the sequel was
not surprising. In the first place although the Locarno Agreements
eased the situation in an admittedly dangerous area they did little or
nothing to strengthen the international system elsewhere. World
War I had broken out in southeastern Europe and World War II
was to begin with a Nazi invasion of Poland. It seems strange now
that anybody could have seriously believed that attacking the problem
in this piecemeal fashion would provide an adequate approach to the
problem of world security when so many unsolved questions in other
parts of the world remained as potential causes of war. In the second
place, the Kellogg Pact while universal in character provided no
machinery to implement or carry into effect its noble sentiments. The
Pact stated principles but lacked any recognized procedures; it failed
to solve the Sino-Russian crisis of 1929.

The period between 1931 and 1939 was marked by the continued effort to serve at one and the same time the two contrasting (or contradictory) principles, that of collective security and that of power politics. In the realm of power politics the break-down of the disarmament conference in June, 1934, after almost two and one-half years of negotiation, the mounting tide of national armaments particularly after 1934, the aggressions by Japan in Manchuria and Italy in Ethiopia, and the successful diplomacy of Hitler's Germany bore witness to the emergence of a feverish struggle. On the other hand, the hopes for collective security died hard and the League of Nations struggled to prevent Japan and Italy from succeeding in their career of conquest. In both cases, however, the collective security system failed to halt the aggressor nations. In the Manchurian crisis the League did not even attempt to apply sanctions partly because Great Britain was unwilling to take a strong stand against Japan. Britain's attitude in turn was due to the economic crisis which in 1931 was causing serious concern in Europe and in Britain itself, to the unwillingness of the conservative government to break from the old idea of localizing a war, and to the uncertainty of the United States policy —for although Mr. Stimson, the Secretary of State, had taken a strong stand against Japan, it was by no means certain that Congress would declare war if matters should come to a showdown. The same attempt to mix the aloofness of neutrality (in practice) with theoretical collective condemnation was to reappear in the Ethiopian crisis where, even after the League had decided to impose sanctions, negotiations were being continued to see whether even at that late hour some compromise could not be arranged between the Italy which the League had condemned and its victim Ethiopia.

The failure of the only attempt to apply sanctions against the aggressor nation can be readily explained. As far back as 1920 many of the League members were trying to weaken the effect of Article 16 by interpreting it in such a way that sanctions could be applied progressively, and therefore half-heartedly. And even the limited embargoes which did not include the all-important item of oil were also half-heartedly applied. Some of the states claimed that internal constitutional problems prevented their full cooperation, and others who were situated near Italy claimed exemption from participating because of their position. Disputes broke out over who should receive compensation for loss of markets due to the refusal to trade with Italy and over how the compensation should be paid, and how much it should be. And worst of all, many people of all countries did not see the larger interests of peace at stake and tried to make their miserable profits by continuing supplies to Italy though they thereby assisted an aggressor to pull down the edifice of world peace.

In 1939 the shooting phase of World War II began. Too late did many people realize it was not merely that a defeated Germany had arisen once more to fight war but that this new conflict fundamentally grew out of the disastrous belief of the victorious powers of the last war that the major problem of peace was to keep Germany down. In reality, the war grew out of the failure of the victors in 1919 to keep the peace among themselves. As a consequence, all the methods which were tried broke down. It is not enough to say that collective security has failed. Power politics has likewise failed. We must, therefore, ask along what lines we can expect to maintain peace now that the United Nations have finally defeated their enemies.

The most far-reaching and indeed the most logical proposals come from those who claim that nothing short of a world federation can guarantee world stability. Proponents of world federalism claim that the first essential to peace is adequate government, and adequate government means control over at least communications, monetary affairs, trade and commerce, and sufficient armed forces to keep order. Anything less than this will mean a return to the practice of a balance of power whatever words may be used to describe the new organization. No system which permits individual nations to maintain armed forces to the limit of their desires can possibly hope to succeed; nor does there seem to be any hope that financial stability can be restored and maintained unless a world government has far-reaching monetary powers and tariff controls.

It is extremely difficult to deny the logic of world federalism in an age when technology has closely interwoven so many aspects of modern life. The intimate interdependence of nations is clearly set forth in the chapters which follow and this interdependence must be made orderly and effective by the development of adequate government or it will degenerate into unparalleled means of inflicting mutual injury. When people come into close dependence they must live a more orderly or a more disrupted life. Only in continued order can life go on in tolerable fashion; hence the quest for world order is the paramount task of our time.

Although in the judgment of the present writers (and of several at least of their colleagues) an objective analysis leads to the conclusion that a strong world government is imperative, we cannot ignore the fact that the great majority of people even in the United Nations are unwilling to forego national sovereignty, and that their political emotions prevent them from seeing the full implications of modern civilization. An analysis of the San Francisco Charter serves to confirm this view and indicates the line along which the governments of the United Nations have sought a solution of the problem of peace.

The principal organs established are a General Assembly, to be composed of members of the organization, each with one vote; a Security Council, the central body of the organization with one representative from each of eleven states, of which the United States, Great Britain, the Soviet Union, China, and France shall have permanent seats, with the other six seats to be filled for two-year terms by election by the General Assembly; an International Court of Justice; a Secretariat; an Economic and Social Council; and a Trusteeship Council. In this chapter we shall concentrate attention on those aspects of the Charter which deal with security.

The title "United Nations" is, as the *New Yorker* points out, a misnomer. "The name should be 'The League of Free and Independent Nations,' pledged to enforce peace;" the associative principle is maintained in the San Francisco Charter as it was in the League of Nations Covenant. The Covenant was part of the Treaty of Versailles and was prepared at the end of the war; the Charter of the United Nations is a separate document, not tied to the peace treaties. In the opinion of most experts, this represents a gain. The preamble of the Charter sets forth more clearly and in stronger terms the purposes and the methods of the Organization than did the preamble of the Covenant, but since a preamble is not normally an operative part of a treaty, we must regard it as a declaration of intention rather than as an expression of legal obligation. The Charter, like the League Covenant, consecrates the principle of sovereignty. The Organization is based on the principle of the "sovereign equality of all peace-loving states." Perhaps the term "sovereign equality" is not synonymous with the word "sovereignty." If it means the kind of equality which the states enjoy within the federal union of the United States, an advance will have been made. If the term sovereign equality as used in the Charter does not go this far, the new United Nations will be at best an uncertain instrument. There is no provision in the Charter for the seat of the new United Nations; Professor Hans Kelson has suggested that territory should be ceded to the United Nations so that it shall not be under the sovereignty of any member state but should rather enjoy a status similar to that of the Vatican City.

While the membership of the League of Nations was at least theoretically universal in character and new members were admitted by the Assembly, under the Charter the consent of the Security Council will be required. In view of the Soviet Union's refusal to join in conferences with Switzerland, Portugal, and Spain, and of the difficulties of voting procedure, the question arises as to whether this provision is a wise one and whether admission should not be made as easy as possible.

In both the League and the Charter the Assembly comprised representatives of the member states, each member to have one vote. But whereas in the League the Assembly and the Council had the same general powers, such is not the case in the Charter. The Assembly will have a wide range of recommending power in political, economic, and social fields; but the major responsibility for maintaining peace and security will be lodged in the Security Council. Decisions in the Assembly will be taken by two-thirds vote on questions of policy and by simple majority on questions of procedure. This step marks an improvement over that in the League of Nations, although several methods were adopted in the League to overcome the rigors of the unanimity rule; and perhaps the advance of the San Francisco Charter is not quite so great as a mere comparison of the texts of the two documents alone would indicate.

In matters affecting peace the Assembly can "discuss" and "make recommendations," but if action is required the question must go to the Security Council. To permit the Assembly to discuss but to have no power to settle disputes is perhaps doubtful wisdom.

The Security Council is the body upon which the success of the United Nations will rest. It alone can take action against a state guilty of war or the threat of war. Indeed, a careful reading of the document will show that the word "war" is not used, for the member states will have undertaken not to use "force" or "aggression." This change of terminology is important, for, as we have seen, the uncertain meaning of the word "war" constituted a grave weakness in the League structure. Now it is not merely the use of force but the threat of force which stands condemned and which will be dealt with by the United Nations on the initiative of the Security Council.

Many people have criticized the relatively weak position of the General Assembly vis-a-vis the Security Council. They claim that the position of the big powers on the Security Council is not consistent with the principle of "sovereign equality of all peace-loving states." They claim that League experience showed that it was the Assembly that put pressure upon the great powers in the Manchurian and Ethiopian crises at a time when the League Council seemed unwilling to take decisive action. Indeed China carried the Sino-Japanese dispute to the Assembly, which body also brought before the world in dramatic fashion the Italian invasion of Ethiopia.

Defenders of this provision claim that it is a good principle of politics to have responsibility for a field of action definitely limited, and that if the Security Council is to have prime responsibility in dealing with aggression, its power should not be complicated by that of another body. But critics allege, and with some show of reason, that although the small nations do not have the same amount of responsibility for maintaining peace, they do exercise a strong moral pressure in that direction and that they have not in practice been arbitrary and unreasonable. Moreover, wars generally arise not out of the disputes of small powers but out of the quarrels of the great. In effect, we see the great powers who are the chief dangers to world peace sitting together (with six smaller powers it is true) trying to find a solution to a crisis to which they themselves will have heavily contributed. For these reasons a great many people hoped that the position of the General Assembly would be considerably strengthened and a provision might be inserted into the Charter that if the Council was unable to reach a decision within a certain time, the matter might be referred to the Assembly. It is particularly important, they urged, that nations with great power should be equally amenable to law so as to ensure that they will exercise force only for the preservation of law and justice and not to further their own interests and to control the instruments of the United Nations.

To those who hold that we should trust to the honorable intentions of the great powers who are now united in their determination to stamp out aggression, the reply is made that not a few differences of a serious character have already arisen among the Allies, and that if they are in fact so united there is no reason why this unity should not have been set down in binding form at San Francisco. Especially, the fear exists that if the big powers are put in this privileged position they may be tempted to settle differences among themselves not according to the principle of justice but by the same kind of uneasy compromise which at Munich led to the collapse of confidence and only postponed war. Moreover, the contributions in war material and economic resources of the smaller powers together will be a substantial contribution to the forces of the international agency and to that degree will lessen the burden upon the great powers. The moral and material power of fifty nations will be more effective than that of four or five.

The animated discussions which have taken place upon the voting procedure in the Security Council constitute a grave challenge to Great Britain, the United States, and the Soviet Union. It would appear that in matters concerning the larger powers Great Britain, the United States, and China were willing to accept the principle that the Security Council vote should be exclusive of the votes of the disputants, but that the Soviet Union held out for the principle that wherever the interests of a great power are involved this power should have the right of veto. At Yalta the Soviet Union accepted a compromise by which it agreed that once a matter was under consideration by the Security Council a decision could be reached over the vote of a dissenting interested party, but that the application of sanctions could take place only if the great power affected agreed.

Critics say that such a procedure would destroy the possibility of joint action against a big power which was bent on aggression, for it is inconceivable that this power would vote to permit the rest of the world to use determined force against it! Defenders of the compromise say that if one great power determines to fight there will be war and that at this stage it is better to play for time. It would appear that this is dangerous reasoning and that in fact we have in the San Francisco Charter a principle of collective security for the smaller powers against whom no such elaborate organization would be required, but that the principle of collective security is applied, if at all, only partially against a great power. It is extremely doubtful whether any substantial disarmament can be achieved by the victorious powers unless greater agreement on the matter of security is reached. And experience suggests that it will be extremely difficult if not impossible to maintain armaments at a given level. They will either increase or be the subject of limitation or reduction according to a general plan.

On the other hand, the provisions for sanctions or penalties against an aggressor are stronger than in the League of Nations. Under the Charter member states will be obligated to accept the decisions of the Security Council and to carry them out in accordance with the provisions of the Charter. Also, they are bound to comply with the call of the Security Council to provide forces, and national air force contingents are to be immediately available for emergency measures.

The provision that each state member of the Security Council shall be permanently represented at the capital of the Organization marks an improvement over the League. For many years grave problems will confront the world; they will require continuous and skillful handling, and it is the part of wisdom to realize in advance the need of continuous deliberations. Within the nations, legislatures sit for extended periods in order to transact necessary business, and we cannot expect that an international system which is being so rapidly brought closely together can escape the necessity for similar continuous consultation and legislation.

In another respect the San Francisco Charter marks an advance. The provision for a Military Staff Committee to advise and assist the Security Council on questions relating to the Council's military requirements and to those dealing with national contingents for combined international enforcement action bears witness to the recognition of the need of immediate power in the hands of the international authority. However, the forces are still to remain under the respective national commands. Presumably the military experts decided that the technical problems involved in establishing an international police force were so great that for the time being at least it would be necessary to rely upon forces under national commands.

The position of the Military Staff Committee may be one of extreme difficulty, for with the end of the war the problem assumed a different complexion from that which obtained where the chiefs of staff might and presumably did exchange highly confidential information and work in closest harmony. With the resumption of peace, national governments have no enemy in the field; and unless there is a widespread agreement the great powers may find themselves unable to effect substantial reductions in armaments and their military staff will have to continue planning the future of their national forces. What will be the position of the heads of these staffs when they meet in the United Nations Council? Will the chiefs be put in a double position, having one day to consider international needs in the presence of other chiefs of staff and the next day to consider at home their own national policies in the light of international difficulties?

The Charter does not, like the League, guarantee as against aggression the territorial integrity and political independence of its members. But since it does provide against change by force, perhaps it will accomplish the same end and indeed provide more adequately for peaceful change. Article XIX of the League Covenant rather ineffectively dealt with the problem of treaties which had become inapplicable or whose continuance might endanger the peace of the world. The Charter does not contain any such statement but does recommend the consideration of questions so as to adjust situations likely to impair the general welfare. Some critics early pointed out that although the Covenant provided that acceptance of membership in the League constituted the abrogation of understandings and obligations among the members which were inconsistent with the Covenant, no such specific statement was proposed for the Charter; the weakness was corrected at San Francisco. The Charter does not stress as strongly as the League Covenant did the reduction of armaments nor does it include any provision for a mandate system for non-self-governing peoples. But it does include a more specific obligation to respect human rights and fundamental freedoms.

Very important too is the absence of a provision permitting member states to withdraw from the Organization. Those who persistently violate the Charter may be expelled (not a sound principle in the judgment of many people), but an alternative procedure is provided by which the offending state may have its privileges suspended even though it will not thereby cease to be a member of the Organization, a provision which in the opinion of one authority has the advantages without the disadvantages of expulsion.

From the above analysis it will be apparent that the Charter contains serious weaknesses. Like the League of Nations, it attempts to make the two contradictory principles, collective security and power politics, work within the same organization. We have seen that a few years after World War I the nations traveled the road of armaments while professing collective security, for it proved impossible to maintain the two principles in prolonged harmony. Without question the nations today will have a much shorter time to clarify their choice than they enjoyed a generation ago. For the rapidity of invention, the astounding powers of organization and the total nature of modern war will make it inevitable that nations will want to know without any possibility of doubt that they have security. Unless they can fully trust the new organization and the great powers can fully trust each other they will seek refuge in skyrocketing increases in national armaments. If the great powers are going to trust each other they must very quickly translate that trust into binding organizational terms. If they do not, they will soon become enmeshed in the fatal Balance of Power system.

Nevertheless, there is no alternative to acceptance of the plan. The only thing to do is to work for the strengthening of the United Nations Organization. Meanwhile there is a danger that the world will be caught in a vicious circle. The members of the United Nations, especially the Big Three, fearing that a collective organization will not be effective may hesitate to embrace the principle of united action. That very fear will tend to cause nations to take unilateral steps for their own security. The Soviet actions in Europe, and the demand on the part of many Americans for universal military service and for the acquisition in full sovereignty of the Japanese Mandated Islands are cases in point.

Such steps, however, will make it even more difficult to effect a reduction of armaments and a successful working of a security system. In that case, power politics, which has demonstrated its complete bankruptcy, will again hold sway and the world will witness an unlimited armaments race, with continuous propaganda directed toward national fears and ambitions and hatreds, and reason will stand little chance. Civilization, in so far as it is a product of reason, will have become still more imperiled. Because of the urgent necessity to be prepared against sudden attack, a universal uncertainty will appear; doubt, suspicion, and distrust will operate not only against foreign nations but against non-conformists within; and, beyond all these things, the grim spectacle of a world wearing out its inhabitants by the over-strain, which will be the consequence of the late war and of the necessity of continuing to produce ever-increasing quantities of weapons of war, will be painfully apparent. Indeed, science has now released a power so appalling that it will bring about the destruction of man's nervous system unless some principle of limitation can operate to prevent that power's being used in unlimited competition in a scramble for separate securities.

It is in the light of these considerations that we must appreciate the problem of organizing the world politically. It has been said over and over again that gun powder and communications rendered the feudal castles out-of-date as sovereign units of power. Modern science has done the same thing to the modern nation, and it will prove to be a literal fact that unless people have a clear vision of what kind of world modern science has created they will perish. Unless world organization can be rapidly strengthened the victor nations will have paid the penalty for not being able to see the true nature of victory which must be not only the conquest of the Axis nations in the field of battle, but also the organization of the power released by science to constructive ends.

The *New Yorker,* in its issue of October 21, 1944, has brilliantly described the essential problem that faces mankind:

The more a man thinks about it, the more clearly he sees that the political world must keep pace with the scientific world. A security league, in the age of flight, is an anomaly. Politically the shape of the new world must be the shape of penicillin and sulfa and blood plasma, the shape of the buzz bomb and the V-2 and the X-903, the shape of the mothproof closet and the shatterproof glass and the helicopter with the built-in waffle iron. This is a shape to conjure with. Mr. Willkie gave us the design in two words. If we try to live with all these majestic and fantastic and destructive gifts of science in a political framework reminiscent of the one-horse chaise, in danger of being upset by the irresponsibilities of diplomacy and the delicate balances of regional alliances and the wistful vetoes of the accused, we will soon enough discover disaster. There is good reason to believe that if statecraft is again caught lagging ten jumps behind science, we will never crawl back to life again as we have done this time. What curious defect it is in us that we should endorse the supercharger and deny the suprastate!

FRANK G. WILLISTON
LINDEN A. MANDER

*Editors' Note:* The atomic bomb has dramatized the *New Yorker's* warning. This latest product of modern industrialism threatens to wipe out industrialism itself; uncurbed, it at the very least implies a rapid decentralization of industry that will effect an unparalleled revolution in human relations, for atomic warfare would spell the death of such easy targets as large cities. Small nations would exist on sufferance only; Great Britain would become intolerably vulnerable; great continental powers like the United States and the Soviet Union would have only a little more latitude. Americans United for World Organization do not exaggerate when they say: "All our standards, our hopes of peace, our ways of curbing war, our political and legislative methods are suddenly out of date. . . . Jobs, profits, ambitions—all mundane things—mean nothing unless the frightful march of science is controlled."

But what shall be the next step? Of two schools of thought, the first argues that the United States should keep to itself as long as possible the monopoly of manufacturing the bomb. Though British and Canadian scientists may have participated in the research, though cooperation in war with our Allies may have been necessary to defeat our enemies, now that we have emerged the greatest single power on earth we should be utterly foolish to share our new inventions with those by whose side we fought, much more with those who may be our potential enemies. It is already possible to point to the emergence of grave issues between nations and to conclude that we must "play safe"; we must get more naval bases and monopolize the bomb.

The second school points out that if we refuse to share the bomb we shall be feared (and soon hated) by the rest of the world; it will be difficult if not impossible for any nation to use such prodigious power fairly. We shall be tempted, whatever our professions, to the type of imperialism which transformed Athens from a leader of the Greek communities to an exploiter of them. Furthermore, the secret of the bomb inevitably will be discovered by other nations, and a deadly race may result. We now know that by the end of the war Nazi research was perilously near and Japanese scientists had made substantial progress in the direction of the harnessing of the atom.

Under these circumstances, Raymond Swing urges that the United States should demonstrate its sincerity in the cause of world peace by declaring that it will use the atomic bomb hereafter only on the authority of a strengthened Security Council and should at the same time initiate a conference of the members of the United Nations for the purpose of so revising the San Francisco Charter as to give the Council powers commensurate with such a responsibility. The new international organization must have *a monopoly of the manufacture and use of the atomic bomb;* the alternative will invite complete disaster for civilization.

Such a monopoly will in turn involve the necessity of international inspection of national armament production. The United States and Great Britain, which accepted the principle of international inspection during the latter stages of the Disarmament Conference 1932–34, should be ready to take this step, even though the inspection must be far more thorough than that envisaged a decade ago.

But "time is" may very quickly become "time was." A declaration promptly made will be moral leadership; delayed, it may well be too little too late. Nothing less than a substantial degree of international government is likely to prevent an all-out struggle between the victors of the late war, especially between the Soviet Union and the United States, a fateful coercion taking the place of any actual *casus belli.* It behooves the governments of the United States, the Soviet Union, and Great Britain, especially, to ponder deeply the implication of the Balance of Power system in the Atomic Age; and it behooves the peoples themselves to insist upon new methods in international relations. If we fail in this we shall richly deserve the consequences of having sacrificed the precious achievements of human history to a tragic intellectual and emotional fixation.

## CHAPTER III

# *Regional Organization*

THE preceding chapter discusses security in its world-wide aspects. This chapter concerns itself with the various patterns of regionalism, the extent to which the regional approach may implement universal security organizations, and the limitations under which it must operate.

It would be both disproportionate and monotonous to consider all the plans of the last two decades. The principal contribution of an exhaustive list would lie in its demonstration that a region is difficult to define and even more difficult to create. However, planners fall into several general categories which should be noted.

First come the gradualists who, looking through the wrong end of the telescope, offer the regional approach as a stepping stone to a universal organization. Because a region is something less than global many assume that the part may more readily be organized than the whole. But, one may justifiably ask, will this gradual step be sufficient for the demands of the immediate future? There is a serious fallacy in assuming that problems develop and reforms gradually expand from a number of centers in a pattern of concentric circles. The sensible approach is to begin with the minimum conditions for success but not to underestimate the possible. The opportunities for advance afforded by social upheaval are historically attested, and we must not neglect them in our era. The world is now emotionally prepared to accept something new.

Second among the regional planners come those who believe that a regional pattern is adequate for solving all international ills. Ranshofen-Wertheimer says that the problem of world security is the problem of Europe. Establish a successful European regional body and world security will automatically follow. Count Coudenhove-Kalergi has also urged a European Federation, excluding England and Russia, the latter for its lack of democracy, the former because of its overseas empire. But both objections could be directed as well to other European powers, some with world interests and others with no more than a façade of democracy; and the impact of England and the Soviet Union upon Europe is too great to be ignored. In effect the Coudenhove-Kalergi plan illustrates the difficulty of devising a region, for cohesion alone is an inadequate test.

John Nicholas Spykman also prefers the regional approach to political problems. "World federation," he says, "is still far off. This is perhaps just as well because the world-state would probably be a great disappointment to its advocates and very different from what they had anticipated." To Spykman a practical foreign policy "should be designed not in terms of some dream world but in terms of the realities of international relations, in terms of power politics. . . . Balanced power is the only approximation to order." This balance in the interests of security is to be achieved by eliminating "wide differences in strength between individual units," particularly within the same power zone. This will necessitate breaking up large states and/or federating or uniting small ones. A balance among regional power zones is also urged. The European power zone is to be organized as "a regional League of Nations with the United States as an extra-regional member." This League is to be "merely an improved balance of power system."

Spykman's proposal is glaringly inadequate both in the light of the inherent weakness of all balance of power systems and in the

naive conception that States will divide power in a harmonious manner. Friction rather than harmony is likely to be the outcome, and if
the differences which inevitably will arise are settled it will be at the
expense of the smaller nations. Spykman merely changes the units
of an unstable world from the nation to the region; the essential
anarchy remains unchanged.

Others within this group rebel at an organization more inclusive
than the one to which they have become attached. The organizational
horizons of many Americans, for example, having been permanently
conditioned by Washington's Farewell Address and the Monroe Doctrine, extend no further than the western hemisphere. There is
an assumption of hemispheric solidarity that does not exist in fact.
The absence of internal cohesion and the existence of strong
roots and branches from and to the old world, is either missed or
ignored.

The establishment of a world-wide regional network would be
comparatively simple if geography were the only conditioning factor.
Following lines of longitude and latitude that divide the earth's surface into equal parts might satisfy an architect or mathematician but
not a political scientist. Because the world was created with five
major regions, separated in most instances by vast expanses of ocean,
a glance at a world map suggests that North America, South America,
Africa, Europe, and Asia should be the major subdivisions. Geography,
however, is only a minor factor in establishing a region, and often
a misleading one as we shall shortly see. Economics, legal systems,
language, race, political ideology, all form their own "boundaries,"
often far removed from the purely geographic.

Because North and South American nations had common origins
in their revolutionary divorcement from other countries in Europe
and a common interest in maintaining their independence, frequent
proposals and attempts, dating as far back as 1823 when Simon Bolivar
presented the first plan, have been made to unify politically the entire
Western Hemisphere. But in spite of these affinities there are many
divisive forces, and the Isthmus of Panama is not the point of separation. Central America and Mexico share a religious, linguistic, political, and legal heritage with South America. The great transportation
barrier of the Amazon and a mountain range to the north isolate

northern South America from her neighbors to the south. Historically the Caribbean Sea has proved a unifier. Northern South America, Central America and the Southeastern United States have some elements of regional unity, though no effective political organization has resulted. Mexico is contiguous with the United States and is a part of North America, yet her relations with the United States have varied greatly from those between Canada and the United States where a common boundary and common continent likewise exist. Racial differences and antagonisms, the contrast between British common law and Roman law, catholicism and protestantism, economic factors of exploitation and creditor-debtor relationship—all these have minimized the importance of contiguity.

Moreover, the distances from Europe to Southeastern United States and to the bulge of Brazil are roughly equal. Transportation follows sea routes between the United States and Brazil because of the previously mentioned barrier to land travel. South America below the Brazilian bulge is in terms of distance closer to Europe than to the United States and in cultural ties it is much closer. If proximity were the dominant factor Brazil and the western bulge in Africa would be closer to each other than to either Europe or the United States; and with the development of long-range air power the African bulge looms much larger than before in relation to the security of the Western Hemisphere.

British, Dutch, and French dominion and colonial interests in the Western Hemisphere also affect the regional pattern. While often small in area, many of these foreign possessions play a strategic part in the defense of the Americas, as the destroyer-base deal well illustrates. Differences in the power of individual states within the hemisphere have frequently prevented unity of action. Fear of domination by the United States prompts smaller powers to maintain a high degree of unilateral action. Many within the United States fear that a number of small powers might outvote the United States where her vital interests are at stake and so oppose any substantial union.

Regional organization in the Old World faces similar barriers, some of which are extremely formidable. Water masses in the Mediterranean and Southeast Asia areas are unifying forces bringing southern Europe and Asia into relations with Africa which are closer than with many sections of the same continents. Religion in the Middle East, North Africa, and parts of Asia has encouraged the idea of a Pan-Islamic Union. Such a region would trace its boundary in the pattern of an irregular belt long and relatively narrow through parts of Europe, Africa, Asia, and many insular territories. The threat of such a union to non-Islamic areas is viewed as ominous for minorities and a threat to peace rather than a harbinger of security. Africa presents a pattern differing from both Europe and the Western Hemisphere. Liberia and Ethiopia, both weak in terms of power, are the only independent states; Egypt and the Union of South Africa are semi-independent; and the major area of Africa is colonial territory. There are several extra-continental powers with either territory or special interests in Africa. American interest in Liberia and Dakar brings the Western Hemisphere as well as Europe into the affairs of Africa.

Until recent years Europe was the aggressive center of world-wide political and economic expansion. The great powers were all European and the relations between them had repercussions throughout the world. Because security has appeared to be primarily dependent upon stability in Europe, proposals for the regional organization of Europe have been more numerous and more vigorously urged than for any other region. It is the smallest of the five major land masses yet has the greatest number of independent states with congested populations, and racial and cultural antipathies that are ancient and strong. England is not physically a part of the continent yet has been closely related to it. Though Russia, because of her size and the drive to isolate her, is frequently proposed as a regional unit in itself, her geographical position and traditional interest make her a necessary component of both European and Asiatic regions. Because of the peculiarities of Europe, proposals for the creation of several minor regions are legion, with opinion regarding their boundaries extremely divided; and it is often difficult to determine where regional organization is merely a façade for a balance of power system.

The divisions which are most commonly made include: 1) the Scandinavian states, 2) the Baltic states, 3) the Balkans, 4) Eastern Europe, 5) Central Europe, 6) Western Europe, sometimes including the British Isles. Many bilateral unions have been proposed, such as of Czechoslovakia and Poland or of the Netherlands and Belgium; and in 1940 the British proposed an Anglo-French Union with a common cabinet and parliament, though France was unresponsive to the invitation.

Granting the existence of strong pressures for European federation and the theoretical justification of such a goal, one nevertheless cannot expect federation in the light of the substantial forces against it. Internally there is a strong fear of German hegemony. Many small-power leaders have voiced a determination to avoid federation. The U.S.S.R. still fears encirclement and sees in a federalized Europe a real threat to her security. Externally the impact and interest of peripheral states, particularly of Great Britain and the Soviet Union if they are not included, and of the United States, will tend to break down regional solidarity. Although the United States has a special interest in seeking security through European stability, our traditional policy of non-involvement in Europe's problems makes our adherence to a European political body less likely than adherence to a universal organization.

Problems of regional organization in the Far East are no simpler than in Europe. Differences of opinion are very strong concerning the participation of the U.S.S.R. in the Asiatic political structure. Diversities in size, population, culture, political maturity and other factors among Russia, China, Japan, and India demonstrate a serious lack of cohesiveness. The colonial areas in Southeast Asia, the special interests of other powers in the area, and the problems, particularly of defense, of regional orphans like Australia and New Zealand also show the unreality of sharp regional boundaries and the difficulties of establishing security within the region.

The obvious conclusion is that regions are extremely fluid and transitory and their internal and external relations so interrelated that it becomes extremely difficult if not impossible to bring them into any substantial form of political organization. The higher the degree of authority proposed for the regional government, the more apparent becomes the lack of a compelling regional unity and community of interest.

Will nations be any more willing to subordinate their positions to a regional body than to a global one? It is conceivable some nations might prefer the smaller unit, but there is evidence to indicate that most would prefer a universal structure. In peacetime the United States, Canada, and Argentina have been unwilling to accept subordination in the Western Hemisphere, nor are there indications of a reversal of attitude. On the other hand Argentina and Canada joined the global League of Nations with little hesitation, and the United States came much closer to adherence than it had ever come to a similar body in the Western Hemisphere. There are two principal reasons for this attitude which will operate with even greater force in the future than in the past. They both relate to the point we have attempted to establish, namely, that a region is not a unified and independent entity. Argentina has been considered the principal stumbling block to Western hemispheric solidarity and organization. This opposition is based, not upon an antipathy to supra-national organization, as her membership in the League of Nations will testify, but rather to the power position of the various countries on the American continents.

In the Western Hemisphere there is no state which even approximates the power of the United States, nor any combination which could successfully oppose her. The fear of domination by the United States has discouraged participation in a regional organization with the "Colossus of the North," in spite of the fact that the military potential of the Old World is estimated by some to be seven times that of the Western Hemisphere. However, in a universal body there would exist states with relatively equal power which could act as a check against United States domination in the Western Hemisphere and could minimize the possibility of a clash of the two hemispheres. Many small powers feel more secure in the larger body than in the lesser.

Strangely enough the large state or states within a region fear being outvoted by the smaller powers, particularly if all votes carry equal weight. This has prompted suggestions that voting in supra-national organizations be weighted, not by population alone but by all factors contributing to the power position of states. These proposals turn the small states further from regional organization and fail to assure the large powers that their authority will be commensurate with their strength.

The second principal reason why the large powers particularly are unwilling to submit to regional decisions is the possibility that their power positions *vis-a-vis* extra-regional powers will be impaired. A program of regional disarmament might contribute to the security of a region, but by the same stroke might jeopardize inter-regional security. An extra-regional nation might have sufficient objection to some intra-regional action to lead it to intervene. Regional action in Asia, for example, might clash with British or American interests in the area. A regional blockade might have to be enforced against the opposition of other powers. The punitive effect of non-intercourse within a region would be negligible if the punished nation could trade elsewhere. The probable effect of intra-regional punitive action would be the disintegration of the region in a political and economic sense, by the withdrawal of the punished member.

Regional application of security measures is valid only to the extent that extra-regional interests do not enter the controversy. Recent experience should have proved that only minor regional conflicts are without global repercussions. Pan-American failure to establish an effective neutrality zone has often been noted. Regionalism as a pattern for security was later discarded by most of its proponents, particularly the United States, when domination of the Old World by one power appeared imminent. An elaborate regional security system is likely to prove a serious disappointment to its advocates, and is dangerous to the extent that it establishes a false sense of security.

In spite of serious weaknesses in political organization on a regional scale, however, regional units established on a functional basis within a universal organization have a valid and important role to play. Under the League too little attention was given to remote areas or to problems which did not immediately touch the interests of the major powers. This weakness has often been misinterpreted as a weakness of the universal principle of security. Rather it was the failure adequately to decentralize universal machinery, to make allowances for regional diversities, and to utilize the judgment of those living at the grass roots.

Confronted by similar difficulties resulting from westward expansion and from increase of federal services, the United States government developed a successful system of decentralization. Regions, instead of being allowed to grow "like Topsy," were formed from the national capital on a flexible functional basis to improve administration of national legislation. For example, there are nine Army Service Commands; thirteen Naval Districts within the continental area, and four in outlying territories; ten Federal Circuit Courts; and twelve divisions of the Federal Reserve Bank. There is little if any justification in setting up the same boundaries for Naval Districts and Forest Service, for Army Service Commands and Federal Reserve Banks.

Many other nations, unitary in character because of size or other factors, use regional devices. While Paris is the capital of France, and there are no subdivisions comparable with our 48 states, the nation is divided into departments with regional offices to facilitate administration. The Spanish Constitution of 1936 in Article 11 provided for regional organization: "If one of several contiguous provinces with common historical, cultural, and economic characteristics agree to organize into an autonomous region to form a political and administrative unit within the Spanish State they shall submit a charter. . . ." consistent with the national constitution. Though the Spanish Republic did not live long enough to show how Article 11 might develop in practice, the constitutional provision for regional emphasis is novel and significant.

Early attempts were made to modify the exclusively universal nature of the League of Nations, but unfortunately they tended to weaken the League rather than to supplement it. The 1922–23 Draft Treaty of Mutual Assistance proposed a "supplementary defensive agreement," an application of the regional principle, with close coordination with the League. A strong and justifiable fear developed that such bilateral and regional guarantees of assistance would degenerate into military alliances and act at cross purposes with the League in spite of the avowed intent to the contrary. The Locarno Agreement of 1925 was a further attempt in conjunction with the League to apply a regional principle guaranteeing boundaries in western Europe by providing mutual assistance when violations arose. Though temporarily successful, the inadequacy and false sense of security created by Locarno were revealed in a most unhappy manner, as was indicated in Chapter II of this book. The assurance of the regional *status quo* depended upon more than regional considerations.

Since flexibility must be the keynote of functional regionalism, no organizational blueprint for all international agencies can or should be set forth at this time. But this consideration does not preclude an outline of the services regionalism may render in the postwar world, and of the general principles of organization on which they should be based. Though no attempt is here made to classify these agencies on the basis of their degree of importance to security, the following passage proposes a rough and incomplete pattern for international agencies under a universal body and decentralized into functional regional units:

A PERMANENT COURT OF INTERNATIONAL JUSTICE. Though the American Bar Association Committee on International Judicial Problems, the Inter-American Judiciary Committee, the authors of The International Law of the Future, the United Nations Organization, and many other organizations and individuals emphasize the necessity of a universal court, substantial disagreement exists on the practicability or possibility of a regional court system. Objections to regional courts decrease, however, in proportion to their acceptance of minimum universal standards of international law and in proportion to the opportunity to appeal from regional court decisions. Regional judicial decisions may have strong extra-regional interest in a particular dispute, there may be universal interest in the decision to the extent it establishes a general rule of law. The precedent it establishes may later affect States not parties to the dispute, or if followed in other regions may create serious conflicts in international law. Because of the peculiar nature of law, the primary emphasis must be universal rather than regional in judicial organization.

INTERNATIONAL POLICE FORCE. The administrative problems in international policing are relatively simple compared with the political. The physical impossibility of policing the world from a central station is readily apparent. How many regional police stations are necessary is a question for military experts to decide. To a military novice, one for each continent or major region appears inadequate. The number of bases would need to be increased to the degree that air and sea power would need the aid of the less mobile infantry for enforcement. A minimum requirement would seem to be the establishment of regional bases where coordination of the several national contingents would be facilitated *in advance* of a combined police action. In the event of a "three-alarm fire," it is conceivable a coordination of one regional unit with others would be necessary. The direction of national or regional forces is rightly placed by the San Francisco Charter in the hands of the universal Security Council. Autonomous regional police forces could not conceivably be adequate for the tasks ahead.

COLONIES AND OTHER DEPENDENT AREAS. Regional development of backward territories has been receiving increased favor and the trend will undoubtedly continue. Lord Hailey, the eminent British authority, has supported the idea, and on July 13, 1943, Colonel Stanley proposed in the British House of Commons "that welfare and development of the colonies be undertaken on a regional transnational basis." Responsibility would remain with the present colonial powers in close cooperation with neighboring territories. Joseph M. Jones in *Fortune Magazine* for October, 1944, says of Colonel Stanley's proposal: "(1) it postulated a positive, dynamic approach by the colonial powers to the basic problems of backward peoples—security, health, education, economic development, etc.; (2) it offered to colonial powers a common-sense method of attacking these problems and to colonial peoples the unheard of opportunity to enlarge their horizons and work with other colonial peoples in the solution of common problems; and (3) it offered to yield to an international group the privilege of planning for the region, of assisting in the execution of the plans, and the right to judge results." Coordination with a universal colonial commission is not precluded.

An Anglo-American Caribbean Commission was established in March, 1942, and has already achieved a substantial success. The Middle East Supply Center, though a war agency, was an example of the regional approach. The Canberra Agreement of January, 1944, anticipates a South Seas Regional Commission. Plans for other colonial areas are less if at all developed but remain susceptible to an application of the same principle.

Minorities. Minorities problems are both national and international, regional and universal in character. A minorities problem may involve the determination of political boundaries in Eastern Europe, but the security of Europe if not the world may also be at stake, as the Munich Pact so tragically demonstrated. Though national sovereignties have insisted that many minorities problems are solely matters of "domestic jurisdiction," the treatment of minorities within a State is becoming the increasing concern of the international community.

As previously noted international civil rights related to the subject of law should have a universal emphasis; but because of the complexities of more than average difficulty due to conflicting ideas and customs, regionalism may play an important role, as a reference to the Pan American organization for the rights of women, described in another chapter, illustrates.

HEALTH. Here, since so many health problems are global in their impact, a strong universal body is desirable. However, some health problems are regional and should be decentralized. Degrees of latitude, altitude and climate rather than territorial boundaries often confine diseases to a particular area. Canada in the north temperate and arctic zones is not directly concerned with tropical diseases. A health subsection on malaria should include those areas where malaria exists. The regional or universal approach should be determined by the extent of each health problem. Already a Pan American Sanitary Bureau has been established and a similar agency proposed for the South Pacific.

COMMUNICATIONS AND TRANSPORTATION. International cooperation has had a long and productive experience in this area. There remains room for progress in the old and the need for development in the newer instruments of communication and transportation. Railroad operation in its technical sphere tends to follow land masses. A standard-gauge railway assures continuity of transport within a continent. River and road problems are generally regional in character. Air transport, however, requires the establishment of universal standards for signals, airport regulation, etc., in a manner similar to that established on the high seas, a subject that is dealt with in our chapter on transportation. The American proposals at the International Civil Aviation Conference in Chicago call for universality in respect to the technical factors but reject the idea of immediate universal control of the commercial.

LABOR. Accomplishments of the International Labor Organization are so generally recognized that its continuance in the postwar world seems assured. The I.L.O. 1942 publication, "Towards Our True Inheritance," recognizes special regional problems but says, "The responsibilities of the International Labor Organization are world-wide, and the experience of twenty years has shown that in order to enable it to discharge those responsibilities in a manner which takes due account of the interests and problems of all its Members it must have direct and intimate contact with all parts of the world and specialized machinery for handling, within a general international framework, the special problems of particular regions."

As pointed out in the chapter on the International Labor Organization, regional conferences have been held in Havana and Santiago. The I.L.O. has also cooperated with the first Inter-American Social

Security Conferences. Proposals have been made for I.L.O. conferences and either offices or conferences for Asia and the Middle East.

The United Nations Relief and Rehabilitation Administration is an example of a universal body—there are currently 44 members—decentralized into regions for the purpose of administration. The fluidity of regional boundaries is vividly illustrated in this organization which establishes boundary lines in some instances where they have never existed before. With the exception of limited relief for Italy the service extends only to friendly territories liberated from their conquerors. In the Far East two regions have been established: the first, with offices in Chungking, is to serve all China; the second, with offices in Sydney, Australia, is to serve all other Far Eastern territories.

Consideration of other international agencies would lead to revelations and conclusions similar to those already set forth. The problem is not to choose between regionalism and universalism, but to utilize in each particular instance the appropriate advantages of both. A balance of operations among State, region, and universal agencies must be sought. The principle of administration at the grass roots should be encouraged where possible, but regional agencies related to subjects of concern to extra-regional States or to the world at large should be supervised by a universal organization. The degree of supervision should vary as the exigencies of each case demand. The purposes of regional agencies must be consistent with the general principles of the larger body. In respect to those matters immediately affecting security, action in the region should be subject to authorization in advance or directed by the central organization. As activities are more remotely related to security, greater freedom of action, subject to review by the central body, may become the pattern of supervision. Regional commissions should include representatives of the central body as well as the territory in which they operate. Technical experts should be utilized without reference to boundaries or organization. Centralization should not go so far as to destroy the interests in, or knowledge of, local problems; decentralization should not preclude the utilization of the technical and correlative services the universal body is in a better position to render.

But that the reconciling of regional and universal methods is not easy has been shown by recent events, one of which may be briefly noted here. Though the Act of Chapultepec resulted from an Inter-American conference ostensibly aimed at integrating the Inter-American system with the United Nations Organization, it sought to accomplish this end by attempting to force an adjustment of the system proposed at Dumbarton Oaks to the Inter-American system. Its most advanced step, providing for substantial enforcement action including the use of arms, stemmed from the fear that Russia might veto action by the Security Council against an aggressor communist government; and it emphasized the desire of many in the Western Hemisphere to maintain either autonomy or a high degree of independence in this area for the pacific settlement of disputes. Indeed extremists have gone so far as to declare that problems within the Western Hemisphere are not within the competence of the Security Council because they are not international problems.

The impact of the Chapultepec Conference on the San Francisco Conference produced, in the Charter, revisions of the Dumbarton Oaks proposals in several important respects. It is true that the Charter emphasizes the superior authority of the Security Council. No enforcement action is to be taken under regional arrangements or by regional agencies without the authorization of the Security Council. Moreover, the Security Council is, at all times, to be kept fully informed of activities undertaken or in contemplation under regional arrangements or by regional agencies for the maintenance of international peace and security. But enough regional and national autonomy remains to offer a potential obstruction to action by the Security Council. Two evidences will suffice: the unity of the Western Hemisphere in pressing for recognition of its continental machinery and the inclusion of Argentina at the San Francisco Conference. Both helped to excuse unilateral action taken by other powers within their spheres of influence and to perpetuate those spheres of influence. Some time later widespread anxiety greeted the letter sent by Senator Vandenberg to Secretary of State Byrnes early in August 1945, in which he suggested that exclusive responsibility for the policing of the Western Hemisphere should be kept in the Americas. Senator Vandenberg disclaimed any intention of weakening the position of the general Security Council, but we may anticipate that the problem of regionalism will yet create perplexity and misunderstanding.

However, a sound utilization of the regional principle will make a substantial contribution to world organization and hence to peace and security.

KLINE SWYGARD

# CHAPTER IV

## *The International Law of the Future*[1]

IN THE recent past, a number of authors have amused themselves by writing on the "future of international law," assuming, some in derision and some in jest, that it has had no existence in the past; that any semblance of it has now disappeared from the world; and that no future for it can be discerned on the international horizon. Everyone who looks forward however to an ordered world where men are free from want and nations from fear is interested in "the international law of the future." As a matter of fact, even though incomplete and defective, there has been for centuries a body of jurisprudence called international law. Inadequate as it has been, the society of nations has created a favorable response to its restraints and has provided a measure of enforcement. The informal and occasional methods of the past are, however, no longer adequate to meet the demands of our present international order. Just as the industrial revolution made basic changes in the economic and social systems of the newly industrialized countries, so also our mechanized society and our technological age are dictating new approaches to the problems of international peace, order and security.

Some have complained that international law is not law. The answer to this question, as former Chief Justice Charles Evans Hughes once sagely remarked, begins and ends with the definition of law. It is true that one school of thought holds to the view that nothing is law

---

[1] a) *Author's Note:* The title is the same as that of a statement of a community of views by North Americans on this subject, of which group the author was a member. It is published in *International Conciliation,* No. 399, for April, 1944.

b) *Editors' Note:* The United Nations Charter, adopted subsequent to the writing of this Chapter, incorporates to a large degree the principles advocated by Dr. Martin. In the matter of regional international courts (not included in the Charter), the Statute of the International Court of Justice would appear to authorize the Court to establish regional chambers if it should so desire.

which does not enjoy the physical sanction of a political superior—a sovereign power—and accordingly concludes that only the municipal (i.e. national) law of the sovereign state is entitled to this designation. This school of thought has had some success in establishing in the public mind the primacy of municipal law over so-called "international law." It has never succeeded, however, in limiting the field of law to the principles covered by its definition. The sanctions of society have doubtless been as convincing in the maintenance of law as the sanction of force. Even many lawyers seem to forget that our courts are important, not for the cases they actually decide, but for the cases they do not have to decide because the courts are open. Moreover, the more recent direction of instruction and research in jurisprudence is to regard law not as a mere mandate or command from a political superior who must be obeyed, but as a result of many forces—social, economic, and political—which contribute to the good life in the great society.

Others, while admitting international law to a legitimate place in jurisprudence, have contended that international law is nevertheless not so well or so uniformly enforced as municipal law. There is truth in this contention, even though neither field of law is in a position to point with pride to a high record of acceptance and enforcement. It is well to recognize that the subject of municipal law is a natural or corporate person and that the subject of international law is the sovereign state; that municipal law flows from a political superior to a citizen or subject and is based on *mandate,* whereas international law flows from the custom and agreement of equal and sovereign states and is based on *consent;* that one is a relation of *subordination* of the subject of the law to the source of law, while the other is a relation of *coordination* between equal units in an international system. The most rigid constitutional system, however, has never made impossible a civil war, nor has the rise of the sovereign and national state denied with any effectiveness the right of revolution.

Still others, agreeing to a reasonable measure of application and enforcement of international law, complain that it is difficult to find out what the law is and, once found, to say what it means. In other words, international law is indeterminate, while municipal law is determinate. It is true that international law has enjoyed little legislative declaration, and has had no elaborate system of courts to interpret its meaning. Its sources are varied and include custom, agreement and consent, the decisions of municipal and international courts, diplomatic papers, treaties and conventions, national legislation declaratory of international law, treaties and commentaries, and the modern conduct of nations. Nations, like individuals, have sought a statement of the law which would absolve them of their obligations under the law and have sought interpretations of the law which would invalidate a charge of violation. However, the demands of our international society and the facts of our international life require not that we neglect international law but that we remedy its defects, for we must reject anarchy as the sole condition in the community of states. We have sufficient history and experience on which to found the international jurisprudence of the future, as well as the machinery for its application and enforcement. Though significant national gains were made by the American people under the weak and nebulous Articles of Confederation, the exigencies of the national situation compelled the Articles of Confederation to yield to a more "adequate" system which took the form of our federal union under the Constitution of the United States. The nations have also made significant gains in international law and order, through the informal Family of Nations and the definitely organized League of Nations. Both have been tried, the first for centuries and the second, to be sure, only for a generation. We cannot risk their inadequacies again.

What, then, are the new directions which international law and its institutions of enforcement must take to render the substance of the law "substantial" and the system of states "adequate," in the sense of preventing and suppressing aggression?

1. THE INTERNATIONAL LAW OF THE FUTURE MUST BE POSITED ON AN AFFIRMATIVE PHILOSOPHY

The approach must spring from positive rather than negative premises. The deficiencies of our international system have come not so much from missing the mark, but rather from the low aim. We have too readily assumed that little could be accomplished; therefore little need be expected. As a result, little has been undertaken. The prevention of war and of aggression, and the punishment of the aggressor are the more spectacular functions of an international society. "To keep the peace," as a continuing, day-to-day, permanent task, is the less engaging but more effective contribution. The tests of domestic order are not the putting down of revolution and the defeat of civil wars, but rather in the just and stable administration of law to the end that a satisfied and secure people will have no reason to revolt. Our approach in international law in the future must not be that of winning frequent wars, even just ones against an aggressor, but that of so administering and enforcing a just system of law as to render global war improbable if not impossible.

In the future, we cannot rely alone on agencies calculated to even up the injustices of the past. Remedial functions alone will not suffice. Preventive functions must also be assumed. Central and regional planning agencies, with the consent of the nations concerned, must be established, not alone to deal with such contingencies as they arise, but to anticipate them, and to take such action as may prevent the happening of new abuses, and the recurrence of old ones. The purely dispute-adjusting international system is as out-moded as is the exclusively peace-enforcing, tax-collecting state. The more affirmative international system, preventing aggression rather than fighting its results, is as necessary today as the social service state, with its manifold positive ministrations to mankind's economic and social well-being. The law of this community of states is international law. The community of states is concerned by and must take notice of (1) a failure by one or more states to carry out their obligations under international law, and (2) any use of force or threat of force by one or more states in their relations with other states. Rather than sudden changes which interrupt peaceful relations, international security requires orderly procedures under which international situations, whether political, territorial, humanitarian, may be adjusted as the occasion shall require.

## 2. THE INTERNATIONAL LAW OF THE FUTURE MUST EMPHASIZE THE LEGAL DUTIES OF STATES AS WELL AS THEIR LEGAL RIGHTS

States have been eloquent in the defense of their rights, often silent and indifferent, and at times defiant, in respect of their duties under international law; like the individual the state seldom fails to find some right it seeks to invoke in its own behalf and against its adversary. International institutes and conferences, both unofficial and private and official and public, have made impressive declarations of the rights of nations. These are excellent as far as they go. Unfortunately duties and obligations are seldom codified and systematized with the care and precision of rights and privileges. Moreover, the obligation or duty must assume a "legal" status. It must be clothed with ultimate sanction. While nations "ought" to do certain things, the gulf between "ought" and "must" has been too wide and is too convenient a means of escape of the gangster nation from its obligations, express and implicit, under international law. International obligations have been allowed too long to remain in neutral zones: the "may" of policy and the "ought" of ethics. They must enter a more positive climate: the "must" of law.

3. THE INTERNATIONAL LAW OF THE FUTURE MUST MAKE THE SOVEREIGNTY
OF THE STATE COMPATIBLE WITH ITS OBLIGATIONS UNDER
INTERNATIONAL LAW

The doctrine of sovereignty goes back to Jean Bodin, who declared in 1576 that the king of France was supreme within his own dominions and was free from all external control. "Supremacy within his own dominions" was absolutism in internal sovereignty. Under the feudal system, there had been an ascending series of allegiances, from the lowest serf to the highest over-lord, heading up in the king. However, with the dissolution of the feudal system, allegiance was direct from the serf and baron, direct to the king, all indirect allegiances having disappeared. It was the exercise of complete, absolute, sovereign power within the state and squared with the facts of history. "Free from all external control" meant factually freedom from the restraints of the Papacy in the ecclesiastical field, and from the restraints of the Holy Roman Empire in the temporal field. It did not mean license in external affairs without let or hindrance. It simply meant that the development of Europe, instead of being under the aegis either of the Church or Empire, with the resultant continental unity and the reduced status of the national state, would be international in character, with the national sovereign state as the basis of the international system. The absolutism within was never intended to mean anarchy and license without. Indeed, the very basis of the inter-state system thus established assumed equality, negotiation, agreement and independence, rather than unilateral or group defiance of the will and the welfare of the inter-state society. The absolutist Austinians, who hold that positive law is in the nature of a command, springing from a definite political superior and binding on citizen and subject, have made of the doctrine something it was never intended to be and which the facts of history do not bear out. For example, absolute national sovereignty is compatible with the federal guarantees of our states as autonomous units in our federal system. Despite the tendency toward centralization in the United States, there is little prospect of our emerging from a federal to a unitary state.

If national sovereignty is susceptible of modification from within, in behalf of autonomous units such as the states of Washington and California, is it not also susceptible of modification from without in the interest of peace, order, and security? No less an authority than John Marshall has said so. In the case of *Schooner Exchange* v. *McFaddon* (7 Cranch, 16), John Marshall subscribed to the traditional doctrines of the absolute sovereignty and the exclusive jurisdiction of the national state. This was *within its own territory* and not in external affairs, as the absolutist Austinians would contend. Here all limitations and exceptions must flow from its own consent. In the interest of international convenience and mutual intercourse, a nation could, expressly or impliedly, relax "that absolute and complete jurisdiction within their respective territories which sovereignty confers." Indeed, the surrender of such sovereignty from within, for the sake of mutual convenience and intercourse, was the greatest evidence of the possession of sovereignty. Thus the surrender of a measure of sovereignty within is upheld as consistent with the doctrine of absolute and exclusive sovereign power.

If a state may surrender sovereignty in certain matters in a field which is regarded as absolute, may it not assume certain functions in the external field where sovereignty is regarded as relative? Certain forms of power must be developed and used for peace purposes which cannot be set aside by the whims of a single power. This does not involve a "surrender of sovereignty" in the internal field where it is absolute, but rather an exercise of sovereignty in the external field where it is relative. It is really a matter of "new uses of power" which has been within our constitutional and international authority all along but which has not hitherto been altogether necessary.

4. THE INTERNATIONAL LAW OF THE FUTURE MUST HOLD STATES UNILATER-
ALLY TO DEFINITE OBLIGATIONS TO KEEP THE PEACE. SOME OF THESE
ARE POSITIVE; SOME ARE MATTERS OF SELF-RENUNCIATION

On the positive side, a state must assume the legal obligation to employ only peaceful means in settling its disputes with other states. Failing settlement by such means, each state must accept the settlement of the dispute by the competent agency of the community of states. On the negative side, the state must yield the use of force or threat of force, unilaterally, in relations with another state, save where considerations of legitimate self-defense dictate another course.

The use of force may be authorized in two cases. One is the case of a duly ascertained legal right, consistently violated, and the means of peaceful settlement ignored or rejected. Then the injured state, with the authorization of the international body and doubtless with its support, may well proceed to use force against the injuring state.

Legitimate self-defense, in cases where the international authority cannot act, or cannot act soon enough, or cannot act adequately, is the right of the victimized state. Such action as is taken should be such as the international authority may be deemed to approve. Reference to and approval by such an authority should be an essential and immediate undertaking by the state moving suddenly and unilaterally against an unauthorized use of force.

5. THE INTERNATIONAL LAW OF THE FUTURE MUST CHANGE THE BASIS
AND THE LEGAL STATUS OF WAR

War as an institution is deeply rooted in the past. The prospect of its complete eradication seems somewhat remote. However, the basis of war must be changed and its legal status altered if civilization is to survive.

In the past, the conditions of peace and war were legal conditions, investing the countries of the world with certain rights and duties. And in case of war the status of neutral and belligerent conferred both rights and duties consistent with each status. World wars, however, every twenty or twenty-five years, with an intervening period of peace, become merely a race between wars and a long armistice. At long last one will bring on the other. The distinction between peace and neutrality, *for purposes of security,* falls to the ground.

The old distinction between belligerent and neutral becomes meaningless and the maintenance of neutrality becomes virtually impossible. The small state, staking its neutrality against possible violation by an aggressor, has, relatively in World War I and almost universally in World War II, either been invaded and occupied by the aggressor state or involuntarily brought into its orbit by domination or by threat. The large state, having some independence of choice between war and neutrality, has in both World Wars found it necessary to abandon neutrality and its defense of neutral rights to defend itself as well as others against actual and possible aggression. The United States in World War I sought to maintain its position as a neutral and to safeguard its rights under international law. This failed. Prior to World War II, the United States sought to isolate itself from war and to insulate against war by surrendering its neutral rights through unilateral legislation. Such action played directly into the hands of the aggressor. The old conditions of peace, war, and neutrality, with their legal distinctions, while serving a purpose in the past, do not seem compatible with the new obligations states must assume in preventing and suppressing aggression.

The aggressor must be deprived of his legal status of belligerent, possessed of definite rights, and protected by a status under the law. I appreciate the difficulty of dividing wars into just and unjust or legal and illegal ones. The offending belligerent, no matter how unjust his cause or how illegal his course, nevertheless has had in the past a status equal under the law to that of his injured adversary and was seised of the same rights and obligations. This legalized respectability now open to the aggressor must be closed to him. Any act by him in pursuance of his unjust cause and illegal course must be regarded as on the level of the acts of the gangster in pursuit of his invalid enterprises. Acts by the community of states, authorized by the competent agency of that community, must be regarded as on the level of such force as is used by the FBI agent against the gangster.

To make this authority effective, states cannot limit their participation merely to seeking peaceful means and to the abstention from force in respect of their own disputes. In the language of *The International Law of the Future,* "each state has a legal duty to take in cooperation with other states, such measures as may be prescribed by the competent agency of the community of states for preventing or suppressing a use of force by any state in its relations with another state." For the future each state must agree to cooperate in defining aggression, in determining when an act of aggression has been committed, in determining who has committed an act of aggression, and in prescribing and enforcing the penalties against the aggressor. Nothing short of this will result in peace. Unilateral self-renunciation, so abundant in the League Covenant, the Washington treaties, and the Kellogg Pact, works no magic against the state determined to be aggressive.

The measures, even the forcible ones, employed by the community of states against aggression, should not be called acts of war, threats of war, or a state of war. They should be referred to as acts of force and threats of force. They must be kept within the realm of police measures designed to discourage and deter the aggressor. Should sustained force and resistance result, the aggressor must not be allowed to dignify his status as legalized belligerent. Under proper authorization and control, "might" may be employed to establish "right."

6. THE INTERNATIONAL LAW OF THE FUTURE MUST RESULT IN A MORE DETERMINATE SYSTEM, ENACTED AND RENEWED FROM TIME TO TIME BY A COMPETENT INTERNATIONAL LEGISLATIVE BODY

The international system of the past has been somewhat indeterminate. It cannot remain so. Something must be done to secure the speed and certainty of the legislative body together with the authority and the representative character of the conference and the process of ratification. The body on which states have equal representation might well have the power to enact new rules of international law by a two-thirds or three-fourths vote, with the understanding that each state may, within a given time, accept or reject the new principle. The same course should obtain as regards the modification of existing rules of international law. This suggestion is a compromise between central international legislation on the one hand and international negotiation and unilateral ratification on the other. It seems well designed to bring the substantive international law up to modern standards. It is not intended to apply to the procedures which would put these rules into effect and especially those which involve the use of force against aggression.

In this way, the law itself could be as modern and practical as the means of its enforcement. We cannot provide machinery which will be put in motion with certainty and dispatch, without the means of knowing definitely what the law is in each case which may arise.

### 7. THE INTERNATIONAL LAW OF THE FUTURE MUST PROVIDE COURTS OF INTERNATIONAL JUSTICE, REGIONAL AND UNIVERSAL, TO SETTLE INTERNATIONAL DISPUTES OF A JUSTICIABLE CHARACTER

Disputes of a political character can be settled only by conciliation, mediation, or direct negotiation. Nevertheless the enlargement of the category of justiciable disputes should be encouraged and arbitration in all its phases should be retained as an international legal process. The Permanent Court of Arbitration at The Hague, tribunals established under general or multilateral treaties of arbitration, bilateral treaties providing for general arbitration, and treaties, bilateral and multilateral, providing for arbitration in special cases, are included in this category. In moving to the fixity of a regime of international justice through permanent international institutions, we should omit no procedure which has been found useful in the legal field. Arbitration will sometimes be resorted to when nations would be reluctant to try the more rigid and fixed process of international point of view on the tribunals. The hearing of cases lying in a twilight zone between law and policy; the utilization of a simpler and less expensive process; the hearing of cases of a particular, regional, or specialized character; the use of arbitration by states declining membership in international courts of justice—these and similar needs suggest the retention of arbitration.

But definite provision should be made for institutions of international justice. The Permanent Court of Justice, or a new court like it, should become the general and universal court, hearing appeals from regional courts, and having original jurisdiction in certain classes of disputes. This court must have a definite personnel. It must sit continuously. It must have a comparatively wide jurisdiction. It must have a representative character. It must be a truly international and universal court. It should provide a model for all courts of the future in international jurisprudence. Its judgments should be regarded as authoritative interpretations of the meaning of the law of nations on any question before it. By adherence to a new "Optional Clause," the states should refer certain classes of legal disputes directly to the Court, without special negotiation in respect of each case as it arises. The classes of disputes so referred should be progressively increased as the consent of states will permit.

Regional courts of an international character might well be established also in the major regions of the world, serving as courts of original jurisdiction for intra-regional justiciable disputes, and possibly as courts of appeal from the decisions of bilateral tribunals and commissions constituted within the region itself. International law, to be such, must be universal. There is no European, American, or Asiatic international law as such. Yet there are continental and hemispheric doctrines and practices, as well as interpretations of international law. The Inter-American Treaty of Arbitration of 1929 could easily be developed into such a regional court for the Americas. One could also be established for the Pacific and Asiatic areas. The treaty law of this hemisphere flows from the Pan-American conferences, and that of the Pacific Area stems from the collective system established by the Washington Conference treaties of 1921–22. Such treaty systems could maintain their own regional courts, below the Permanent Court of International Justice. This court, while serving as the general and final tribunal for the community of states, could also serve as a court of original jurisdiction for Europe. Judges for the European section of the court would come from European states alone, while judges of the final and general court would be drawn from all countries and regions.

The balanced system of judicial arrangements in the United States, both constitutional and statutory, offers some good suggestions for a world judicial system. Our jurisdictional arrangements, original, appellate, final, and exclusive, offer lessons of practical value for any successful scheme of international justice on regional and world bases.

In the background there must be the possibility of ultimate enforcement. There is no magic about courts of justice, municipal or international, which guarantees acceptance and the carrying out of awards, without something stronger than a moral sanction. The suggestion that courts of unlimited jurisdiction might be substituted for the political and military authority which states may be called upon to exercise is not only a perversion of the judicial process, but it also divests that process of the sustaining influences without which it is of no effect.

CHARLES E. MARTIN

# PART TWO: Political and Human Rights

# CHAPTER V

## *The Problem of Dependencies*

THE problem of dependencies in the postwar world is part of the larger problem of realizing in a deeper and truer sense than ever before the rights of men. Opportunities for living as contrasted with merely existing must be granted to people in all stages of advancement and in all parts of the world. Any program for improving the way of life of colonial peoples, after making allowance for widely differing physical conditions and for marked variations of capacity among the groups concerned, will provide for a rising standard of living, for expansion of social services, and for increasing participation in government. First there must be for each region an economy which shall steadily raise the level of subsistence for the native peoples; in some cases this will call for expansion of individual holdings for production of food, in others for cooperative in place of capitalist plantation systems, in others for industrialization on a steadily increasing scale. Experimentation in production and processing of raw materials must be furthered in every possible way, and since many commodities will be able to meet postwar competition of synthetic materials only if efficiency in production and marketing is at the highest possible level, there must be aid and guidance for the development of export trade. To accomplish these things capital must be attracted toward colonial areas in increasing amounts—a task which may require the services of some international agency but which will be made easier as conditions among laborers improve. Finally, trade and opportunities for proper exploitation of the resources of colonies must be kept open to the people of all nations cooperating in maintaining world order. Such a program will, by increasing consuming power, aid in improving living conditions for workers in advanced countries; but outside this wider scheme it cannot function.

The two most essential social services are health and education. When we compare the 1850 doctors having "professional qualifications of the standards accepted in Great Britain," who Lord Hailey says serve for the 61 million in Britain's whole colonial empire, with the some 54,000 considered too few for Britain's 45 million and take into account the environment in which the 61 million colonials live, we can get some idea of the need for more extensive medical aid. But even more urgent is the need for the attack upon disease through improvement of nutrition and the expansion of preventive medicine. Education, which is at present available to only a fraction of native populations, not only must be greatly extended but so changed in character as to be a leaven working first in individuals, then in groups, and finally in an entire area to stimulate worth-while activity and help break down anti-social and unhygienic customs.

Again, dependent people must be aided in gaining a steadily increasing share in their own government. But here we must bear in mind that forms of governments are means to an end, namely the good life for the common man. It is often assumed that because Americans in the eighteenth century and Greeks, Belgians, and a score of other peoples in the nineteenth and early twentieth centuries could not achieve individual liberty and promote general welfare without independence, the same will be true for advancing peoples in the latter part of the twentieth. Fortunately, most colonials in the less advanced areas who are interested enough to agitate on behalf of their own improvement, recognize their economic and social needs to be so great that standing alone they cannot hope to satisfy them, and may use the right of self-determination to vote for remaining in or entering a larger political community.

Whether autonomy or complete independence is the ultimate goal, the form of local self-government must be that most likely to raise the standard of life. For example, representative government in any one of many European and American states where there is no deep gulf between sections of the people has led to steady improvement in the lot of the individual; but in the West India colonies with white planters determined to hold power it has brought little progress to a great negro majority. Likewise, in colonies like present-day Kenya, or New Guinea, with a small white settler population, or West Africa with a small educated native class, representative government can mean only the tyranny of the few over the many; and in the Malay States, the Straits Settlements, and British Guiana where there are several different national groups, it may well lead to bitter conflicts, deferring to a distant future real government by the people. Before legislative assemblies can succeed in colonial areas of Africa and Southeast Asia, experiments in local self-rule through native institutions must be continued on a wide scale. Indirect rule through native chiefs and headmen, in spite of its dangerous tendencies toward irresponsibility on the part of colonial officials and stagnation in local conditions, offers the most promising training for the duties of citizenship at the higher level toward which all policies should be directed. But political policy in general, except as a matter of good faith in providing this training, must be subordinated to economic and social policy. If native life is made more secure, if there is better health, nutrition, and education, and if administrators are honestly determined to hasten, not retard, the day when natives will govern themselves, the necessary political institutions can be developed probably in large measure by the natives themselves.

Among the possible institutional arrangements that have been suggested are: (a) the placing of all dependent peoples under the direction of an international agency responsible to whatever world organization may develop; (b) the expanding of the mandate system to include all dependencies; (c) the continued administering of the empires of the allied and friendly neutral states under the present systems, with safeguards for achievement of individual rights and for access of all the United Nations on equal terms to the resources of these areas. The great variety of conditions that will be found in dependent areas after this war makes it probable that no one set of institutions can serve effectively in all. Therefore it is wise to examine each of these plans to see in which area or areas it is likely to prove the most competent agency for carrying out policies essential to human welfare.

At first glance a direct international administration of all dependencies seems promising. It would guarantee, its proponents have argued, equal opportunity to all nations for investment and trade, thus putting an end to the international friction to which imperialism has given rise. Such an administration, staffed by experts drawn from both colonial and non-colonial countries and not subject to pressure of national interests, would be better able to protect and promote native rights. But examined in the light of the situation from which we must start, the objections to this plan are numerous. Colonial peoples themselves, insofar as they are vocal, do not favor it and the small groups of Europeans in such colonies as the Belgian Congo and Kenya will definitely oppose it. The natives most in need of enlightened administration have become accustomed to the particular system under which they live, and with their aversion to change it seems unlikely that their progress would be hastened by the introduction of a new organization. The very disinterestedness of direct international administration might leave the people with a sense of being exploited by an efficient but unsympathetic committee. The reservoir of experience and skills accumulated by French, Dutch, British, and Belgian administrators would not be duplicated by an international staff in any foreseeable future. However unsatisfactory the ties between Africans or Asiatics on the one hand and western nationals on the other, they are ties not lightly to be cast aside in a world in which there is so much to drive us apart.

It is of importance that British leaders in the long fight for native rights, leaders like Lord Hailey, Marjory Perham, and Bertrand Russell, and such an organization as the Anti-Slavery and Aborigines Protection Society have been unanimous in opposing this scheme.

We cannot expect the colonial powers to abdicate in favor of direct international rule. All of these states will be haunted by fears of declining status, while their nationalism will be heightened by the memories of their sufferings and by pride in their contribution to victory. At the same time they will be confronted by a gigantic task of restoring and adjusting their economic life. Bearing in mind that these states will be influential members of the United Nations (not defeated countries to be dictated to by some hypothetical power) we shall be unrealistic if we assume that they will vote away the empires which they have always regarded as essential to their economic life and which they have cherished as evidence of national prestige. It seems equally improbable that the United Nations organization can, without endangering its very existence, assume this burden along with the tasks of rehabilitation, of safeguarding the peace, and of maintaining order.

Though direct international administration for all dependencies which would involve difficult, drastic, and for the most part unwelcome changes does not seem feasible, such an administration for a few areas and on an experimental scale may be decidedly advantageous. Among such areas might be included the present mandates of Togoland, the Cameroons, and Nauru, and territories formerly held by Italy and Japan. Under international supervision as distinct from direct international administration might be placed waterways of high strategic and commercial importance, such as Suez, Panama, the straits of Gibraltar and the Dardanelles; also parts of Portugal's colonial empire and in due time newly independent states like the Philippines, India, Syria, Ethiopia, and Burma.

If an International Colonial Commission actually functioned in regard to even two or three areas, either as supervisor or administrator, it might be voluntarily resorted to in a variety of circumstances. Portugal, hampered by lack of trained colonial officials and especially by lack of funds for developing the resources of her colonies, might conceivably share administration of one part of her empire with the Commission if by this arrangement that part would participate in an International Development Fund and become in general more attractive to investors. New states, like India, or states like Iran long regarded as spheres of influence by stronger governments, fearful of too great dependence on any one power, might find the advice of such a commission to their liking and profit. The acceptance of such adjustments, however possible, is highly problematical, but contemplation of the difficulties involved may lead to a more realistic consideration of the plan for international administration of all colonies.

Except for changes suggested above, the mandate system should be continued for dependencies now under its control, but should be strengthened at several different points. To prevent such a sluggish economic policy as Great Britain fostered in Tanganyika, the Permanent Mandates Commission, in consultation with the mandatory powers, should be authorized to work out schemes for economic development and to enforce their execution in good faith. This would in turn call for the right of inspection of all aspects of colonial administration and the right and obligation to receive complaints and petitions from colonial people in contrast to the present arrangement whereby such communications must be presented through the mandatory. But to extend this improved system to include all dependencies would meet with many of the same objections as the establishment of direct international rule. There seems to be at present little or no public opinion in its favor. It carries with it an implication of inferiority likely to be resented by native leaders with their rapidly developing race consciousness. It is significant that the British Labor Party, which in 1937 made extension of the mandate system to other colonies a part of its platform, in 1943 declared in favor of rapid realization of partnership between Great Britain and her colonial peoples, including acceptance of principles of international supervision and accountability. While there would be twenty years of experience with a small group of dependencies to draw upon, the very large staff necessary for supervision of the greatly increased number of mandates would be hampered for some time by inefficiency. And even if the staff were efficient, the inherent weakness of the system, as indicated by Lord Hailey, would still persist, namely, that the "power of supervision is detached from direct responsibility for administration and its consequences." Since it is obvious that success in achieving the objectives of any just postwar colonial policy can be further extended and failure effectively retrieved only if responsibility can be fixed, the mandatory system would fall short as an over-all arrangement.

The third proposal, that of leaving administration of the empires of the allies and friendly states under the present system with the safeguards noted above, seems to the writers of this chapter to offer the best hope of a steadily progressing way of life for colonial peoples. Such a method of dealing with colonial dependencies requires, first, that the powers concerned are thinking in terms of human rights and world order, and next that the proposed safeguards will be practical and effective in holding the colonial powers to a program for which millions of people have fought.

In the case of the Dutch dependencies, at the instigation of religious groups organized politically, the "Ethical Policy" directed toward the social advancement of the natives has been an ideal set before colonial administrators since 1901. The realization of this ideal—slow and halting as it has been—has led to the granting of political rights to a small group in Java and to higher standards of indirect rule throughout the Outer Islands. Official announcements by Queen Wilhelmina and H. J. van Mook, Netherlands Minister of Overseas Territories, during the recent war, guarantee self-government to the two parts of the Kingdom outside the Netherlands and leave no doubt that human rights will continue to be in the forefront of Dutch colonial aims.

During the depression, within the limits of funds available, this colonial government made a little progress in the East Indies in improving food supplies, in promoting industry, in protecting labor.

France in West Africa has discouraged plantation economy and promoted the cultivation of subsistence crops, and has, throughout her empire, avoided with better success than any other power discrimination against colonial people on account of race. Until recent years the home government has not visualized autonomy for any colony but rather has assumed that the goal should be assimilation of the colonies to the life and culture of France. Recently, however, the French Committee of National Liberation, the Colonial Conference held at Brazzaville in 1944, the persistent policies of the religious and leftist parties, and assurances from the supporters of General de Gaulle give definite promise to French colonial peoples of a new political status involving self-government and a recognition of their civilization and tradition.

As to the Belgian Congo, an English anthropologist, Dr. Lucy Mair, who is an intelligent and forthright critic of modern imperialism, finds evidence that Belgium, in spite of the evils of King Leopold's irresponsible and ruthless policy before 1909, is "the only colonial power to have taken a strong line in defense of native interests." Belgium's colonial department has "squarely faced the disparity between the demands of European enterprise and the resources of the native population and has met the situation by the strict regulation of European expansion." Local officials have trained Africans for participation in all possible types of technical employment and through study and experimentation introduced better diet, better housing, and more adequate health services.

Great Britain's record in recent years for putting human values first is outstanding. Following World War I Great Britain interpreted the obligation of trusteeship as involving government activity on behalf of native welfare. Beginning with the Empire Development Act of 1929 she has expanded agricultural service through studies of plant pests and diseases, has experimented in the introduction of new crops, and has shown an increasing concern for health and housing which culminated in 1940 in an Act providing for expenditure of £5,000,000 annually over a period of ten years. But probably in no aspect of the social and economic development of her dependencies has Britain shown more advance than in that of labor. Between 1937 and 1943 laws encouraging and regulating trade unions have been passed in thirty-three colonial territories, laws for conciliation in labor disputes are on the statute books of five colonies, and workmen's compensation is provided in thirty colonies.

Most encouraging too are the experimental attitudes toward well established policies to be found today among colonial administrators in general. For example, control of tribes and villages by their own chiefs through indirect rule, which British colonial leaders have long accepted as an effective and desirable method of giving natives a share in their government and aiding them to adjust to the present-day world by way of their own institutions, is now being subjected to critical evaluation. In some instances, it is said, it has become a shelter behind which unworthy tribal leaders are oppressing their followers and carrying them back toward savagery; and it is urged that where this abuse has developed the only answer is direct and responsible rule. At the same time we find French colonial authorities, who have heretofore emphasized the advantage of direct rule in centering responsibility and furnishing direction for the advancement of natives, now deeply concerned in helping natives first to become good citizens in their immediate communities and then to progress toward a "higher level," in the "shadow of their own traditions." To this end, M. Lapie has recently stated, the introduction of indirect administration is "imperative."

Proposals for the achievement of the rights of colonial peoples and their consequent orderly and continuing progress, as well as for the assurance of the rights of every law-abiding nation to share in the proper exploitation of undeveloped areas, include a Colonial Charter, Regional Councils, and an International Colonial Commission. Every national state governing a colonial empire must publicly accept as a basis of its colonial policy a Colonial Charter, which will include pronouncements that colonial dependencies are not possessions but areas held in trust and that the primary aim of trusteeship is to help the colonial peoples toward self-government. There will be guarantees also for preparing and admitting natives to the civil service and for giving equal economic opportunities to all nations adhering to the principles upon which the charter is based.

On Regional Councils will sit representatives of the colonial peoples and of non-colonial powers with definite interests in the area as well as representatives of the colonial power itself. Each Council will furnish the opportunity for consultation as to ways and means of promoting decent living, for hearing complaints and criticism of these matters together with new proposals both by the peoples immediately concerned and by outsiders with interests likely to be affected. To the Council can be presented evidence of discrimination against investors, employees, and business and commercial men of any country. In view of the tremendous need for research in all matters pertaining to health and to increase of production, here may be coordinated the efforts of the various powers, thus avoiding duplication and insuring that the funds available will be wisely expended.

The International Colonial Commission would be charged with international colonial administration and supervision. If and when it is set up, it would recommend to the various national colonial administrations means of speeding up native progress. It would supervise the general administration to see that it keeps within guarantees given, and would act upon complaints of actual violations of the terms of the Colonial Charter.

Back of all these safeguards must stand, of course, some central United Nations organization and to the latter must in the end come questions not successfully handled by individual powers or by Regional Councils or by the International Colonial Commission. Such eventualities, however, present a possibility quite different from burdening the international organization with the overwhelming task of governing all dependencies. The evidence that these proposed safeguards are practical and likely to be effective lies in the fact that in tentative forms they are already in existence and have brought results. Every colonial power has agreed to the Atlantic Charter and has given assurances that constitute the beginning of a colonial charter.

The Anglo-American Caribbean Commission may well be a forerunner of both Regional Councils and an International Colonial Commission. Here there has been active cooperation between the United States and Great Britain in handling problems of food supply, unemployment, and political dissensions; and, in the future, it is planned that conferences including representatives of the West Indian peoples will be held to deal with long-range politics. The Havana Conference provides an example of participation of non-colonial powers which is lacking in the Caribbean Commission. The Permanent Mandates

Commission in the immediate field of colonial affairs and the International Labor Office in handling comparable problems furnish abundant precedents for successful international cooperation and for national acceptance of policies suggested by responsible international bodies.

While Spain and Portugal have heretofore been decidedly backward in their colonies, their shortcomings in regard to native welfare seem to have been due largely to lack of the means for carrying on social services. As a way of obtaining funds necessary for the economic development of their empires these nations, especially Portugal, may welcome a large measure of international supervision.

India may well be the acid test for any plan for dealing with dependent areas. Britain has given the people of that country a solemn promise that they can choose whatever status they desire as soon as they shall among themselves agree upon a constitution. In view of the Indians' widely expressed lack of confidence in Great Britain, perhaps no better means than a Regional Council can be found for aiding the Indian people to formulate a constitution and hold Britain to her word when that instrument is drawn up. Certainly a body in which all interested parties are represented has a better chance of determining the governmental arrangements that will best serve the welfare of nearly 400 million people than have India and Great Britain in their present state of mutual bitterness; and Britain's record of cooperation with at least one of the interested parties, the United States, offers hope that she will in good faith enter into consultation on the matter. The alternative, that the United Nations as a body or any member of that group should attempt to give orders to Britain, would imply that there is no international cooperation. In that case all hope of this or any other system of dealing fairly with dependent areas is at an end.

We advocate a national colonial administration with effective safeguards for most dependencies because it seems likely to give a decided impetus to improvement of conditions among native peoples: it will develop techniques already tried out; it will make fuller and more effective use of personnel familiar with basic problems; and it will avoid resistance on the part of members of the United Nations to what may well seem to them a blow to their prestige and to their economies. Moreover, it gives consideration to certain assumptions on the part of colonial powers that have apparently received general acquiescence. We must begin not where we wish we were, nor where we intend to be, but where we are.

We are then concerned primarily not with matters of abstract justice or with condemnation of the imperialism of particular nation-states, but only with hastening the day when men and women everywhere will be living on terms of self-respect and social responsibility. We shall, therefore, remember that for millions that day must in the nature of things be far distant, and that for people in even the most advanced dependencies alteration of their status within closely integrated imperial units will demand cautious procedure. With such an approach it is entirely possible that some complicating problems may disappear without being subjected to direct attacks and that, consequently, nations will favor delegating a steadily increasing share of colonial administration to an international organization. If, for example, we develop an expanding world economy, as we must if we are not to return to the insecurity and instability that brought on two world wars, the exaggerated and sometimes erroneous idea of the value of a dependent empire and the pride felt in it as adding to national prestige will both tend to disappear. With markets and sources of raw materials more accessible the determination to cling to colonies as economic assets will be lessened; and prosperity may well weaken the desire to have them as evidence of national greatness. A period of world peace too may remove another condition that gave importance to colonial empires in the eyes of the people of the mother countries, namely, the possibility of war; control is not readily yielded in regard to areas considered strategic or producing material essential to military operations. Furthermore, if we concentrate on making a decent life for ordinary people everywhere, the expense of doing this may lead some nation-states to welcome sharing responsibility either with other nations interested in a particular area or with some international agency.

To let the obstacles of national need and national pride be thus pushed aside in the course of meeting the larger problem, instead of going against them head on, may not furnish a dramatic crusade for justice. But progress in the development of western civilization has come by subordinating perfect justice in individual cases to general community order. If we are to insist upon the most complete justice for all dependent peoples we may prepare the way for such world disorder as will deprive individuals everywhere of even a minimum of rights. This is not to deny that again and again Dutch, British, French, American, and all other colonial officials have fallen far short of their duty toward subject peoples; it is rather to question the wisdom of trying to obtain the performance of that duty by means that are unrealistic and dangerous. There is no final solution for a great social problem; there can only be adjustments in the direction of a final valid aim, and these adjustments must take into account the varied factors that enter into the problem.

EDITH DOBIE<br>LESLEY M. HEATHCOTE

*Editors' Note:* The international trusteeship system set up under the Charter of the United Nations at the San Francisco Conference follows substantially the pattern set forth above. Article 76 lays down the basic objectives which include the advancement of native peoples "and their progressive development toward self-government or independence as may be appropriate," to encourage respect for human rights and fundamental freedoms, and to insure equal treatment in social, economic, and commercial matters for the members of the United Nations.

The trusteeship system is to apply to territories now held under mandate, to those territories which will be detached from the enemy states as a result of the Second World War, and to territories voluntarily placed under the system by states responsible for their administration. The terms of trusteeship for each territory are to be agreed upon by the states directly concerned.

Under Articles 82–84 strategic areas may be designated to include part or all of any trust territory; the Security Council is to exercise all functions related to these areas. In all other trusteeship areas the functions with regard to trusteeship are to be exercised by the General Assembly. A Trusteeship Council to comprise an equal number of representatives of the administering and non-administering members of the United Nations is to be set up. It will consider reports from the administering authority, accept petitions, provide for periodic visits of inspection, formulate a questionnaire on which the annual report to the General Assembly is based, and take such other action as is needed.

No reference is made to any international control over existing colonies of the member states. In some respects the trusteeship system goes beyond the mandate system, as for example when it provides for periodic visits to trusteeship areas; in other respects it avoids some of the legal difficulties of the mandate system established at the end of World War I. Much discussion has taken place concerning the justification of the division into strategic and non-strategic areas. This question falls outside the scope of the problem of administering dependencies as such. At the moment of writing the meeting of the Foreign Ministers of the Big Five is discussing the question as to the administration of the former Italian colonies and wrestling with the difficult problem of defining which are the states directly concerned that should draw up the terms of trusteeship for these areas.

# CHAPTER VI

# The Protection of National Minorities

THE history of nineteenth and twentieth century Europe cannot be told without constant reference to the minority problem which had taken on a peculiar degree of complexity, because in the course of centuries scores of peoples had intermingled and no clear-cut boundary lines separated one national group from another. The extremely mixed nature of such states as the Austro-Hungarian and the Turkish had caused the minorities problem to become international in character. The Serbs in Serbia, for example, could not remain unaffected by the treatment of their national compatriots in Austria-Hungary; and Bulgarians responded to the sufferings of their fellow nationals under Serbian rule. There were similar situations throughout much of Europe. Clearly so vital a question demanded some answer, and during the nineteenth century several attempts were made to prevent national emotions from reaching a point dangerous to international peace.

The first method was by internal constitutional guarantees, as in Austria in 1867 and Hungary in 1868. Such guarantees however proved insufficient. In many cases they were ignored and remained a dead letter upon the statute books. A second method, that of international action, was therefore resorted to. Several States signed bilateral treaties to ensure reasonable treatment of political and religious minorities. But when this procedure likewise failed, the great powers intervened sometimes diplomatically, sometimes by a show of force, and on one or two occasions imposed a limited international supervision, as they did over the Turkish administration in Macedonia in 1903.

Before World War I, however, international measures for the protection of national minorities met with relatively little success. No permanent agency existed to provide continuity of supervision. The great powers intervened not primarily for humanitarian reasons, but in order to take political advantage of troubled situations. The methods were political rather than judicial, and no satisfactory method of enforcement as a normal routine had yet been devised. So the fifty million people who represented the national minorities in Europe constituted a continuing menace to the peace of Europe and of the world. The explosive character of the minorities problem combined with the dangers inherent in the balance of power system contributed in a large measure to the outbreak of war in 1914.

During the war Allied statesmen increasingly laid emphasis upon the rights, and philosophers wrote eloquently of the cultural value of small nations. Self-determination became the slogan of the day, and peoples who had memories of bygone glories when they had existed as powerful and influential states looked forward to resuming their proud station in the world community. But the task of unscrambling omelets proved difficult in international politics. Strategic interests and the inextricable mingling of national groups made it impossible to redraw the map of Europe so as to place every national group within its own national setting. Twenty or thirty millions of people remained as national minorities, some of them under the rule of newly liberated countries like Poland or Czechoslovakia. Those who had been masters were now subjects, and in many cases the hitherto minority group became the dominant nationality with all explosive elements which such a reversal of fortune might have been expected to bring.

The Peace Treaties, however, reduced the minorities and introduced a comprehensive system of international guarantees. The general Minorities Treaties contained a number of rights guaranteed to minorities, such as the right to life, nationality, personal liberty, freedom of worship, equality before the law, and the use of minority languages; also the right to public employment and public honors and the exercise of professions. The signatory states undertook not to impose restrictions on minority languages in any branch of public life, whether in commerce, religion, the press, or public meetings, and to insure that minority subjects should obtain an equitable share of financial assistance in setting up educational, religious, and charitable institutions. These rights were recognized by the signatory powers as obligations to be embodied in their fundamental laws, to be modified only with the consent of a majority of the League of Nations' Council, and the minority groups were to have the right of petitioning the League if they believed that their rights had been violated by the government under which they lived.

Thus the obligations became a matter of international concern and the League guarantees appeared to have made a substantial advance upon the nineteenth century machinery, first by providing a permanency of control, second by providing for collective international instead of separate national intervention, and third by introducing a judicial procedure which it was hoped would remove minority questions from international power politics.

It may appear curious that some of the new governments accepted these obligations only under protest: Poland which had suffered so much under Austrian and especially under German and Russian rule vehemently objected to the conditions which the Principal Allied and Associated Powers imposed upon it. It argued that the treaties infringed Polish sovereignty, humiliated Poland's national dignity, and constituted "an unwarranted interference" in Polish national affairs. Critics of the Minorities Treaties claimed that they tended to encourage minorities to exaggerate their complaints and thus to make the position of the government more difficult. The treaties by promoting a state within a State would intensify and not mitigate disunity. Moreover, only a few governments had had to accept obligations toward minorities. Why, asked Poland, should some states be singled out for this treatment and others go free? Why should not the Minorities Treaties by generalized and international guarantees be given to minorities of all countries including the Principal Allied and Associated Powers themselves?

While the governments claimed that the Minorities Treaties went too far and imposed intolerable obligations, the national minorities, as time went on, complained of the ineffectiveness of the League machinery. They alleged that many petitions remained unanswered, that too much secrecy surrounded the whole procedure, that the League Council was too concerned to conciliate governments and sought compromises instead of justice. They charged that statesmen appointed to the committees of three were too busy to give adequate attention to minority questions, and that they had to judge on inadequate evidence since the League had no authority to send officials to the scene of discontent to investigate the situation at first hand. Why should not permanent commissions be established such as existed in Upper Silesia under the German-Polish Convention which lasted from 1922 to 1937? Moreover, the League authorities could only deal with particular complaints and were not empowered to consider the more deep-seated factors which could be adequately treated only by a stronger and more permanent body.

One can readily see that the success of this experiment would depend upon the effectiveness of the League machinery, "including not merely carefully devised procedures but also a fine sense of tact and a deep feeling for justice on the part of the League officials." It would require a liberal and even generous attitude on the part of governments, a freedom from excessive preoccupation with "sovereignty," "national dignity," and "prestige," and a genuine desire to promote justice among all subjects irrespective of race, nationality, or creed. It would demand on the part of minorities an acceptance of their subordination to governments of alien nationality, a willingness to recognize differences and difficulties, and an ability to conduct themselves with restraint; "for if they maintained a persistent attitude of hostility to their governments and indulged in disloyalty and even pin-pricking activities, they could easily wreck the fine balance of the new international experiment."

Above all, the success of the League machinery for the protection of minorities would depend upon the successful working of the League in its major task of preventing war. If the foundations of peace collapsed, little hope could exist for the continuance of enlightened and liberal treatment of national minorities who, as international tension mounted, would in all probability become elements of danger in view of their sympathy with those of similar nationality across the borders. Specifically the Sudeten Germans in Czechoslovakia could not expect the full benefit of Minorities Treaties if the danger of war increased between Germany and Czechoslovakia; for Sudetenland would constitute a possible spearhead of attack upon Czechoslovakia itself, and would therefore have to be put under precautionary restrictions for security purposes. These restrictions necessarily abridged the rights of the Sudeten Germans and furnished additional excuse for German criticism and agitation.

Indeed, the Nazis began systematically to exploit the grievances, real and imaginary, of the discontented minorities in Europe for the purpose of promoting disunity within Germany's neighbors as a prelude to military conquest. While Hitler forcibly suppressed minorities at home in order to build up a powerful army capable of striking quickly, his agents abroad were utilizing the freedom of discussion permitted to political parties and national minorities (where, indeed, they had not already been restricted or suppressed by dictatorships as in Poland and Yugoslavia) to widen the gap between governments and their subjects.

After war had broken out in 1939, Nazi Germany and Fascist Italy set up puppet regimes in Croatia and Slovakia and by assigning territory in Transylvania to Hungary kept alive the old grievances between the two countries, each of which had laid claim to Transylvania after the last world war. In order to strengthen Germany at home, the Nazis repatriated hundreds of thousands of Germans from surrounding countries although opinions differ as to how thoroughly this process was carried out in certain areas. They forcibly and in many cases brutally uprooted thousands upon thousands—indeed millions—of non-Germans and transplanted them to other places. This action has complicated the solution of the minorities problem after the recent war, for whereas in 1919, apart from any refugees from Russia and Turkey, the minorities comprised relatively stable groups, today they represent an uprooted and bewildered people.

What should be the principles governing the international society of the future? The answer to the question "Can an adequate security system be developed to prevent another war?" will determine the kind of answer to be given to the question "Can the minority peoples be granted justice, and if so, what institutions will enable them to give expressions to their legitimate political, economic, and social life?" Without an adequate international security system there can be little or no hope for minorities as distinct groups, for they will be forcibly assimilated into political units whose prime purpose will be to strengthen military power; and, as has been conclusively shown elsewhere in this volume, preoccupation with military security will leave little room for liberty and culture even of the dominant national, let alone the minority, groups.

Many schemes of a federal nature both for the continent of Europe as a whole and for regions within the continent have been proposed. These have been dealt with in the chapter on Regionalism and Security. If these federal arrangements in the Balkans or elsewhere can be effected, the question will arise whether such divisions as Slovakia, Croatia, Macedonia, Ruthenia, would have a special position in such supranational organization or whether representation would be confined to larger national entities. If the prevailing opinion should decide against such regional groupings it might incline to functional organization, in which case minority representation might be devised. Within the International Labor Organization we have representatives of capital, labor, and government. Is it fanciful to hope that in international organizations devoted to conservation, public works, power development, and intellectual cooperation the minorities could be represented?

If one cannot at present lay down in hard and fast terms a regime for protection of national minorities very different from that of the League, it is because the fundamental pattern of world organization has not yet appeared and because the cataclysmic events in Europe have wrought such devastation that much experimentation will be necessary before even the new framework can be erected, let alone the subordinate arrangements within that framework. Certain policies may, however, be suggested.

Where substantial national groups exist plebiscites might be held to determine the choice of the people and international commissions should be appointed to delimit the boundaries as was done in the case of Upper Silesia following the plebiscite after the last war. Those who wish should have the right to move should the area come under the rule of a nationality not to their liking. Where areas contain extremely mixed populations and neither separation nor mass transfer is practicable a strong case can probably be made for the apppointment of international representatives on the spot to deal with complaints as they arise. Precedent for such action exists. Between 1922 and 1937 impartial representatives resided in both German and Polish Upper Silesia and did excellent work in protecting the interests of the respective minorities. If the minority should be sufficiently large but so located that it cannot be incorporated into the nation which it would like to join, provision should be made for a large measure of autonomy such as was granted to Memel which with its majority of German-speaking citizens was placed under the rule of Lithuania in the period following World War I. Another method is that of direct international control. As this book goes to press we learn that the foreign ministers of the Big Five have agreed to the international administration of Trieste, claimed by both Italy and Jugoslavia.

Larger and more politically self-conscious minorities might be incorporated on terms of equality within multi-national units. The Sudeten Germans tended to resent being classified as a minority in Czechoslovakia; many loyal Sudetens wished to be regarded as partners in the new state and as not a mere minority. What we now know as Jugoslavia first had the name The Kingdom of the Serbs, Croats and Slovenes. Unfortunately, internal differences prevented the formation of a federal or multi-national state and the Slovenes and Croats had to endure the harsh rule of the centralizing-minded Serbian faction.

Students of European affairs, at least those of liberal tendencies, believe that if the problem of general international security can be satisfactorily solved and boundaries lose their military and strategic importance a number of multi-national states or even sub-regions may be formed in which the more powerful and politically conscious "minorities" may become partners while the less numerous and less politically conscious minorities will be satisfied with a large measure of local self-government along the lines, perhaps, of the millet system which existed in Turkey for several centuries. Above all, given international security and an adequate amount of economic collaboration, nationality groups, whether large or small, should enjoy a considerable amount of "cultural decentralization"; they should be able to continue to speak their own languages, observe their own customs, celebrate their national holidays, and recall their national heritage in story and song. The reason is obvious, for whereas the determination of national and regional political, military and economic policies and their effective organization often require expert deliberations which do not necessarily involve every-day discussion on the part of the average citizen, matters of language, dress and other social customs do touch individuals in their daily life. They enter intimately into family and small group experience and, therefore, deeply affect the sentiments of artisan, peasant and middle class alike.

The terrible uprooting of millions of people during the last ten years, while in many ways complicating the problem, may in some measure assist the statesmen and people of Europe to transfer some of the uprooted peoples into more homogeneous areas and thereby lessen the friction which has too often developed among contiguous and intermingled nationality groups. Authorities on minority problems have in earlier years remarked that the transfer of populations involves so much drastic separation of people from places which have had all the associations of home, and so much economic and legal confusion and painful readjustment that it should be resorted to only when all other methods have clearly and unmistakably failed. Perhaps the wholesale redistribution of population in many parts of Europe by Nazi Germany will have rendered this objection somewhat less powerful, but we should not underestimate the terrible price which this surrender to the hysteria of nationalism involves.

Some writers find encouragement in the predominately peasant nature of eastern and southeastern Europe where the minority problems have frequently appeared in an acute form. If an effective international organization can remove the danger of war, and regional or other economic agencies can assist this area by capital investment and the promotion of more efficient farming methods as well as small scale industrialism to raise the economic standards of living, perhaps the natural community of peasant interests will do much to offset the exaggerated political nationalism of the nineteenth and early twentieth centuries. So much will depend upon whether man can cease being hypnotized by the nationality aspects of his life and come to see issues in a broader light that will harmonize the political, economic, and cultural relations of his existence and their interdependence with those of other countries.

The establishment of democracy in these areas within a strong framework of international organization, should help in this direction. Hitherto, monarchies and oligarchies in Hungary, Rumania, Jugoslavia, Greece and Bulgaria have not only discriminated against minorities of other nationalities within their borders but have in no small measure been responsible for inefficiency and corruption within their governments and consequently to some degree at least for the unusually low standard of economic life of the masses. Preoccupation with defense against neighboring nations and against democratic movements within have given the army in association with the oligarchies an unfortunate amount of power. The conclusion seems to be inescapable that effective democratization of society must be achieved for unless the landed aristocracy of Hungary and the dominant group in Rumania, the monarchy in Greece and the reactionaries in Serbia are overthrown, unrest will continue in eastern and southeastern Europe. If the "old gang" is permitted to resume control we may expect to see a continuance of "divide and rule," of setting group against group and of exploiting national, class, and cultural differences. Hence the problem of national minorities cannot be divorced from the major policies adopted by the great powers in Europe, and a peculiar responsibility rests upon the statesmen of Great Britain, the United States, and the Soviet Union to see that the peoples of the smaller countries can enjoy political and economic freedom and not again become pawns in the balance of power system or mere hewers of wood and drawers of water for descendants of feudal and dynastic rulers. Though it is not contended that democratization of Europe will settle the minorities problem, it is clear that without such democratization no solution will be possible.

Finally, if national minorities are to receive sufficient protection international society must claim and obtain a much more explicit right of intervention in what have thus far been largely considered "national" questions. There should be written into the new international charter or covenant or whatever name is given to the document which will embody the rights and obligations of all nations in the post war world (and not a few only as in 1919–20) a clear statement of the principle that whenever so-called domestic issues which have hitherto lain within the sphere of national sovereignty affect the welfare of international society the latter will have the undisputed right to take cognizance of the matter and to take such action as it deems right and proper. Some two hundred leading North Americans including judges, practicing lawyers, professors, government officials, and men of special international experience have proposed that this principle be incorporated in the international law of the future. In a document bearing the title the *International Law of the Future, Postulates, Principles,* they set forth six postulates, ten principles and twenty-three proposals. Principle Two reads:

Each State has a legal duty to see that conditions prevailing within its own territory do not menace international peace and order, and to this end it must treat its own population in a way which will not violate the dictates of humanity and justice or shock the conscience of mankind.

They then make the comment that although international law is principally concerned with relations between states, nevertheless, on frequent occasions the community of states has prescribed standards for a state's protection of aliens within its territory and, as pointed out above, many treaties have made provision for protection of minority groups. Moreover, The Eighth International Conference of American States in 1938 declared that "any persecution on account of racial or religious motives which makes it impossible for a group of human beings to live decently, is contrary to the political and juridical systems of America." In 1937 the Council of the League of Nations declared that attacks had taken place in Spain during the course of the Civil War "in violation of the most elementary dictates of humanity underlying the established rules of international law," and that such attacks were "repugnant to the conscience of the civilized nations." It is, therefore, correct to say that precedent exists for including this principle in the international law of the future to the end that a minimum of justice may be secured to all persons within states and that because such persons will be under the general protection of the community of states no excuse will remain in this connection for any state to intervene on its own authority in the affairs of another state.

LINDEN A. MANDER
SVERRE ARESTAD

CHAPTER VII

# International Protection of Individual Freedom Within the State

DURING the nineteenth and early twentieth centuries the idea of progress made considerable headway. Men believed that history revealed a great movement toward human freedom. Nations were throwing off the tyranny of irresponsible rulers; science and education promised to banish superstition; and trade and commerce to lead to the material welfare of mankind. Political and social institutions seemed to reflect man's increasing emancipation. Serfdom and slavery were disappearing, discrimination on grounds of race, sex, and religion was on the decline and Magna Cartas, Bills of Rights, and National Constitutions in many countries had placed hard-earned human rights in a seemingly impregnable position.

The World War of 1914–18, waged in order "to make the world safe for democracy," led to the freedom of many nations from former imperialist rulers, and the newly constituted governments adopted democratic institutions with special mention of safeguards for individual rights.

Not only in national constitutions but in international relations, the liberal movements appeared to gain ground. During the nineteenth century certain of the great powers intervened in an attempt to prevent Turkey from ill-treating her minorities. The United States protested to Rumania against the latter's ill treatment of Jews. And in one or two instances international agencies were established in the Balkans to ensure that peoples received a minimum of humane treatment. International cooperation took place to prevent slavery and slave trading and to establish better treatment of colonial peoples. After the war of 1914–18 the Minorities Treaties, the International Labor Organization and other agencies, some of which are described elsewhere in this volume, gave evidence of greater preoccupation with the status of welfare of the individual, although he was still regarded primarily as a citizen of the State and not as an individual in his own right.

The advent of the dictatorships caused a serious set-back to democratic movements based upon the philosophy of the worth of the individual. Fascist Italy, Nazi Germany, reactionary Hungary, and other countries overthrew the ideals of freedom, and the world witnessed an outbreak of persecution and destruction of liberal institutions which within a few years had thrown democracy on the defensive. Wilson's fourteen points, which emphasized the rights of nations rather than the rights of the individual (on the assumption "that the nation, if free, would assure personal freedom to its nationals"), did not touch the heart of the problem. Sovereign independence and internal freedom did not always go together: indeed, several of the sovereign nations proved to be not the promoters but rather the enemies of the freedom of their subjects.

Hence a new note has appeared in the recent utterances of statesmen and representatives of important institutions and organizations. On January 1, 1942, the United Nations' representatives spoke of the necessity of preserving human rights and justice "in their own lands as well as in other lands." On March 24, 1944, President Roosevelt stated: "The United Nations are fighting to make a world in which tyranny and aggression cannot exist; a world based upon freedom, equality, and justice; a world in which all persons regardless of race, color, or creed may live in peace, honor and dignity." At Teheran President Roosevelt, Mr. Churchill, and Marshal Stalin declared themselves for a world family of democratic nations, "whose peoples in heart and mind are dedicated, as are our own peoples, to the elimination of tyranny and slavery, oppression and intolerance." The Catholic bishops of the United States in November, 1943, issued an impressive statement concerning the requirements of the new world order; the part dealing with human rights declares:

We hold that if there is to be a genuine and lasting world peace, the International Organization should demand as a condition of membership that every nation guarantee in law and respect in fact the innate rights of men, families and minority groups in their civil and religious life. . . .

Surely our generation should know that tyranny in any nation menaces world peace. A nation which refuses to accord to its own people the full enjoyment of innate human rights cannot be relied upon to cooperate in the international community for the maintenance of a peace which is based upon the recognition of national freedom. Such a nation will pursue its own selfish international policies, while paying lip service to international cooperation. . . .

These extracts illustrate the growing conviction that more is needed than *national* freedom; the individual must count in his own right; he must not be regarded merely as a unit of national society. Nevertheless, the task is one of peculiar difficulty and will demand the most careful consideration if the lofty purposes expressed above are to be transformed into effective realities.

Before analyzing the desirability or possibility of future international action, it may be wise to look at the fate of national bills of rights incorporated within national constitutions of the nineteenth century which were designed to assure equality before the law, the inviolability of the person and dwelling, the need of warrants before arrest, the elimination of *ex post facto* legislation, freedom of the press, of speech, of conscience, and rights of association and public petition. With the growth of new functions of government the national constitutions after 1920 included other rights such as social insurance against accident, old age, and unemployment; regulation of hours of labor; protection of the family; and assistance to the peasant. These new social rights were not easily compatible with the traditional rights of the nineteenth century; the latter implied little or no public interference; the former called for a substantial measure of government control.

The changing emphasis upon rights and duties shows that it is difficult to define in specific terms what are universal and what are relative human rights, those that are negative and those that are positive.

Since rights and duties are in large measure the results of the ideals of the "good life" which communities have, we can hardly expect to formulate in advance a philosophy of or even a complete list of rights which all nations would accept. Take, for example, freedom of trade mentioned in the Atlantic Charter. Obviously a socialist society cannot allow any such freedom to an individual without abandoning its goal of socialism. By contrast, the Atlantic Charter contains no reference to freedom from discrimination on account of color, religion, or sex, probably because its inclusion (especially if "guaranteed" by coercive international authority) would have seriously embarrassed several of the great Allied Powers and even endangered their unity during their common fight against the enemy. It would, therefore, seem difficult, if not impossible, to create an international organization capable of enforcing an international bill of rights. Only when conditions within a country have reached an intolerable degree of injustice or when they threaten to disturb the peace of the world is it likely that these methods will be called into play, at least for some time to come. The chapter of this book dealing with national minorities shows how difficult it was for the League of Nations to do a great deal for these national groups. How much heavier will be the task of internationally protecting individual rights in view of the great difference of social ideals and levels of civilization. Nor does the experience of national attempts in the United States to induce the Southern States to lessen discrimination against Negroes give much ground for optimism.

One is, therefore, inclined to suggest that little progress in safeguarding individual rights will be made if we approach the problem along the lines of abstract moral or legalistic analysis. This does not mean that we should do nothing, for if the victorious democratic nations confess their inability to make effective the freedom of men and women the recent war will appear to be little more than a mockery. It is not a question of denying the possibility of attaining and guaranteeing freedom; it is rather a question of finding the organization and procedure which will best help to achieve our desired ends. We believe that we shall find in the International Labor Organization the pattern upon which the future organization to protect individual rights can be built. The I.L.O. had a charter which set forth its objectives in general terms; it did not approach the problem of labor standards with a theory of capitalism or socialism or the place of government regulation. It began with a number of specific problems, the eight hour day, the employment of women and children in industry, night labor, etc. Year after year in annual session it considered two or three or four items which had been agreed upon by the Governing Body, and the evidence for which had been carefully surveyed by the permanent officials in the International Labor Office. In the course of a generation the Organization passed more than sixty conventions and recommendations; from a consideration of particular problems it was led to an examination of the wider principles and implications of modern economic life, for the profound economic depression which afflicted the world could not be ignored nor could it be dealt with without giving attention to the basic problem of unemployment. Gradually a philosophy of social welfare emerged, a philosophy which was not connected with the particular methods advocated by particular schools of economic thought. Equally significant was the activity of the non-governmental groups whose participation gave vitality to the I.L.O. and afforded a guarantee that those with immediate interests at stake would be on the alert to see that their governments gave consideration to the conventions and recommendations adopted at the conferences.

May we not see in this institution a possible model in the matter of protecting human rights? Without question a general charter should be drawn up which sets forth, as did the Preamble of the I.L.O., the generally accepted rights and duties which international society regards as universally desirable of attainment. Annual conferences should be held, attended by governmental officials and representatives from organizations concerned with civil liberties and minority rights. Within the Secretariat of the United Nations there should be a section devoted to Human Rights which would provide the continuity of administration necessary to carry on the detailed and organizational work which is involved in planning international conferences and in following up the conventions and resolutions there adopted. A Governing Body similar to that of the I.L.O., or an agency like the Permanent Mandate Commission, could insure continuity of policy. The Commission to Study the Organization of Peace writes:

The United Nations Commission on Human Rights would be a quasi-autonomous body of experts—not only jurists but others experienced in public affairs. It would be vested with powers of investigation and advice. Its function would be the continued development of human rights and of measures for their effective safeguard.

The development of standards would result from comparative research, special studies and inquiries, and the deliberations of conferences in the light of changing social conditions, increasing world solidarity, and democratic progress.

This method would not be entirely new in the realm of human rights. In 1928 the Sixth International Conference of American States created the Inter-American Commission of Women for the purpose of gathering information on the position of women in the Americas and preparing resolutions for the Pan American conferences. Since that time substantial progress has been made. Pan American conferences have formulated a declaration of ideals, passed resolutions in conference, and utilized a Commission to prepare information and reports, but they have not attempted to pass direct international legislation enforceable by international police measures. In the light of this experience it seems pertinent to suggest that the United Nations establish a section to deal with the protection of human rights in the proposed Economic and Social Council and that the purposes of the organization be briefly stated in a preamble which should have the same appeal, the same idealistic tone as the Declaration of Independence or the French Declaration of the Rights of Man and Citizens. Such a preliminary declaration of principles was attached to the Charter of the International Labor Office, and was very useful in defining the ideals of the organization. A similar preamble for a section on Human Rights should have a no less valuable function. The organization should have as its agencies an Annual Conference, a Governing Body and/or a Permanent Commission on Human Rights, and a Secretariat or International Office of Human Rights.

The proposed International Office of Human Rights should fully cooperate with the educational agencies of the United Nations and of the member states, for progress in the field of individual freedom will, as we have pointed out above, depend upon persuasion and agreement rather than upon legal coercion. Education and publicity are particularly necessary in the present age of highly developed means of communication in which propaganda plays so important a part in molding public opinion. If democracy is to flourish there cannot be too much discussion of justice and human rights; nor too much dissemination of relevant information whether by school, press, radio, or other organs of popular education. Both the League of Nations and the International Labor Organization failed to appeal to the imagination of the average person in large measure because of the relatively little attention given to propaganda methods for winning widespread public support in all countries. The proposed Office of Human Rights must not commit the same mistake; it must make use of the most effective educational and publicity methods and not be content to become well known among a relatively limited circle.

In conclusion we cannot emphasize too strongly that without an effective system of international security in which military aggression is rendered impossible, the movement for safeguarding human rights by national or international action is doomed to failure. If a renewed armament struggle breaks out, the energies of nations—with the Soviet Union, Great Britain, and the United States setting the pace—will be absorbed, at an accelerated rate, in preparing for increasingly total war on a psychological, economic, and military basis. Governmental power over individuals and groups will have to be increased in order that the nation may be armed to the teeth and that the element of surprise may not again put democracy at a disadvantage; for aggressors will strike quickly in a desperate effort to gain a decisive initial victory.

Free discussion of international affairs and of governmental measures will in such case become increasingly difficult, for each government will hide behind secrecy on the plea that certain information cannot be given to its own people since its publication might be of more value to potential enemies than to its own citizens. Government by discretion will increase, and the rule of law will decline. Criticism of the government will be rendered more difficult because fifth column methods will have roused uneasy suspicions as to whether the critic is loyal or disloyal, whether his purpose is to remedy abuses within the government or to discredit the government in the eyes of its own people.

One of the essences of freedom consists in the exchange of cultural and scientific information, and especially of news, but little interchange of such information will be possible if the fear exists that the exchange of valuable knowledge will be used primarily for military and only incidentally for welfare purposes. Nor will democracy long be able to retain freedom of collective bargaining, the right to strike, the right of free political discussion, even the right to form international associations among religious and scientific bodies if the safety of the state may be threatened even indirectly by such agencies. Those familiar with the devious and ingenious methods of psychological warfare will not underestimate the danger to civil liberty which a renewed outbreak of international rivalry will bring.

One may conclude, therefore, that in order to make nations safe for freedom a system must be devised in which ideas cannot be used so as to form the prelude to military attack as was done in Europe prior to 1939. Liberty of opinion must not carry with it the hazard of external attack. The encouragement of thought must be safeguarded; the perversion of thought to serve sinister ends must be prevented. These purposes can be attained only within a world where international organization has become so effective that ideas can remain instruments of culture and not become weapons of psychological warfare to be followed by the threat or actuality of military force. Freedom and human rights can be maintained only on an international basis; they can no longer be realized within an exclusively independent national state. We can have civil liberties or national sovereignty. We cannot have both.

LINDEN A. MANDER
MELVIN M. RADER

NOTE: The subcommittee which prepared the report which forms the basis of the present chapter comprised Linden A. Mander (Political Science), Harry Cross (Law), Merrill Jensen (History), and Harold Eby (English). The excellent report *International Safeguard of Human Rights* issued by the Commission to Study the Organization of Peace had not come to our notice before our study was completed for the central Universities Committee on Post War International Problems. We are happy that our proposals substantially coincide with those of the Commission.

# CHAPTER VIII

# National and International Aspects of Race

IN THE present war the question of race has come to occupy a prominent place. Reluctantly we have had to face it, not merely in order to increase the solidarity and effectiveness of the home front but also to counteract the effective use of race as a major weapon by our enemy. The conviction which came to Wendell Willkie on his journey through Russia and the East was that we might not win the war, and would certainly be barred from winning the peace, unless we could understand and appreciate the terrific power of the awakening consciousness of racial groups. Dr. Gunnar Myrdal, after a four-year study of one segment of the "race" problem, reached the same conclusion. We could not win the war, he declared, without convincing our colored allies—"who are most of our allies"—that we were not fighting to maintain our advantage over colored peoples. "The deep patience of colored peoples is at an end."

Though few Americans are ready to attach so much importance to the question, the enemy did force an acknowledgment of its vital relationship to victory. After discovering the importance to the war effort of our great pool of negro labor we took unprecedented steps to remove racial friction in order to increase our industrial and agricultural production. Because even the most obtuse among us recognized that Jim Crowism was hardly a help in this situation we took to using unfamiliar words and practices. As one negro leader in the Northwest put it: "We Negroes don't feel quite the same about the war as some of you. We have discovered that only when war comes do you admit that you need us, and needing us, you are ready to grant us the justice you deny us in peace time."

Recognizing that we could not trust to individual good will alone, the government set up a Fair Employment Practice Commission.

Though few powers were granted to the body its creation was at least an official recognition both that racial discrimination was practised in American economic life and that "something should be done about it." We began a movement to lift the many state restrictions upon the suffrage of the Negro. While the results were varied, a Supreme Court decision declared existing restrictions illegal, and the drive against the poll tax though unsuccessful in Congress met with such public support that its leaders have pledged continuance of the fight. In the elections of 1944 Negroes voted in many an area where they had hitherto been easily and persistently barred.

Less dramatic but equally significant efforts have been made in the setting up of inter-racial committees in scores of communities where the whole question of racial discrimination has until now only evoked an uneasy silence or a few mutterings from a handful of citizens. These informal and unofficial attempts have been most successful in the South where greater progress toward racial understanding has been reported than in any previous period. Some real gains have appeared in the extension of educational rights for Negroes. The wide disparity between per capita expenditures for negro and white children remains a tragic acknowledgment of the travesty of race equality, but the gap has been narrowed. This year a number of state universities, such as Missouri, have admitted Negroes for the first time.

We have even talked of eliminating Jim Crowism in the armed services and some gestures have been made in that direction. But each of us can correct by a brief conversation with any negro soldier the widespread idea that here at least racial equality is in a fair way to being achieved.

We have also made a bid for the good will and loyal support of one of our allies by the repeal of the Chinese Exclusion Act. But here, too, the gesture was made only after we had learned how our enemy was exploiting our exclusion of Orientals. A glance through the testimony presented before the Congressional committee reveals our shocked realization that the repeal was necessary for the winning of the war in the Pacific. All other considerations were incidental. A similar gesture to the Philippines followed our return to the islands. No action has been taken as yet, but the arguments are the same: we need the good will of the peoples of the islands and this is one simple yet effective way to get and hold that friendship.

These moves of ours were prompted not merely by a desire to obtain the help of colored groups at home and abroad but also by a belated recognition that Japan in its propaganda for Asia was playing up every real and seeming act of racial intolerance in this country. Race riots such as the one in Detroit were treated as representative of the real attitude of white America. The testimony of the American Legion and other groups opposed to the repeal of the Chinese Exclusion Act had barely been completed before the Congressional committee when transcripts of it began showering down upon the Chinese lines in propaganda leaflets. The wearied Chinese soldiers were told that despite the alleged friendliness of their leader for the Western Powers the American people were willing to permit the Chinese to die for them but not to live near them on terms of equality.

Though evidence from occupied Asia is both meager and conflicting there seems to be common agreement on one point. While the brutalities of the Japanese belied their professions of sympathy for other Asiatics, their propaganda cry "Asia for the Asiatics" had an appeal that few Allied leaders cared to admit. The spate of books appearing shortly after the loss of the Philippines, Malaya, French Indo China and Burma all indicated that but for the single exception of the Philippines the rest of Eastern Asia scarcely lifted a finger in the defense of the white man's empire. There were notable personal exceptions, but the general experience was everywhere the same. Filipino leaders such as Romulo have said quite bluntly that the destruction of Western prestige in Asia was short of being complete only because the United States had treated its colonials as human beings rather than as chattels. Reports filtering out of occupied Asia indicated that the few statements made by allied leaders were too vague and infrequent to serve as an adequate counter-offensive to the persistent and insidious Japanese propaganda; and although the sullen indifference of even open hostility of native populations which helped in the rout of the white man from Asia was later directed against the newer Japanese conquerors, there is no evidence that the resentment against Western imperialism diminished appreciably.

But it is not only in this area of total war that we must admit continuing defeat. Ugly rumors and reports would indicate that our own colored populations have been torn by a new rivalry for their loyalties. Forty years ago we were told that the Negroes in Harlem and in Central Africa had been strangely stirred by the Japanese victories over the white Power, Russia. This was the first reversal in modern times of the monotonous defeats of the colored peoples at the hands of the white. There was no indication that the former understood the causes or the character of that war. A colored race had beaten the white race! That was sufficient to create a stir of a sort which has now become more general and infinitely more menacing to our complacency and our security.

Spengler insisted in the revised edition of his *Decline of the West* that not Germany but the West had lost the war, when the West lost the respect of the colored races. Without that respect the white man's rule was at an end. What would Spengler say now? Much more than a British bastion was lost when Singapore fell to the Japanese. With it went the centuries-old prestige and authority built up by superior power, weapons, strategy, and economy. Though we have defeated Japan we shall not quickly make up or cancel out the effects of our own earlier defeat. Long after we defeated our enemy and imposed our peace upon him, the story of his amazing conquests of the American, British, Dutch, and French Pacific empires in those few tragic weeks of the winter of 1941–42 will remain a legend in hundreds of millions of Asiatic homes.

A glance at the military record is equally embarrassing to the racist. First, to paraphrase freely Churchill's famous phrase, never have so many whites owed so much to so many people of varied races and colors; as one American negro soldier put it, "Simply put on my tomb, 'Here lies a black man killed fighting a yellow man for the protection of a white man.'" Second, we have stripped from ourselves quite deliberately the means by which our dominance over colored races has been made possible in the past: We have been forced to grant to colored peoples access to the technical skills and equipment by which we have both won and sought to justify our supremacy. The colored races have thereupon in a relatively short time demonstrated an ominous facility in the use of our instruments. By grim necessity we have discovered that the most primitive peoples in the Pacific can be taught to understand and handle some of our most intricate equipment, and our colored allies have witnessed and dimly understood the shattering of the long-held assumptions that only the whites could master the highly complicated machinery of modern civilization.

In the face of the dawning but reluctant acknowledgment that race has become a terrible weapon in the hands of our enemies, what has been our own record in terms of defense or counter-offensive? Though there is no one answer and honest citizens will disagree widely, certain judgments can and must be made.

Negro comments on the platforms of the two major parties in the campaign of 1944 indicate how far we are from meeting minimal demands for political and legal equality. The drive for the lifting of the poll tax and a federal law to wipe out lynching foundered on the resistance of southern die-hards and of some Republicans who found too inviting the temptation to play politics with such an issue. Jim Crowism remains an established part of army and navy procedure although some gains have been noted. A young Canadian Negro who joined the American army to see for himself the racial discrimination of which he had heard, but which he had never experienced in his own country, found his evidence in the labor battalion to which he was assigned. Racial discrimination remained in many industries, even in the north, and even in industries producing strategic war materials. Some of that was to be found in union practices. While the F.E.P.C. remained largely an expression of irresolute good will some Americans loudly proclaimed by their strikes against the use of negro labor that they put racial advantage above the opportunity to marshal all our workers in the war effort.

A few months ago a group of negro soldiers in a typical labor battalion in an army camp in the Northwest asked a morale officer quite bluntly why they should fight for the rights of Czechs and Poles when they themselves were denied rights at home. The Negroes put the question courteously yet with a persistence and an understanding of their position that swept aside the attempted reassurances of the young officer. On another occasion negro soldiers from the same post rallied to the defense of a Japanese American who was contesting the legality of certain parts of the evacuation order. The Negroes insisted upon contributing to the payment of the legal fees and collected from their own handful several hundred dollars. This too was their fight, they said—the issue was one of color, and yellow and black were in it together. Well may Gunnar Myrdal insist that "caste is becoming an expensive luxury of white men." It may yet prove little short of suicidal.

Our racial conduct abroad has been even more dubious than at home. We have, it is true, repealed the Chinese Exclusion Act, but the Chinese are not so naive as to interpret the repeal as other than an emergency measure. The bitterness of those who fought against it was more eloquent and revealing than the arguments of those who supported it on grounds of elemental decency and good will. If any of us are still inclined to over-confidence, Lin Yutang's bitter book, *Between Tears and Laughter,* ought to indicate something of the extent of our failure thus far. Whether one regards the book as an expression of petulance or as the matured judgment of a Chinese scholar, it is a grim indictment of our handling of the "race problem." We may deny sturdily and with proper indignation his judgment that "neither in the United States nor in England has any political leader said or done anything to bid for the support of Asia's millions or given them an incentive to better fighting morale," but we shall be hard put to it to find in Churchill's or Roosevelt's speeches anything to refute that claim.

Future historians may give a large place to the re-opening of the Burma Road in their account of our war with Japan. We are beginning to learn of the part played by Japanese-American, American negro and Chinese troops in that epic. We have had similar lessons in Italy and elsewhere. Yet certain communities on the West Coast have attempted permanently to deny the parents of some of those boys the right to come back to their own homes. One small town whose Japanese-American and white sons were supporting each other on the Burma Road and elsewhere, placarded the entire community with signs warning all Japanese away from that area—forever. Certain labor groups, American Legion posts, newspapers, and isolated organizations and individuals joined in the campaign to make the war a race war. We may yet discover how white prejudice prolonged the war in the East, but we shall never know how many American boys we have sacrificed to the exploded racial myth.

But if we have failed to sense the importance of racial justice to the winning of the war we have failed more tragically to see its significance in the winning of the peace. Lin Yutang's statement that "It is white insolence that will ruin any world cooperation," however true or distorted it may be, is ominous for the obvious fact that a considerable part of China's leadership shares his conviction. And when Gunnar

Myrdal writes that "it will be impossible to make and preserve a good peace without having built up the fullest trust and good will among the colored peoples," though he approaches the problem of our role in the peace from a different vantage point, he comes to the same conclusion as Lin Yutang.

There is another consideration much less apparent but no less important. Perhaps the greatest tragedy of the war lies in the exhaustion or paralysis of our will to act. Some of us have learned how much we owe to a Filipino scout, a hillman of India, a Chinese coolie, a Korean guerrilla, an American negro naval hero, the American Japanese sergeant from Seattle who died of his wounds—these and the hundreds of millions of their compatriots! Will we remember the way in which our lives have been identified with theirs, our lives saved by their sacrifice? Will we be ashamed to mouth again the old prejudices, fears and shibboleths, or will we be too tired to stand up against war weariness and sudden revulsion?

The problem of race presents itself persistently in every honest consideration of the winning of the peace. We can note but a few of the specific issues involved. Perhaps the only item on the agenda of the Paris Peace Conference in 1919 on which the Chinese and Japanese delegates could agree was the clause providing for racial equality. The odds were against them. Japan had sacrificed little in the war, and for that little had been amply repaid. In addition, she had other objectives which she was even more anxious to attain. China's part in the war, for different reasons, had not been too impressive. Torn by civil conflict she was in no position to make demands. Today—tomorrow—the situation will be very different. China and Russia will not easily be turned aside from insistence on racial equality as one of the principles upon which the post war world shall be built. A certain Dutch Colonial official understood this fact when he spoke against allowing the Chinese and Russians to aid the Netherlands in the re-conquest of their colonial empire. And Chiang Kai-Shek has told us repeatedly although politely that China has a profound sense of responsibility for the peoples of the Pacific. Nehru, the Indian leader, has even more firmly warned us that the Orient will never tolerate the re-assumption of the white man's control of Asia.

If we seem here to have drifted away from consideration of our domestic race problem, we need only recall the warnings given us by so many of our leaders that the domestic aspect of the race question has had and will continue to have implications for every aspect of our international relations. A studied refusal to be realistic and in-formed about the local situation means that we shall be quite as obdurate when called to make comparable decisions on a world scale. If we cannot and will not build an economic and social system within the United States which more nearly conforms to our professed loyalty to the ideal of democracy with its "liberty and justice for all" we shall be to that extent disqualified for world leadership.

There is thus a close and dangerous connection between the attitude which produces chest-thumping congressional demands for "white supremacy" and that which prompts lusty American cheers for pro-posals that we take over the Pacific Islands—and thereby fall victims to the very imperialism we are asking American boys to destroy. On the other hand, great possibilities for American leadership in the world of tomorrow are open to us if we can but demonstrate a capacity to solve the race problem within the limits of our own social, political and economic order.

Carey McWilliams thus rightly urges that if we Americans would but take this initiative "we might be in a position to assert real world leadership in relation to these same problems after the war. On the other hand, by continuing an ostrich-like-do-nothing policy at home, we are certainly writing another Versailles." And he concludes his argument with the story of the *New York Times* correspondent who was killed in New Guinea and buried at Port Moresby in good company with a negro sailor, an Australian sailor, and a native Papuan infantryman—an incident which led another American re-porter to remark that "he had the firm conviction that all men would one day be brothers, or they would be slaves." "This," adds Mr. McWilliams, "is the lesson which America must learn, for it is not only the color of America that has changed; the color of the world has changed." (*Brothers Under the Skin,* Little, Brown and Company, p. 325)

But America may yet discover that the question is not merely one of leadership but rather one of survival. The racism which has pro-duced increasing tension in this country is not basically different from that which has brought to Germany defeat and universal condemnation. Its incompatibility with internationalism is evident. Its incompatibility with the continued existence of the American state, while it is less apparent, is demonstrable. The premise of racism nullifies the very principle upon which the American commonwealth is based.

FRANK G. WILLISTON
FRANZ H. MICHAEL

## CHAPTER IX

# An Anthropological View of Colonial and Race Questions

### I. COLONIES

In CHAPTER FIVE of this book, which deals with the problems of dependencies, the reader will find a persuasive argument for a more conservative policy in the treatment of subject backward peoples than that which follows. The careful reader will observe, however, that the two arguments are in complete agreement as to ultimate objectives, which are the extending of maximum justice and maximum opportunity to the exploited and retarded darker-skinned citizens of the world in order that they may as soon as possible assume their equal status and make their important potential contribution to the progress of mankind. The difference between the two arguments lies in the degree of confidence of the writers in the prospects of an adequate program for the subject peoples under a continuation of the colonial system and in the capacity of such peoples to make a more rapid progress toward independence and equality than popular opinion has hitherto considered possible. The present writer has, as will be observed, little of the former faith and much of the latter.

In the post-war period we shall doubtless hear much discussion of the relationships between the economically advanced and the economically retarded areas of the world. Over a billion human beings now live in the latter—that is, in areas which, except for China and the Latin American countries, are nominally colonies or dependencies of the wealthiest nations. The consequences are now generally recognized as unhappy and the issue is exigent.

Hundreds of socio-economic systems and cultures in the backward areas of the world have deteriorated rather than been advantaged by contact with the expanding economy of the Caucasians. In general the colonial or imperialist system of the past half century has not substantially improved living conditions for others than members of the native aristocracy. In some areas, as in parts of the Congo and of India, living standards have actually deteriorated during the development of European enterprises and controls, while everywhere the ideological and artistic heritages of the colonials have been in process of decay. It is safe to say, furthermore, that the competitive pursuit of cheap investments, colonial labor, raw material resources, and colonial markets for factory products has been important among the causes of recent international wars, that the colonial-mandate system is an essential factor in the imperialist policies of the last fifty years, and that if colonies, mandates, and dependencies are even partially responsible for conflagrations as destructive as the Second World War, they are luxuries more expensive than we can longer afford.

In this connection it becomes necessary to make note of two recent scientific affirmations each of which disposes of an ancient superstition about the darker-skinned peoples. The first (which will be stated more fully in the second part of this chapter) is that, so far as is known and for all practical social, educational, or political purposes all the peoples of the world are of equal capacity, that the brains, central nervous systems, glands, and physiological characteristics of all peoples are hereditarily so similar as to warrant equalitarian social treatment. The second is that there is no evidence supporting the theory that tropical or humid climates are enervating or impose limitations, under modern conditions of hygiene, to the potential achievement of populations who live in them.

In other words, we cannot suppose with present evidence that either racial or geographic inferiorities of any moment exist. If there still be some geographic handicaps, as for example on small Oceanian atolls, these handicaps do not alone justify a dependent political relationship *in perpetuum*.

How rapidly can the technologic, economic, and social heritages of such peoples develop into patterns of life of a kind to justify political independence and equal partnership in the affairs of the world? This question can be answered if we study the present highly variable patterns of life of the retarded peoples. Only confusion will ensue if we lump together all colonial and dependent peoples and deal with them according to one master plan. These peoples differ markedly in their economic, political, and cultural heritages. A tentative delineation of their socio-economic systems under three major headings will serve as an illustration of the variety of problems to be solved.

### 1. HUNTING-FISHING-GATHERING SOCIETIES, DEMOCRATIC, AND LACKING SURPLUSES

There are many scattered but basically democratic social systems of hunting-fishing-gathering type, numbering only a few hundred thousand persons in various colonial regions such as the Pygmy districts of Central and South Africa, the Andamans, and Philippines. Their food production is unequalled in primitiveness. They have neither surpluses of foods nor production of commodities for market. They have no heritages of trade, use of money, or specialization of labor. Their communities are only tiny bands which live in sparsely populated districts. Strategic production is largely by band committees, and distribution of the products of such work is always potentially by sharing. There are no significant inequalities in wealth or in ownership of the major productive resources, since such resources are community not private property. Within limitations of custom, marriage is by freedom of choice and polygamy is rare. Government is thoroughly democratic— by town-meeting, elected committees, elected functionaries, or respected elders subject to veto or recall by the majority; there are no self-perpetuating headmen or chiefs. The sexes have equal status and participate equally in government. Fighting is infrequent; it is of feud-vendetta character and never for plunder. All the people participate in religion and ceremonial, which feature many individuals, shamans, who possess special supernatural power. All the people participate in complexly developed arts of non-material kind: oral literature, sung music, and dance; plastic and graphic arts are usually meagerly developed.

### 2. SOCIETIES WITH PRIMITIVE AGRICULTURE, HAVING VERY SMALL SURPLUSES AND DEMOCRATIC

A second and larger category is of comparably democratic social systems which are of most primitive agricultural type. They number

in all no more than a few millions of people found spottily in a few
districts in Africa and Asia, and here and there on the smallest, or
in some interior districts of the larger, Oceanian islands. Most of these
systems acquired agriculture in the latest centuries or millennia. With
their present agricultural techniques they can neither produce surpluses nor support larger populations. Their villages are small, rarely
exceeding a thousand persons. There is slight division of labor, with
a very few specialists in crafts such as pottery, weaving, and woodwork.
Since strategic resources, such as agricultural lands or fishing areas,
are the property of the village and are only let out in long term assign-
ments to lineages or individuals, there are no significant inequalities
in wealth or status. The sexes are equal in status. There are few surplus
products and only the most primitive beginnings of commodities and
trade. There are no markets, and no money, except where such
systems are on the verge of envelopment by wealthier social systems
that lie in contiguous districts. Strategic production is by individuals,
lineages, or voluntary work committees, but there is always potential
sharing of strategic products in case of need. Government is of many
kinds but all are essentially democratic, by town meeting, elected committees, respected elders, or functionaries subject to veto or recall by
majority will. There are no self-perpetuating headmen or chiefs.
Marriage, which is by freedom of choice within special patterns of
custom, is rarely polygamous. Fighting is rare, never for plunder, and
largely in self-defense or in pursuit of minor feuds. Elaborate magico-
religious ceremonials are participated in by all, and there are many
religious functionaries who are primarily laymen. Plastic and graphic
arts are often beautifully developed, and all the people participate in
rich heritages of oral literature, sung music, and dance forms.

### 3. AGRICULTURAL AND PASTORAL SOCIETIES, UNDEMOCRATIC AND HAVING LARGE SURPLUSES

The third and by far the largest category includes a tremendous
array of social systems all of undemocratic kinds. The numbers of
people who live within such social systems run into the hundreds of
millions. As soon as possible anthropological research should be con-
ducted with a view to clarifying the main subdivisions of this category.
One obvious subdivision includes the many agricultural-pastoral social
systems of tens of millions of people from Rio de Oro along the Atlantic

Coast of Africa eastwards along the Gulf of Guinea Coast to Abyssinia. A second subdivision includes the vast Congo districts. A third, the East African areas from Somaliland south to beyond the Zambezi. A fourth, the great millet-pastoral populations of the Anglo-Egyptian Sudan. A fifth, the innumerable peoples of Malaysia. A sixth, the varied Melanesian communities. A seventh, the larger islands of Micronesia-Polynesia. Several large subdivisions may well be blocked out for Indian and other areas of southern Asia. Still further significant subdivisions should be noted within each of the above larger groupings.

In spite of their diversity in institutions, these areas display the following generalized features in common: Populations are large, and they vary from tiny villages to cities of considerable dimensions. Specialization of labor is highly developed in many crafts; there are often specialist villages and specialist tribes or castes. Strategic productive resources, in lands, herds, and slave or serf-like lower classes, are the private property of hereditary aristocrats. There are great inequalities in wealth, and often rigid class or caste stratifications. Production allows large surpluses. The specialist groups produce many different commodities, some for direct market sale. The feminine sex everywhere has lowly status, and is purchased in marriage; forms of prostitution sometimes appear; the wealthy are polygamous; human beings tend to be equated with commodities. Government is everywhere the vehicle of aristocracy supported by tribute and tax collectors and by vast land, animal, and human properties, and is defended by arms, more lately by the European empires in control of the area. Religions are vested in more or less wealthy priesthoods. Until European imperial controls were established there was much native warfare fought for plunder, lands, herds, or slaves. Plastic and graphic art work of many kinds and of highest quality is carried on by specialists and often reaches the market place.

In the pre-war years prevailing colonial or mandate administrative policy operated on the premise that none of these peoples could or should rapidly develop levels of technology, economy, and political structure equivalent to our own, that it would inevitably take many generations to effect the change. No exception was made for the several millions whose heritage was relatively democratic, because their economy seemed especially lowly. There is, however, much direct evidence that the native peoples of all backward areas are capable of rapid advance, granted adequate educational and financial assistance and full opportunity to acquire techniques and knowledge.

We now know that non-literate peoples have frequently learned and applied technologically advanced skills within a generation. Numbers of Eskimo youths of both sexes have become experts in communication and flying since 1941. Numbers of Polynesian youths have lately learned radio communication. Fijian Melanesians have learned as much of medicine and nursing as Europeans have chosen to teach them. African natives have advanced to high posts in the French colonial service. Mexican Indians have become as skilled as white Americans in the operation of complex electrical and mine equipment. Native Siberian folk of scores of languages and tribes have become literate and mastered hundreds of advanced technical operations in Soviet war and civilian industries during a decade. The same Siberians have become participants in the elaborate modern machinery of government of the special type developed in the Soviet Union.

In short, popular beliefs in "inherent incapacity," in the insurmountable laziness, ineptitude, clumsiness, stupidity, apathy, indifference or passivity of peoples of backward economies have neither scientific basis nor historical support. Just as millions of housewives in America have in only two or three years mastered a thousand technical skills and taken on many administrative responsibilities, from airplane engineering and draughtsmanship and executive posts of varied kinds down to the simpler skills, jobs from which tradition had so long excluded them, so too the peoples of darker skin, with similar assistance, encouragement, and wage inducements, can be expected rapidly to take their places beside us as producing specialists and executives, as well as unskilled workers, in modern industrialized culture.

In an important sense, therefore, the progress of colonial and other dependent peoples is contingent less upon their capacities than upon their opportunities. The responsibility is upon us. When we give them the chance, the healthy youths of the darker-skinned populations will display as great an avidity for science, technology, culture, democracy as do our own. Some anthropologists might be found to favor the theory that Oceanian and African natives display more eagerness for knowledge, if not for democratic patterns of living, than do our own people.

There is then no incapacity of subject peoples to prevent the abandonment of the old colonial and mandate systems or their early replacement by a more efficient, more democratic system—and one which, incidentally, will be more profitable to us because it will raise the levels of the backward peoples and increase their ability to purchase our products. Neither economic advantage nor political expediency will be served by any long continuation of the old imperial colonial-mandate system. Any practical program for the dependent peoples in the postwar years must be based upon guarantees of a democratic and peaceful world, a world in which the benefits of industry, both in its products and in its operations, can be extended to hundreds of millions of those who until now have been its victims rather than its beneficiaries. There will of course be many and strong pressures to maintain the prewar status in these respects; but if yielded to they can lead only to unnecessary limitations of trade, intensified imperialistic rivalries, greater social and cultural deterioration of the many now subject peoples, and a resumption of international war in the not distant future.

It is the opinion of the writer that a democratic international organization is, on the contrary, the only agency which could now assume administration, in any just and profitable way, of the world's present colonial or dependent areas. Only such an administration could be sufficiently freed from the pressures of imperialistic economic rivalries to guarantee a continuation and extension of economic enterprise in the retarded localities, the raising of their material conditions of living by the return of a just share of the rewards of industry to all who participate in it, and the development of democratic ideology and institutions among the native peoples. The international organization should furthermore determine as soon as possible, as did the United States for the Philippines, the approximate dates when areas of dependent status, which are advancing in economic level and democratic procedures, shall attain a dominion-like status, under a program which shall aim at their ultimately achieving equal partnership in the world order itself.

There are, of course, strong political and economic forces opposed to the dissolution or even the effective modification of the British, French, Belgian, Dutch, or Portuguese empires. This writer believes that the realistic way to deal with this opposition is to demonstrate that a reform of the imperial system promises both immediate and long range economic gains for all concerned. As soon as the leaders of empire recognize that the internationalization of dependent areas is good for business the old imperialistic system can be expected to fade out to the tune of nothing worse than a diminishing chorus of romantic regrets.

The essential point to keep in mind is that progress toward democracy, toward higher standards of living, and toward local independence in the economically backward parts of the world can best be served by joint international action to enhance the purchasing power of the native peoples. International loans of the type envisaged at the Bretton Woods Conference are a necessary beginning. If international action, safeguarding the interests of the producing people in native areas, at the same time shows that it serves the interests of those investors who have legitimate enterprises there—as it surely can—then the imperial powers will have no incentive to retain a unilateral military dominance over the existing dependencies. The colonial can thus make way for a more profitable as well as an infinitely more humane system.

A formidable part of the task before us is that of education; for surely the need of developing cooperation in the entire field of human relationships is as much a challenge to education as to any other of our institutions. The history of imperialism, the study of the cultures and potentialities of the world's darker-skinned and economically still backward populations—these and kindred subjects must come to be stressed by political science, sociology, and anthropology, and be expanded and intensified in their service to human needs. The revamping of narrowly technical subjects into subjects of broad educational and humanitarian value is a major problem for the social sciences, as it is for both formal and extra-school education in general, during the post-war years. If education, framed thus broadly, does its job, we can trust the peoples who constitute the great powers to prevent their governments from continuing to plunge into suicidal imperialist ventures. We shall be safe if people learn what racism means to our generation. We shall be safe if people acquire knowledge of and sympathy and respect for the hundreds of millions whose technological level, by one or another quirk of fate, is still beneath our own. Such are the popular bases of democratic action.

We have no choice other than to forge some sort of democratic international system which will raise the buying power, the standards of living, and the cultural level of the world's areas of retarded economy, which will develop many new, modernized, and democratic nations where only "backward peoples" have been before. And the supposition that such a change need take many generations is dangerous. Everything that we know of the plasticity of human beings, of their still but slightly explored potentialities, of their eagerness to improve themselves flies in the face of such counsels of despair. The responsibility is upon us to do what all our sciences, all our social theory, all our historical knowledge indicate as not only possible but necessary for the prevention of accumulating disaster.

Whatever opinions there may be concerning the administrative authorities who should govern dependent territories, there can be no question but that much more is required of anthropological skill and training in the day-to-day government of native peoples. Although in recent years advances have been made in certain parts of the South Pacific and of Africa, nevertheless applied anthropology has not yet played the role which it must play if the so-called advanced peoples are to rectify the errors of the past and truly assist the dependent peoples to become self-governing.

Trained anthropologists are necessary to enable alien governments to win the cooperation of the inhabitants; for these experts who know native life and custom can advise officials in many ways which will avoid foolish and tactless action. The anthropologist, who has lived with these people and knows their language, their customs, their background, their way of life, will, particularly if he is not identified with a government, gain the confidence of the tribal groups and thereby facilitate the application of sound policies. He can become the spokesman for people who have grievances. He can estimate the consequences of a proposed step in the light of the old traditions and the impact of new forces, and he can prevent undue disorganization which has so often accompanied the impact of Western civilization upon other cultures.

In the realm of public health, for example, the anthropologist can render great service in assisting the study of causes of de-population and the many factors which have affected the birth and death rates—factors which go beyond those of diet and the purely biological aspects. As Felix Keesing, in *The Science of Man in the World Crisis*

(Columbia University Press, 1945), points out: In addition to the medical ideas and practices of dependent peoples, their beliefs and customs, bound up with religious fundamentals of their culture, play an important part; and in the sphere of myth and magic, ritual and sorcery, the anthropologist alone can be trusted to "move with certainty." Moreover, the anthropologist can assist in introducing new crops, new work habits, adjustment of land titles, and in estimating the importance of work patterns as economies are changed. He can advise on the wise limits of direct and indirect rule, pointing out where chieftains may be using their power in an undesirable way. His advice will be necessary in helping to smooth over the serious strains which accompany the changing customs in tribal societies and bring undue difficulty in the normal problems of understanding between generations, the problem of "fathers and sons" of which Turgenev wrote many years ago. Especially may the anthropologist be of service to the missionaries, many of whom in the past, and perhaps in the present, have underestimated the good in native religions and have unduly disrupted the working faith of the natives. And, of course, on such questions as fundamental purposes of native education, how far it should be severely practical, how far secondary and advanced instruction should be given, the relation of native dialects to European languages and their respective uses, the advice of anthropologists is required.

The element of timing is important. Many principles, sound in themselves, may not work out because of the lack of skill in knowing just when and at what points reforms should be introduced. Above all, if we are to deal justly with native peoples, to whom the white race has brought so much suffering and even misery, we must be prepared to spend much more money in colonial administration, either under a mandate system or a trustee system or under direct international administration. This should not be impossible, for if we achieve a world order, part of the many billions that will be saved as a result of the reduction of armaments may be applied to the task of assisting native peoples to attain their fullest status and realize their best destiny.

## II. RACE

Professors Williston and Michael, in the preceding chapter entitled "National and International Aspects of Race," have effectively stressed some of the immediate social and political consequences of racial discrimination. The following, supplementing their conclusions from an anthropologist's point of view, will be based upon the present major scientific postulates on the subject of race and race differences. The most important of these postulates—insofar as they affect our judgments regarding minority problems—are as follows:

Racial purity is a myth. There is not now, and there is no available evidence that there ever was, a pure race within the larger human group. All the major geographical populations of human beings of today are themselves blends or amalgams of earlier geographical populations, which in their turn were doubtless also mixtures. The anatomical features of these earlier geographical populations are hardly if at all known; nor can the percentage components from earlier populations, which have blended to make up the modern, now be ascertained. Thus all modern geographical populations of human beings—popularly termed races—constitute mixtures whose components cannot be estimated or described. For hundreds of thousands of years all the human populations have been in constant process of intermingling, largely as a consequence of community to community intermarriage, and the process has accelerated with advances in technology, and in intercommunication during the latest millennia. There has never for any long time been a pure, inbred, or isolated community, and there has never been a pure geographical population or race.

The most distinctive geographical populations—more often and popularly termed races—today are Caucasoids, Mongoloids, Negroids (Africa only), Congo Pygmies, Bushmen-Hottentots, Eastern Pygmies, Melanesians (they are not Negroes), Australoids, Ainus, Micronesians-Polynesians. The first three named appear to be in many subdivisions, but scientists do not find it possible to agree as to these. Only the Mongoloids are readily and rather clearly subdivisible into East Asiatic Mongoloids, northeast Siberians, Eskimos and Amerindians, and Indonesians or Malaysians. There are scores of other more or less distinguishable populations, most of which amount to blends of very recent formation—for example, the American Negro or various populations of India.

No scientific proof of sufficiently exacting kind has even been given to justify the setting up of a supposed Nordic or Aryan race, or an Alpine race, or a Mediterranean race. Patently there never were, and there are not now, a German race, English race, French race, Italian race, Slavic race, Philippine race, Japanese race, and the like. These are national or linguistic groups, not populations so distinguishable in hereditary features that the term race can properly be ascribed to them.

Jewish people are anatomically identical with those populations (in Europe, Africa, and Asia) among whom they have long been resident. There never was and there is not now a Jewish race. The Jews are overwhelmingly the descendants of converted or proselytized residents of the countries, mostly European and Mediterranean, where they now are, plus minor admixtures from various other countries. The Jews comprise, in short, only special kinds of socio-religious communities that treasure a common ideological and religious heritage. Jewish behavior, where there is a distinctive pattern, of response, is a special type of minority behavior, not hereditarily or racially determined. It is analogous to the special response patterns or behavior of any minority, tribal, regional, class, or national population, and these patterns of behavior are, by the general if not unanimous agreement of anthropologists, determined by socio-historical rather than biological causes.

Granting this postulate, we must judge all populations—though not all individuals—equal in biologic heredity: brains, central nervous systems, glands, or hereditary determinants of mentality, character, and temperament. There can be no master race, because there are no known hereditarily determined superiorities or inferiorities between modern populations. As far as we know, all populations, including those of dark skins and pygmy stature, have the same potentialities for creativity as have any others. In the light of present knowledge most scientists will insist upon an equalitarian position, for any immediate purposes in the post-war years, regarding the potentialities of all populations or races.

Because there is no evidence, let alone proof, of any instinctive basis for antisemitic or other such notions, we must suppose that reactions or feelings of a racist kind, such as enmities or discomforts in the presence of dark-skinned persons, are learned, taught, acquired. Until tutored, youngsters and adults entirely lack such responses or feelings. Racism itself has developed its characteristic features only since the time of Columbus. It interconnects principally and orginally with the rationalizations that developed to justify the use of purchased African slaves who were employed to open up the Americas. Its twentieth century variety, a heritage remaining from an older racism, was further developed as the deliberately forged weapon of a Fascist minority which has sought to divide the democratic majority by developing irreconcilable splits within it.

A continuation of racist maltreatment, humiliations, and discriminations in the United States can only contribute to the early development of an American brand of Fascism and a third World War. A continuation in America of antisemitism alone will have the same consequences.

In the United States an ideology and practice of racism directed against the Negroes carries with it analogous animosities to other American minorities such as Jews, Puerto Ricans, Mexicans, and Orientals. Similarly, an ideology and practice of racism directed against the American Jews means retention of American racism directed against Negroes and other minorities, including other religious groups. As a social process, racism is indivisible, for if it is directed against any one minority within a nation others already affected will continue to suffer. In other words, all American minorities now subjected to racist accusations and discriminations share a common agony, of varying degrees of intensity. Such minorities need to associate themselves one with another, as well as with other anti-racists, in a common drive that will finally eradicate racism from our life.

Nothing is more tragic than the spectacle of Jews who discriminate against Negroes or of Negroes who express antisemitism. Such internecine animosities, which are nothing short of suicidal from the point of view of these two minorities or of any democratic Americans, serve only the ends of Fascism.

A continuation of racism in the United States, even if directed against only the partially African ten per cent of America's citizens, promises the ultimate crystallization of an armed alliance of most or all of the darker-skinned peoples of the world against us. Whatever we become politically, our American economic system will participate in the post-war years in the modernization and industrialization of many of the areas of darker-skinned populations who at the present moment are economically backward. And when hundreds of millions of darker-skinned peoples of Asia, Oceania, Latin America and Africa achieve economic power they may well unite to destroy us if we continue to insist that we are a master race. Apart from any matter of justice, the need to oppose Fascistic trends in the next generation requires us to accept the equalitarian principle in dealing with minorities.

In order to render democratic progress possible, democratic organizations and the organizations of the minority groups themselves must publicize the danger in this connection of the propaganda for "States' rights"; no state or group of states should be permitted the dubious enjoyment of discriminatory practices which can only serve to imperil the safety, the security, and the democratic institutions of the rest of America. And we must train the existing personnel of the teaching profession in the scientific evidence on race and race differences and in the history of the treatment of minorities. This training should reach teachers all the way from the elementary to the adult education levels.

In the field of legislation we shall find the situation putting responsibilities upon legislative agencies ranging all the way from those of small communities, such as counties and municipalities, through state legislatures to the national Congress. For the latter, we find that two things at least are already on the order of the day. One is the need to make permanent and to grant sufficient funds and power to a Federal Fair Employment Practices Commission. Discrimination against the employment of members of minority groups must be eradicated from enterprises that render any broad service, or that produce for a large market.

And, to return to education for a moment, a second main objective for federal legislation is the assistance of counties, municipalities and states in providing adequate education for all and in outlawing discriminatory practices, such as racial or religious quotas, in schools or colleges of non-denominational type. Educational organizations have long advocated federal aid to education in backward districts. The Negro people will benefit especially from increases in funds for the education of their younger generation. Still other federal legislation is needed to eradicate Jim Crowism in public places and vehicles and to eliminate the Poll Tax as a voting qualification. Other and valuable work in this general cause can be carried out by people and organizations that until now have done relatively little: churches, service clubs, women's clubs, P.T.A.'s. The Kiwanis Clubs, the Lions, the Rotary

Clubs, the Junior Chamber of Commerce, are composed largely of small business people and professionals who want to get along with their neighbors. Mayors' and Governors' Committees on Race Relations— Civic Unity Committees, or Committees on Minorities—can often be set up, composed of leading representatives of industry, government, labor, education, the churches, and of minority elements in the population.

Already there are signs of progress in democratic directions in other parts of the world. The experiences of years of Fascism and war in Europe, and the remarkable unity of formerly antagonistic groups forged in the European undergrounds that operated under Fascist domination, promise improvement in the treatment of minorities on the European continent. Sane Europeans have learned from the horrors of the past eleven years that maltreatment of minorities returns no profitable dividends. Segregation and discrimination never pay. They return only terror, insanity, and death. The hypocritical treatment of the Jewish minority in the Near East, the wretched mishandling of Croat and Slovene minorities in Jugoslavia, must make way for a democratic living-together comparable to that long witnessed in Switzerland. Such developments toward democracy in Europe can in their turn exert an influence upon the ideology of Americans, and in one or another way assist in the equalization of opportunities for those so long discriminated against within the United States.

MELVILLE JACOBS

PART THREE: Economic and Social Welfare

# CHAPTER X

## *The Economics of Peace*

THE minimum economic goal of a peaceful world is a world in which everyone who is able and willing to work can find work that will enable him to earn enough to feed, clothe, and house his family at a level of health and decency. Such a goal has been almost within the grasp of mankind ever since the industrial revolution unleashed the economic power to overcome poverty. Simple as this objective seems, it has never yet been achieved universally, nor in any particular nation, for any extensive period. Many factors have contributed to this failure, but the greatest, perhaps, has been ill-advised interference by both government and business with economic activity.

Since the rise of independent states during the eighteenth and nineteenth centuries there has been a tendency toward self-containment and self-aggrandizement based upon a false sense of national welfare. Populations of the world have grouped themselves together for ethnical, linguistic, or geographic reasons or because of historical accidents. No corresponding grouping of the natural resources of the world has been found. Actually, nature has distributed soil, climate, waterways, minerals, forests and all of the items upon which economic well-being is based, with no respect for the makers of national boundaries. No nation has ever been self-sufficient in economic resources. Even such well-endowed states as the United States and Russia must look abroad for many essential raw materials and finished products. On the other hand, very few nations are wholly devoid of economic wealth. Each nation has its specialties which it has been able to develop because of the particular combination of natural resources, climate, and skills which it enjoys. Thus, we naturally link Brazil and coffee, Bolivia and tin, Germany and chemicals or optical instruments, England and woolens, the United States and automobiles.

Restrictions imposed during the early flush of national consciousness, following the industrial revolution, gave way to an era of less government interference with economic activities. Freer trade became the fashion following the doctrines of Adam Smith. It was recognized that each nation stood to gain in wealth and well-being in proportion as it specialized in doing what it could do best and in trading its specialties for those of other nations. Great Britain, for example, found that she could get more cloth and wheat, not by trying to produce both, but by making cloth and trading cloth for wheat. Trade, freed from unsound restrictions, such as tariffs imposed by governments, contributed to the end that each nation became more prosperous in proportion as it specialized and exchanged its goods for those of other nations.

World War I marked the end of an era and ushered in a reversal of the trend toward relative freedom in economic development and intercourse. Following the conflict, the imperfect political machinery for peace left the door open for a further political force working against economic progress, the fear of war. Responding to the rising tide of democratic liberalism as expressed in the philosophy of self-determination, the Versailles Treaty had re-drafted the map of Europe, making many small nations where a few larger ones had lived before. Almost from the first, these countries exercised their newborn sovereignty to build trade barriers and reshape their economic structures on restrictive lines.

The upsurge of nationalism, coupled with the absence of security from aggression, which all too soon became apparent with the failure of the United States to join the League of Nations and of other leading nations to support it, bred fear of war among the small states of Europe. The old German military aggression, moreover, had only been halted, not destroyed. It soon became clear to the small states of Central Europe that another world war was brewing. Thus, the will to war in Germany and Italy and the fear of war in their neighbors stimulated the attempt at economic self-sufficiency where self-sufficiency was economically impossible. Frenzied effort to build up industries, to encourage agriculture, and to reconstruct national economies along lines that would permit aggression at the earliest chance, or provide some measure of protection against aggression became the order of the day in Europe. Nor was the lesson lost on Japan, which also began preparation for fulfilling its own dream of empire.

Meanwhile, in the United States and Great Britain pressures were brought to bear to alter the course of economic freedom. Self-interested groups, such as the farm bloc in the United States, combined with other politically-minded minorities, like the Western silver bloc, to procure the enactment of unsound economic legislation. The Congress fixed prices above the world levels and voted subsidies to enable cotton farmers, for example, to continue to produce high-cost cotton. It passed tariff measures which raised the barriers to imports, forcing other nations to retaliate. Great Britain, abandoning her time-tried policy of free trade, put up tariff barriers and entered into Empire preferential arrangements with other members of the British Commonwealth. The traditional gold standard tottered and fell, leaving in its wake a wave of currency depreciation, barter agreements, exchange controls, blocked exchanges, and general chaos in international payments.

Other developments during the interval between wars also threatened economic freedom. Business itself, often aided by government participation or acquiescence, established or strengthened commodity control schemes and international cartels and subjected such essential materials as rubber, tin, chemicals, and steel to strict regulation of both production and distribution, largely in the interest of producers. Wherever the effect of such monopolistic practice was to limit output and maintain prices at higher levels than would ensue from freely competitive enterprise, economic progress was halted. Such practices are open to the same condemnation as restrictive tariffs.

Not only were there international cartels and control devices, but within such industrial nations as the United States, Great Britain, France, and Germany, there was a tendency toward larger concentrations of economic control in the form of great corporations and corporate enterprises, which, even where not strictly monopolies in the narrow sense of the word, acted like monopolies by exercising control to maintain prices and limit output to what could be sold at the fixed prices. Thus, economic freedom was becoming more and more limited by both political and economic developments.

It is frequently said, "If we could only start with a clean slate, how much better we could do." Now that the war is won, the nations of the world will have a unique opportunity to rebuild the economic framework on a pattern for permanent peace. The dislocation, relocation, and destruction of industrial plants; the shifts of populations; the disruption of normal banking and financial machinery; the forced changes in ownership of business properties, amounting often to thinly disguised brigandage, mean that most, if not all, of Europe's economic structure must be rebuilt. Opportunity will exist for reconstruction on a new and better basis if ancient prejudices and deep-seated fears can be overcome. Likewise, in the East, Japan and other industrialized areas, many of which were only getting started when the war broke, may be able to use war's devastation as an opportunity for reconstruction on a solid basis of specialization for peace. In the United States, Great Britain, and Russia the entire economic structure has been converted from peace to war production. Many industries have been closed down completely and replaced by new plants and equipment; labor has been retrained for new types of work. In short, no less than an industrial revolution world-wide in scope has altered the world's economic life.

Thus, we do have, to a considerable extent, a clean slate on which to draw a new pattern of a world economy of peace. Admitting the over-simplification of such an assumption, and realizing the limitations on free action that will persist, we may, nevertheless, find it worth-while to explore some of the possibilities for economic reorganization which definitely exist now that victory is achieved.

First of all, it is a challenging fact that any effective economic system which emerges after the war must be the result of conscious deliberation—of planning. Recently it has been aptly pointed out by several authorities that the choice which we face is not between planning and an aimless *laissez faire,* but between sound and unsound economic planning.

Planning must be of two sorts, one for the immediate period of transition from war to peace, and another for the ensuing era of peace. Immediate plans must now be executed, with the cessation of hostilities, to find employment, food, clothing, shelter, the bare necessities of life for liberated peoples. Such temporary, piecemeal, but essential planning, unless handled with extreme caution, may well plant the seeds of ultimate economic restriction, leading to poverty in place of plenty. For example, the speedy re-establishment of French agriculture, which the liberation of France makes indispensable, to give employment and food to the people of France, is fraught with danger. During the years between the wars, France encouraged the production of wheat to the point of giving it twenty-five per cent of the arable land. Yet France was a high-cost wheat producer which, without subsidy or tariff protection, could not possibly compete with the great wheat-exporting nations. France had thus penalized herself in a misguided effort to purchase self-sufficiency should war come. The same story can be told of Italy. The question then becomes, should these countries return to the production of high-cost wheat in a world in which Argentina, Canada, Australia, the United States, and possibly Russia must deal with the problem of surplus, low-cost wheat producing capacity? The immediate answer may be yes, for the transition emergency; but the permanent policy must look to more intensive crops better suited to the soil and climate of France and Italy.

A relatively simple example, wheat serves to point up the tremendously complex problems which the victors of this war must solve in reconstructing the economy of the world on a sound basis. Left to themselves, industrialists, farmers, and businessmen could only work out these problems slowly and painfully, if at all. Removal of tariffs, subsidies, and other artificial obstacles to economic freedom would help, but even so it would take time to reorganize the world's economies on a sound foundation with each nation specializing on what it can do best. The process would be fraught with hardship and great suffering. Literally thousands of commodities and industries must be studied to determine those best adapted to particular regions or states, and industries started by accident or by vested interests which seek profit at the expense of efficient production and general welfare must be eliminated.

Government must therefore extend its activities in the economic sphere to a degree that goes beyond the popular concept of *laissez faire*. But traditionally there has existed much confusion over the extent of government control desirable in business and economic affairs, and Adam Smith himself listed a large number of responsibilities of government as quite within the scope of *laissez faire* and, indeed, essential to the successful operation of a "free" economy in the interests of all of the people. What we here propose is merely an extension of the "rules of the game," whereby the government will define more sharply the fouls, offside plays, and blows below the belt. Within the limits of revised rules, business and economic interests should be permitted the utmost freedom of action. The rules would merely prohibit monopolistic practices, cartels, subsidies, and tariffs, and encourage instead specialization in the production of those items in which each nation can compete most effectively without artificial subventions.

From the standpoint of world peace, an argument can be made that the more completely each nation is dependent on other nations for strategic materials, necessities, and luxuries, the less danger there is of any nation starting aggressive warfare. Would-be aggressors might find it difficult to arouse enough enthusiasm for war if the people knew that they were not self-sufficient. Economic specialization and international cooperation should be organized to deter political pressure groups from establishing this or that industry because it may contribute to national defense or be useful in time of war. There is but one choice for thoughtful, peace-loving people and that is to strive, however difficult the task, to destroy the economic, along with the political, causes of war.

Hope lies in the fact that progress has been made in the international handling of certain problems in the past. To mention a few successful examples, one recalls the International Postal Union, agreements on the allocation of wave lengths for radio broadcasting, the Canadian-American fisheries pacts, the control of opium and traffic in drugs, and cooperation in the fields of agriculture and labor.

The League of Nations accomplished a great deal in the direction of better understanding of international economic problems through the researches and publications of its staff; but a fundamental weakness of the League lay in the failure of its framers to think in economic terms. Primarily a political structure, the League included no provision for dealing with economic problems at the policy level. Had there been a strong Economic Council, coordinate in authority with the political divisions of the League, the policy of applying economic sanctions against Japan in 1931, for example, might have had more serious consideration. The first step toward the aggression which culminated in World War II might thus have been averted.

Looking backward on failure is pointless unless it helps prevent the repetition of blunders. Fortunately, there is some evidence that we are beginning to profit by our errors. A number of encouraging developments may be cited.

In the first place, a brief but sound guide to future economic action appears in the Atlantic Charter, the fourth article of which states:

They [the United States and Great Britain] will endeavor, with due respect for their existing obligations, to further the enjoyment by all States, great or small, victor or vanquished, of access on equal terms, to trade and to the raw materials of the world which are needed for their economic prosperity.

Later accepted by all of the United Nations, this statement of policy is a decided step forward, though it is to be hoped that such "existing obligations" as Empire preference, high United States tariffs, pressure bloc legislation, and encouragement of cartels will not prove too binding. It is essential also that the "equal terms" of access to markets and raw materials shall in practice become liberal and moderate terms rather than terms equally obstructive to economic expansion.

The fifth article of the Atlantic Charter is also a heartening statement of policy, expressing as it does the

desire to bring about the fullest collaboration between all nations in the economic field with the object of securing, for all, improved labor standards, economic advancements, and social security.

These principles, formulated and agreed upon by the Prime Minister of Great Britain and the President of the United States, were reiterated and strengthened in the Master Lend-Lease Agreement of 1942; and tucked away towards the end of the 1944 Dumbarton Oaks Charter for a general international organization of the United Nations is Chapter IX, "Arrangements for International Economic and Social Cooperation." Appearing almost as an afterthought, the latter may offer, nevertheless, greater hope for the peace of the world than all of the other provisions combined.

Indeed at the San Francisco Conference the delegates conferred extensive powers upon the Economic and Social Council, which is to consist of representatives of eighteen members of the Organization. The states to be represented for this purpose are to be elected by the General Assembly for terms of three years. Each such state is to have one representative who shall have one vote. Decisions of the Economic and Social Council shall be taken by simple majority vote of those present and voting. Through this machinery, which is to be integrated with the "various specialized economic, social and other organizations and agencies," presumably such as the International Labor Office and the monetary, banking and financial agencies, the "solution of international economic, social and other humanitarian

problems" is to be sought. Within the framework of this new approach
to the world's economic problems, sound solutions can surely be discovered. But the will to succeed, coupled with the necessary intelligence
and energy, must first be assured by each and every member of the
United Nations.

Traditionally, though the domestic economic policy of the United
States Government has been *laissez faire,* its attitude toward international trade has been highly restrictive. Preoccupied with the vast
task of settling and developing a continent, the American people tended,
after the nation had become firmly established as a world power, to
turn their backs to the old world and concentrate on building a strong
domestic economy.

The earliest American international economic policy was a continuation of the free trade attitude of colonial days, the economic
expression of that abhorrence of interference which had been a contributing cause to the American Revolution. A more restrictive attitude
emerged soon after the Revolution, however, and the first tariff act,
passed in 1789, paved the way for future emphasis on the principle of
protection of domestic manufacturers. Though there is perhaps some
justification for such a policy in the argument that manufacturing
could not even get started without protection of "infant industries,"
the whole theory is of doubtful validity and was greatly overworked
in any event. It remained, however, for Alexander Hamilton's "Report
on Manufactures," made to the Congress in December, 1791, to set
American tariff policy definitely on the road to the restriction of
imports for the protection of "infant industries." A rising tide of
restrictions on imports followed until the "tariff of abominations" was
passed in 1828. A reaction followed, which reversed the trend for a
few years, and a revised policy of "tariff for revenue" lowered duties
substantially. By 1861, however, the business interests which profited
by high tariffs had regained control, and protection once more dominated our commercial policy and continued to do so until 1913. The
Underwood Act of that year brought the first relief for over half a
century, relief, however, which was short-lived. World War I and
the subsequent change in administration brought back a high tariff
policy which culminated in the second tariff of abominations, passed
over the protest of American economists in 1930.

Since 1933, the culmination of years of liberal thinking has resulted in a flood of long-delayed legislation which has altered substantially the policy trend both on domestic and on international economic problems. Coincidentally with the most severe depression in our history at home, and a rising tide of autocracy and totalitarianism abroad generated in part, at least, by the world-wide effects of the collapse of the American economy, the New Deal was faced by a combination of problems that defied sound and speedy solution. Improvisation of varied policies, often conflicting or contradictory, and reflecting the total absence of clear and integrated economic thinking among American leaders whether of business, of government, of labor, or of agriculture was the result. One proposal followed another in the hectic effort to regain economic stability and eliminate unemployment. Business was given its head in the ill-fated National Recovery Administration, which dominated the central stage of the multiple-ring circus which was Washington after 1933, until the Supreme Court ended its efforts in the Schechter decision in 1935.

More serious because of its repercussion on foreign policy was the effort to bolster agriculture by applying a straitjacket of restriction on production coupled with artificial price stimulation and government purchase of surpluses. The basic difficulty with agriculture was excess capacity stimulated by World War I and aggravated by curtailment of markets at home and abroad. Home markets were hit by the depression while world markets had been shattered by blundering and misguided policies of governments following World War I. First was the high tariff policy of the postwar years, which made it impossible for impoverished nations to buy our cotton, wheat, meat, and other farm products; second, the ill-advised efforts to raise prices for United States' farm products above world market levels, which drove other peoples to plant cotton and other crops instead of buying from the United States; and third, the growth of national self-sufficiency by would-be aggressors and those who feared aggression, which circumscribed foreign markets. A more realistic farm aid program would have had two planks; first, active international cooperation, through membership in the League of Nations, and second, drastic reversal of high tariff policy. In other words, the United States failed to refrain from aggressive economic warfare.

Though the Secretary of State did, indeed, launch his excellent reciprocal trade policy, it was "too little and too late" to save either the nation or the world from war. Had the New Deal launched a bold and forthright program of world cooperation and in 1933 asked for Senate approval of adherence to the League as a road to recovery, great progress toward sound foreign policy might have been made. A low tariff policy might even have been extracted from a jittery Congress which, though it passed a multitude of drastic ill-planned laws, did not really know which way to turn.

However, harassed as the nation was by the utter collapse of business, banks, trade, and commerce, domestic problems were so insistent that longer-range foreign policies were neglected until too late. Nor should we assume that a reversal of restrictive high tariff policy of over half a century could actually have been easily won. Partisan opposition to the rather mild Reciprocal Trade Agreement Program of 1934, which still continues, cannot be ignored. Men cling tightly to economic prejudices and formulas, often to their own undoing.

Two facts commend the reciprocal tariff. First, it substitutes careful scientific analysis for the outmoded system of political "log-rolling" which had degenerated into a vote-trading orgy among congressmen with ever-rising tariffs and with the rights of the American consuming public ignored. Under the reciprocal trade agreement plan, a competent staff of experts, drawn from several government departments, makes a thorough study of the facts about each commodity, holds hearings at which all interested citizens can present their views, and finally arrives at a decision based on the best interests of all of the American people rather than on those of some minority pressure group.

The second fact which commends the Hull program is that it spreads the benefits of its reduced tariffs and its removal of other obstacles to trade to a large number of countries. For example, when the United States completes a trade agreement with Canada, what is called "most favored nation" treatment is required. This means that every nation dealing with the United States receives the benefits of the same low rates granted to Canada. While the United States has no authority over other nations, it has urged the desirability of their also extending "most favored nation" treatment to others. Thus, as nation after nation has signed agreements with the United States (thirty agreements have been completed) the benefits have spread over wider and wider areas. Unfortunately, the outbreak of World War II hampered this program which was in any case inadequate to avert disaster.

Constructive and farsighted was another of the New Deal laws affecting foreign economic policy; the Lend-Lease program adopted by the United States Congress and approved by the President on March 11, 1941. This program functioned most effectively during the war but has now too hastily been abandoned.

In concluding our examination of the economic policy of the United States, we should note two recent developments as evidence of the grave danger we face unless we radically revise our attitude toward international economic objectives. The first of these is the International Wheat Agreements of 1942 between Argentina, Australia, Canada, Great Britain, and the United States. The first definitive economic postwar plan to be agreed upon by participants in the second World War, this agreement leaves much to be desired. Patterned too closely on the restrictive policies of the past, it provides for limitation on production, stock controls, and price-fixing. If this is to be the type of agreements implementing the Atlantic Charter, it augers ill for the solution of pressing postwar economic problems.

More recently, the Congress, in passing the bill for the disposal of surplus war property, has paved the way for future international controversy and possibly for the initiation of another era of economic warfare by subsidizing the sale of surplus farm products abroad. This encouragement of "dumping" is bound to cause antagonism, if not retaliation, by other nations.

In the light of the foregoing brief review of the international economic policy of the United States, what can be recommended for the future?

First of all is the necessity for every American to realize that shooting wars are encouraged and even made possible by economic wars. Hitler could not so easily have roused the German people to start another war had economic warfare not been raging. Economic warfare gave him his theme song, "Lebensraum," with which to rally the support of the German people.

In the second place, the American people must realize that they cannot hope to enjoy their position of economic strength and power without taking commensurate responsibility for world policy. America must continue the world leadership which this war has forced upon it. This leadership she can exercise to prevent future wars by concentrating on the elimination of the economic causes of war. In doing so she must put her own house in order. The American people must insist that their Congress revise or repeal existing legislation which contains the seeds of postwar economic conflict. First of all, the reciprocal trade agreement programs should be strengthened by two amendments: (1) the program should be made permanent, and (2) the existing limitations that no tariff can be altered more than 50 per cent or no item shifted between the free and dutiable list should be removed. But this is not enough. As is so ably pointed out by Percy W. Bidwell of the Council of Foreign Relations, the Trade Agreements Program is too slow and too limited in its scope to be adequate for the task ahead. Bilateral agreements have their place, it is true, but multilateral agreements are also essential. Provision must be made for multilateral economic cooperation. Dr. Bidwell proposes (in the *American Economic Review,* March, 1944) that the United Nations "should at once proceed to the formation of a comprehensive agreement on postwar commercial policy" ultimately to be "open to all countries of like mind." He becomes more specific in recommending that

. . . The founding states should pledge themselves to undertake at once (1) the reduction of protective import duties; (2) the abolition of quantitative restrictions on imports, such as licensing systems and quotas; (3) the removal of outright prohibitions and restrictions on imports and exports; (4) the elimination of all types of tariff discriminations; (5) the abandonment of export subsidies and the suppression of all types of unfair competition in foreign trade.

Dr. Bidwell recognizes that such a program "should be undertaken gradually" and that qualifications of all five proposals may be necessary. He offers it as a point of departure toward the goal of international economic peace.

Other United States legislation which should be repealed or amended includes the Silver Purchase Act setting an artificially high price for silver, and the Surplus Commodity Disposal Act which, as noted above, subsidizes the dumping of surplus farm products abroad. Other means must be sought for solving the farm problem. American agriculture can compete in world markets without subsidies if it will specialize in the production of crops and livestock in which it is most efficient. Instead of asking aid through subsidies, it should seek more efficient techniques or develop new products through research. Cotton serves to illustrate. Texas and certain parts of the lower Mississippi

Valley can produce cotton at low enough costs to compete in world markets without subsidy. Other cotton-growing sections in the United States which cannot compete should either shift to other crops or seek lower costs. Possibly the new cotton-picking machinery may be of assistance. But artificial raising of cotton prices by government action, including subsidies, has not solved the problem. Rather has it stimulated foreign competition by encouraging cotton growing in Egypt, India, Brazil and elsewhere and cut off the markets of efficient cotton growers in the United States. It is likely that as world standards of living rise, the demand for cotton will grow stronger; but in the meantime, if the United States wants to head off trouble abroad, existing legislation should be repealed. It is hoped that the United States will be able to keep most of its people busy and that national income will be as high as $140 billion to $150 billion measured in terms of average 1943 prices. On this basis, foreign trade should exceed $13 billion, as compared with a low of less than $3 billion in 1932, and should be about equally divided between exports and imports. Some observers believe that even larger foreign trade will be necessary if America is to use its greatly expanding manufacturing capacity after the war.

Whatever the figure, there is no doubt that we will have to buy large quantities of goods abroad if we are to sell large quantities of our own. The American people must learn that imports are equally desirable with exports in building jobs and prosperity at home, and more important, in keeping the world prosperous. They must also learn that a great creditor nation, such as the United States has become, must import much more than it exports if it is to be repaid for its loans abroad. Fear of imports must give way to a recognition of their great value to our own wealth and well-being as well as to the prosperity of our neighbor nations. Ignorance must give way to facts.

The efficient farmer must learn that he has nothing to gain and much to lose from protective tariffs. When he supports them he merely cuts off the export market for his cotton, wheat, corn, and pork by making it harder for the foreigner to buy. He only gives misguided aid to the inefficient farmer who cannot compete without tariff subsidy.

Labor should realize that the old bogey of competition with cheap

labor was merely a political "red herring" designed by business interests which sought protection of their inefficiency and wanted his vote
for a high tariff. High wages in the United States are determined by
the high productivity of American labor in the efficient industries.
Protected industries can seldom pay as high wages as those which need
no protection. Ford was the first to pay $5 per day for common labor
in the United States, yet Ford was able to sell automobiles competi-
tively in world markets. Efficient labor at high wages produced a
low-priced car. High wages do not necessarily mean high costs. Low
wages where labor is inefficient may spell high costs. If one man in
a modern American factory can product 200 lamp bulbs a day and
earn $10 for his work, the labor cost of lamp bulbs is 5¢ each. If it
takes 10 men in a foreign factory at $1 per day to make 100 lamp
bulbs, or 20 men at 50¢ a day, the labor cost is 10¢ per bulb. Even if
the cheaper labor could turn out as many as 200 lamp bulbs in a day,
the labor cost would be no cheaper than that of the $10 American
worker.

Above all, the American citizen must realize that buying in the
cheapest market will bring him the most for his money and that any
tariff which shuts out imports tends to raise his cost of living and
reduce his rate of consumption. The tariff on sugar of nearly 2¢ per
pound is a good example. The American people consume about 6
million tons of sugar each year or, on the average, 104 pounds per
person. The United States produces about one-third of the total, or
about 2 million tons. In order to protect this industry, the American
people pay $235 million, nearly 2¢ a pound more than necessary to
get sugar from Cuba and other low cost producing areas. We do this
in order to protect American farmers who raise sugar beets and sugar
cane, and a few American workmen in the beet and cane sugar re-
fineries. In 1939, the total value of sugar beets grown in the United
States for sugar was under $49 million, while $23 million of sugar
cane was produced to make a total of $72 million. Fewer than 15,000
workers were employed in the 163 beet and cane sugar factories at an
average wage of about $1,000 per year, or a total expenditure for
wages of less than $15 million.

In other words, it costs the American people $235 million more than
necessary for the sugar they use, to provide a few farmers and a few
factory workers a total income of $87 million. Of the $235 million,

about two-thirds goes to the Treasury of the United States; the other third, nearly $80 million, goes in higher prices to the protected sugar industry. It would be much cheaper for the American people to put the entire personnel of the domestic sugar industry on direct pensions than it is to pay the present high tariff. In fact, if we add to the $87 million the farmers and wage earners receive, the additional $80 million which the protected industry receives we would still be better off by $68 million a year to pay direct subsidies to everyone connected with the industry. And this has gone on for many years. The same story could be told for other protected industries. Is it worth it?

One of the major problems which the American people must solve now that the war is over is the degree of government control or interference necessary in foreign trade. Practically, it seems inevitable that postwar world trade will be guided rather fully, if not controlled by the governments of the world. Russian trade will continue to be completely monopolized by government and many other nations will closely supervise both exports and imports at least during the years of reconstruction. Reasons for control inhere in the difficulties of rebuilding destroyed or dislocated industries, with limited foreign exchange or purchasing power. If citizens and businessmen are permitted to buy and sell according to their own whims and for personal reasons, the national interest may be sacrificed. Until nations have rebuilt their economies on such basis as to provide surpluses of their specialties for export and consequent income or purchasing power to buy the products of other nations, little freedom can be expected.

Businessmen in the United States are also certain to find that foreign buyers, whether public or private, will require very much longer credit terms than prevail in domestic business. Where a concern does ninety per cent of its business on a thirty, sixty, or ninety-day credit basis, it will be reluctant to extend credit for ten, twenty, or thirty years on the other ten per cent. Yet, if America is to make anything like full use of its great capacity to produce, and if it is to play a part in helping industrialize undeveloped nations, means must be found for extending the long-term credit needed by impoverished buyers. Ways of minimizing and spreading the risk of loss must be developed. The government will doubtless have to provide machinery for this purpose, looking to foreign governments for guarantees and assurances on the return on these long-term transactions. This subject is covered in the following chapter.

Whether or not additional governmental machinery is necessary to further foreign trade is debatable. It may be argued that the United States could strengthen its position in trading with Russia and other nationally controlled export and import departments by setting up a huge government-operated export and import house. This agency would serve as a middleman or bumper between American private business and nationally controlled or operated business abroad. All exports would channel through this agency which would be somewhat like the Lend-Lease organization. American businessmen would sell to the government Export-Import House, which would pay for the goods immediately and in turn sell them to Russia, France, China or wherever they were wanted on whatever credit terms were necessary to get the business. Similarly, this house would serve as the centralized purchasing bureau for all foreign products, buying them on the best terms possible and reselling them to American business firms for distribution within the United States.

Opponents of such a radical proposal argue forcefully that the government would be plunged into business on so great a scale that the advantages of bargaining with foreign powers would be offset by the danger to free enterprise. They would prefer to let private exporters and importers organize their own machinery for dealing with foreigners, asking only for assistance on the credit-granting function and that only as long as necessary to reestablish stable economic conditions throughout the world. They point to the fact that private traders did business with Amtorg, Russia's foreign trade monopoly, before the war, have continued to do business with neutral nations during the war, and are capable of carrying on after the war. All they want from the government beyond credit guarantees is factual information on markets, such as the foreign commerce service provided before the war, and such insurance of equal opportunity to compete with other suppliers as may be worked out through international agreements on commercial policy.

The whole problem of cartels and commodity control schemes raises the question of America's ability to compete without government action unless such schemes are universally outlawed. It is analyzed in a later special chapter on the subject.

NATHANAEL H. ENGLE

CHAPTER XI

# Monetary Policy

## INTRODUCTION

IN THE months following the termination of World War I the general opinion on postwar international monetary policy was fairly well summed up in the Brussels Monetary Conference of 1920 which unanimously resolved that "it is highly desirable that the countries which have lapsed from an effective gold standard should return thereto." For two generations before 1914 King Gold had maintained sway over the principal commercial nations of the world. Though during the eighties and nineties the reign of gold was challenged by bimetallism, before the turn of the century gold had won its victory. Expanding industry and commerce were matched by increased monetary gold stock, and the secular trend of prices was upward. Gold had been a benevolent monarch. In America, recovery from the depression of the nineties had been followed by nearly two decades of prosperity, interrupted only by a sharp but short panic in 1907. The years before 1914 were looked upon as good years; even today "parity" prices in agriculture are based upon the relationship existing in 1909–14.

In Europe, too, the gold standard had been generally accepted, and its wartime abandonment had brought economic chaos. A return to gold appeared to be an essential step toward economic rehabilitation. In England even before the guns had ceased firing on the Western Front the Cundliffe Committee had outlined a program for bringing the pound back to its prewar parity with gold. Painfully Europe returned to gold in the twenties, but the hope that the restoration of gold would bring back economic normalcy proved to be a Utopian dream that was rudely shattered by the international crisis of the early thirties.

A fundamental objective of an ideal international monetary program

130

is to contribute to the expansion of world productivity and world trade. The late war so drove home to everyone the significance of the term *One World* that we know we cannot maintain the "American standard of living" in a world where millions of persons are starving or living on a bare subsistence level. Peace and the sanctity of our own territory depend as much upon equitable economic relations as upon international political machinery or great armaments.

At a minimum, an international financial program adequate for the larger objectives of a better world economic order must accomplish the following:

1. Make financial provision for the relief and rehabilitation of liberated countries,
2. Facilitate international payments by stabilization of exchange rates,
3. Promote and safeguard foreign investment,
4. Contribute to the liquidation of war-created international indebtedness.

The attainment of these purposes will require more of such international cooperation as has already been evidenced by the conference on relief and rehabilitation in Atlantic City in November, 1943, by the Bretton Woods Conference of July, 1944, by the adoption of the Bretton Woods Agreements Bill by Congress in July, 1945, and finally by the adoption of the United Nations Charter.

### RELIEF AND REHABILITATION

The conference at Atlantic City formulated a program for the United Nations Relief and Rehabilitation Administration which is now a going concern. As its name implies, it is an agency designed to promote relief and rehabilitation in the areas devastated by war. The aims and policies of that organization have been stated elsewhere in this book (see Chapter XIII) and need not be repeated. We are here concerned with how UNRRA will manage its finances.

There has been practically a unanimity of opinion among experts that the immediate needs for relief and rehabilitation of liberated countries must be met by large outright donations, and not by credit. UNRRA has therefore formulated a financial system based upon that point of view. The agreement establishing UNRRA has aptly been called a Declaration of Interdependence. All of the nations share in the contributions to the fund, although obviously the principal sources of money and goods must be the nations like our own, which have been spared the loss and burden of invasion.

At the Atlantic City conference in November, 1943, the UNRRA Council adopted the resolution that each uninvaded country be asked to contribute one per cent of its national income for the year ending June 30, 1943. The contribution of that amount will be payable 10 per cent in free exchange and 90 per cent in supplies procured within the country. All purchases for UNRRA will be through national agencies, and those agencies will determine what goods can be spared from civilian and other requirements.

The total overall cost of relief has been estimated at $20 billion, of which liberated nations which possess gold or other assets will pay $15 billion. The member governments had by November 30, 1944, appropriated a total (equivalent in U.S. dollars) of $1,217,091,869.

The UNRRA Council established an administrative budget of $10 million for the calendar year 1944. This amount was to be allocated proportionately among the invaded and uninvaded members, the quotas ranging from $5 thousand to $4 million. By November 30, 1944, a total of $8,370,000 had been received for administrative purposes.

When the army relinquishes control over an allied area, a civilian government takes over. If this government has foreign exchange resources enabling it to buy in the markets of the world, it will cooperate with UNRRA in obtaining the needed food and industrial materials. Governments that have ample foreign resources will bear part or all of the responsibility for financing procurement of relief supplies for their areas, while countries lacking foreign exchange may apply to UNRRA. The governments or authorities will have charge of the supplies in the liberated areas. They will distribute the goods through ordinary channels of commerce whenever that policy is practicable and consistent with a fair distribution of essential goods. The local currency proceeds realized from the sale of such supplies will be used to finance UNRRA's expenditures within those areas. In paying countries UNRRA may be called upon to take a very active part in certain services such as repatriation of displaced persons, health, and welfare.

After investigating the resources available and the needs of the various countries, UNRRA will decide the share each nation will receive. Most UNRRA supplies will be sold locally, and rationing and price control will be required. Black markets will be actively suppressed. When asked to do so by the military, UNRRA may operate in enemy or ex-enemy countries as long as the needs of the liberated countries have been met, and the expenses for such operations are paid for by the enemy or ex-enemy countries.

UNRRA was established as an emergency organization, and will bring its activities to an end through rehabilitation. Though in some areas it may not continue after the harvest of the first crops, in others, where ruin and depletion are greater, rehabilitation will take longer. However, all of the UNRRA activities are expected to come to an end within two years after termination of hostilities on all fronts.

### INTERNATIONAL COOPERATION

Two other problems of supreme importance in any discussion of postwar finance are international monetary stabilization and the promotion of foreign investments. It is vital that a successful plan of cooperation between the nations be worked out in order that we reach a satisfactory solution of these problems. The need for better international monetary cooperation may be revealed by reviewing the lack of adequate collaboration during the inter-war period.

Before World War II many attempts, which we cannot give space to here, were made to obtain international monetary cooperation, but they were intermittent and eventually ineffectual. In the first decade after World War I the international gold standard was resumed, the nations concerned acting virtually independently. A financial world crisis was precipitated in 1931, with the nations of Central Europe as storm center. Only by maximum international cooperation could ruin have been averted. Actually inadequate assistance was given haltingly, with Great Britain bearing the brunt of the battle. After weeks of tension she was forced to abandon the gold standard to which she had proudly returned in 1925. International assistance in her emergency was "too little and too late." More than a score of countries followed Britain off gold and became the "sterling area," with the result that a "gold bloc" was formed on the continent to bring together those nations which, because of extensive devaluation in the 'twenties, were reluctant again to lower the value of their money in terms of gold.

The decline of sterling exchange placed Japanese exporters (e.g., textile manufacturers) at a competitive disadvantage in the markets of the Far East. Because domestic prices in England were virtually unchanged, the East Indian importer could buy cotton goods in Manchester for the same number of shillings as formerly, and his native currency would now buy more English shillings. The Japanese promptly abandoned gold and permitted their yen to go down 50 per cent or even more, as compared to a 30 per cent decline in the British pound. Canada's currency depreciation of approximately 15 per cent gave her producers of basic raw materials, such as lumber, an edge over their competitors in the United States. To meet the exchange differential the United States increased tariff duties, but though this protected the domestic market it did not help us to hold our share of world trade. By 1933 the United States was bounded on the north, east, south, and west by countries off gold, a situation which contributed to our decision in 1933 to abandon the gold standard temporarily, the major causes of which were the domestic price situation and the banking holiday.

The World Monetary and Economic Conference that met in London in the summer of 1933 was barren of any real results in the direction of international monetary stabilization. By 1939 regulation of exchanges on a nationalistic basis was the rule rather than the exception, and the Axis powers had become most aggressive in creating various classes of exchange. Currencies were blocked, to be used only for the purchase of approved imports, and favoritism existed with respect to rates. In the German market several classes of exchange were quoted. To a lesser degree other nations regulated exchange transactions through their exchange stabilization funds. These restrictions proved to be toll gates on the highways of commerce, slowing down and making more expensive the international movement of goods. Nationalism led to high tariffs, bilateral trade agreements, blocked currencies, competitive currency manipulation, multiple exchange rates and other restrictions which hampered the growth of world trade.

Students of international finance today are eager to avoid the pitfalls into which the world fell through lack of cooperation after the last war. In order to find some workable solution for the problems which face us in our postwar financial plans, representatives of forty-four nations met at an international conference at Bretton Woods, New

Hampshire, July 2–22, 1944. Although the conference itself lasted only a short three weeks, a great deal of preliminary work had been done and public discussion of earlier plans had been carried on for more than a year.

The main items discussed at the Bretton Woods Conference were the questions of international monetary stabilization and the promotion of foreign investments. As a solution to those problems, the conference provided for two separate institutions—(1) the International Monetary Fund, and (2) the Bank for Reconstruction and Development, hereinafter called the Fund and the Bank respectively. Unlike UNRRA, these two later plans have not yet been put into operation. Although they were accepted by the representatives of the forty-four nations which participated, they must, to become effective, be ratified by the appropriate agency in each country. It is the conviction of the writer that the agreements represent a workable program.

Readers familiar with the preliminary steps in negotiation prior to Bretton Woods will recall that in April, 1943, the British and American treasuries simultaneously announced plans for currency stabilization. The former was known as a Clearing Union, the latter as a Stabilization Fund. The British plan was frequently identified as the Keynes plan in recognition of its authorship by Lord Keynes, one of Britain's outstanding economists and a dominant figure throughout all of the negotiations. The American plan was alternately referred to as the Morgenthau Plan, for Secretary Morgenthau, and the White Plan, in recognition of the large share of responsibility for its drafting by Dr. Harry D. White, Assistant to the Secretary of the Treasury, under whose immediate direction it was worked out. We make no attempt here to trace the history of the plans during 1943 or the modifications effected in them at the Bretton Woods Conference of 1944, but rather center attention on the programs agreed to at the conference.

Though the two institutions proposed (the Fund and the Bank) would serve different purposes and have separate administrations, they were nevertheless devised to supplement each other. In discussing the two institutions, we shall endeavor to show the purposes of each, to describe how they would operate, and to discuss the extent to which they would meet the desired objectives.

### INTERNATIONAL MONETARY FUND

The major purpose of the Fund as planned would be to facilitate international payments on current account. To achieve this objective it provides for international cooperation, the elimination of competitive currency manipulation, the stabilization of exchange rates, and the making available to member nations resources with which to correct maladjustments in their balance of payments.

Although approved at the Bretton Woods Conference and ratified by the United States, the plan of the Fund has not yet been adopted by the other United Nations. And this nation has ratified, not the actual plan as put forth in the Bretton Woods Agreements, but its own interpretation of that plan, which somewhat restricts the activities of the Fund. However, in order to simplify our discussion we shall treat it here as though it were put in operation. International cooperation is the keystone of the Fund. It manifests itself in the organizational plan; it is facilitated by the Fund's statistical services and its provisions for consultation; it is the basis for the agreement by the signatory nations to refrain from discriminatory currency arrangements and arbitrary changes in exchange rates; it is carried out in the cooperative agreement of each country to make available its "quota" of gold and currency.

The Fund will be located in the United States, presumably in New York City. The administrative set-up insures a measure of consultation and mutual discussion. Annual meetings of the Board of Governors will bring together member bank officials of all participating countries. The Executive Directors, five of whom must under the terms of the Agreement represent the major countries, will meet as often as the business of the Fund may require. The location of Fund headquarters in New York will offer a convenient center where other bank officials may visit and confer with fellow bankers. The terms of the agreement give the Fund an opportunity to become a storehouse of international financial information. Officers of the Fund are directed to assemble extensive economic statistics; they may require members to supply national data on gold holdings and movements, merchandise exports and imports, national income, foreign exchange rates, exchange controls in force, and other prescribed matters. To perform adequately its regulatory duties the staff of the Fund must interpret these data and make them available to the member nations.

The Fund will consist of a pool of gold and currency equivalent to 8.8 billion American dollars, of which the quota of the United States is $2,750 million. The initial payments of the member nations, with certain permissible exceptions, consist of one-fourth in gold and three-fourths in their own currencies. It is contemplated that the participating nations will not physically transmit the gold or currency to the Fund in New York but rather will deposit it in the central bank or treasury of the member country to the credit of the Fund. The total amount of the Fund will remain relatively fixed, but the proportion of dollars, pounds, francs, or pesos will be constantly changing as member countries borrow the currencies of other countries.

In the preliminary drafts of the American plan which was named "An International Stabilization Fund," emphasis was placed upon stability of exchange rates. Later drafts and the Articles of Agreement have retained the maintenance of stable exchange rates as a major objective, although they have put less emphasis upon a new monetary unit and rigid stabilization. Gone are the terms "Unitas" and "bancor," that were used as descriptive names to differentiate the American and British plans. One of the first steps in getting the Fund started is for each member country, subject to approval by the Fund, to fix the "par value" of its currency, which may be measured either in United States dollars or in gold. Since the weight of the dollar is now fixed in terms of gold, this makes gold the index of the par value of each currency, and to this extent the Fund conforms to the basic principles of the international gold standard.

The plan of the Fund requires all members to fix a par of exchange, and it assumes that stable exchange rates will be maintained except when changes are necessary "to correct a fundamental disequilibrium." Recognizing that a rigid exchange rate may be detrimental to the domestic economy, it makes provision for altering rates when fundamental conditions warrant, and makes possible a uniform change in the par value of all currencies. It provides, however, that alterations may be made only after consultation with the Fund, although a change of 10 per cent of the initial par value may be made without the Fund's specific consent—an arrangement that will be useful primarily during the transition period from a war economy to peace. Changes in excess of 10 per cent require the approval of the Fund's directors, but the agreement specifies that the directors will concur if they find that the change is proposed to correct a fundamental disequilibrium. The provisions for altering exchange rates appear to insure against competitive currency depreciation and at the same time allow the members to make necessary adjustments.

In addition to fixing of "par values" and providing for approved changes the Fund must be able to use its pool of $8.8 billion to aid members in meeting adverse balances of payments. It is a fundamental principle of foreign trade that transactions must balance. This does not mean that we must accept goods from abroad in any given year equal to the amount we sell abroad. Services of various kinds—shipping, banking, insurance—as well as foreign travel, capital movements, specie shipments, find a place on the international balance sheet. Gold producing nations (e.g., South Africa) treat gold as a commodity. In gold-standard days, gold was regarded as a "settler" of international balances, but short-term credits were widely used and central bank policy was frequently directed toward influencing gold movements.

Under the international gold standard the rate of exchange (i.e., the buying price of drafts per unit of the foreign money) was free to fluctuate but was held within narrow limits by the right to ship gold freely from country to country. Gold in New York had the same value as it had in London plus or minus the traveling expenses from one country to the other. Transportation, insurance, and incidental expenses of gold shipment normally amounted to approximately $\frac{1}{2}$ of one per cent of the value of the gold. Therefore, the price of drafts drawn in English money could rise $\frac{1}{2}$ of one per cent above or fall $\frac{1}{2}$ of one per cent below the par of exchange, which historically approximated $4.86. As an illustration of how gold shipment served to limit exchange fluctuations, let us assume that British purchases in the United States were in excess of her sales of goods and services to the people of our country and that the transactions between these two countries constitute a completely closed system. In this case the supply of drafts drawn in pounds offered for sale in the United States would exceed the demand, and the rate of exchange would fall. When it reached approximately $4.84 per pound it would become profitable for dealers to buy the drafts, send them to their London agent with instructions to buy gold for shipment to New York where it would be converted into dollar bank balances, at $4.86 less costs and shipment, thus creating an almost unlimited demand for English drafts. Conversely, if drafts sold above approximately $4.88 it would be cheaper for an American importer to ship gold than to buy drafts.

The Fund operates on similar principles, substituting a credit transaction for gold shipment. Private operators—banks and foreign exchange dealers—will continue to buy and sell drafts in the market. Market fluctuations one per cent above and one per cent below the established par of exchange are authorized. As long as the market keeps within this range, the Fund will not intervene. Assume for the purpose of illustration that the British pound which has been "pegged" at approximately $4 during the war is fixed at that rate when the Fund is inaugurated. Under these conditions the price of drafts in the open market in New York may sell for as low as $3.96 or as high as $4.04.

If there is an excess of British exchange in New York and the rate drops to $3.96, the Fund may be called into play. In lieu of shipping gold (as described above) the Bank of England would seek to borrow dollars from the Fund, let us say in the amount of $100 million. If its application were approved, the Bank of England would credit the Fund with 25 million pounds, the pound equivalent of the $100 million borrowed, and would request that the dollars borrowed be deposited to the credit of a New York bank. This latter institution would be instructed to buy in the market all drafts on England offered at the minimum rate, which, according to our assumption, is $3.96. The assets of the Fund now would include 100 million fewer dollars, but an equivalent increase in British currency. If the cause of the fall in the exchange rate in New York or London is seasonal or temporary in nature, the purchase of $100 million of sterling drafts should be sufficient to bring about equilibrium. Three months later there may be a reverse flow of payments. The Bank of England could then buy dollar drafts in the London market and repay the currency borrowed from the Fund. This hypothetical transaction illustrates the manner in which the Fund would meet an adverse balance of payments on current international account—a fundamental purpose for which it is intended.

It is contemplated that the resources of the Fund are to be used to meet temporary needs only, and charges and other restrictions are imposed in conformity with this assumption. The "charges" are graduated on the basis of time and the amount borrowed, the maximum net amount which can be borrowed in any one year being limited to one-fourth of the quota of the borrowing country. For example, since Britain's quota is $1,300 million, the maximum that she may borrow any one year would be one-fourth of that amount or $325 million. No member may become indebted to the Fund in excess of a total of 200 per cent of its quota.

In this manner the Fund provides an institution for facilitating international payments, and it makes credit available for temporary uses under restrictions that allow loans for only the purposes intended. Though a fear frequently expressed is that everyone will want dollars and the Fund will soon be depleted, actually the process of extending credit will be gradual with a responsibility upon chronic borrowers to make fundamental adjustments. If a general scarcity develops, dollars may be rationed. Such a policy is more equitable than discriminatory or multiple currency practices.

Prohibitions upon the activity of the Fund and its members include engaging in discriminatory currency arrangements, making arbitrary changes in exchange rates, permitting capital loans, extending credit that does not conform to the purposes of the Fund, or dictating the type of economy of a member nation. The last of these limitations was inserted primarily to assure that Soviet Russia may continue to have a system of state credit if she chooses and will not find the resources of the Fund denied her for this reason.

The Fund was subjected to searching analysis by informed, constructive critics, and proposals for its amendment were made. Edward E. Brown, President of the First National Bank of Chicago and one of the American delegates, listed six objections which he found have been most frequently made, and discussed them *ad seratim* in an able and dispassionate manner. Stated in abridged form, the objections in the order in which Mr. Brown examined them are:

1. It is premature,
2. It is so large that it will encourage nations to postpone necessary reforms,
3. The Fund will be controlled by the borrowers and will be unable to deny credit to a member,
4. It gives no assurance of exchange stability,

5. It does not do away with exchange controls or solve the problem of blocked currencies,

6. The United States will put up the only currency having real value.

Space does not permit us a full answer to all criticisms, but a brief statement about each of the six objections enumerated above follows:

With respect to the first of the objections mentioned, Mr. Brown admitted that he felt when the conference was called that the world was not ready for the inauguration of the Fund. However, the rapid march of events and the provisions for postponing the Fund's transactions with any country until hostilities ceased convinced him that it should be adopted promptly. This position appears sound.

In answer to the objection that the Fund is too ambitious and that it will encourage nations to delay the painful task of setting their houses in order, Mr. Brown and also Dr. Harry White (*Foreign Affairs,* January, 1945) point out that it must be large enough to meet all needs, though it is not a cure-all and admittedly must be accompanied by sound internal finance in the member countries. For a nation like China, devastated by years of war, the achievement of sound domestic finance must be a gradual process, and such a nation deserves encouragement. To the possibility that the existence of the Fund will encourage laxity, sound administration is the answer, and to the achievement of this we must all give support.

Mr. Brown's reply to the argument that the Fund will be controlled by the borrowers is that extensive control is exercised by the United States and by other nations whose financial policies are as conservative as our own.

The force of the objection that the Fund gives no assurance of exchange stability because of the provisions for alteration of exchange rates, depends largely upon the individual critic's economic philosophy. Changes in exchange rates were harder to make under the original American plan than under the present Fund, but British critics opposed any program that would make changes in the gold value of sterling too difficult, and the present Fund provisions are the result of a compromise of conflicting views. As now proposed the Fund offers a workable program, and those who favor relatively stable rates may content themselves with the hope that after the adjustments of the immediate postwar years, further changes will be infrequent.

The failure of the Fund immediately to abolish blocked balances and exchange controls has given rise to criticism. We shall discuss blocked sterling balances which are so large as to create a special problem in the section of this study which deals with war-created indebtedness.

The sixth objection has caused more anxious concern in this country than any other. Those who undertake to allay this fear call attention to the general and special provisions designed to assure the soundness of the Fund. The amount of credit that can be extended to a member nation in any one year is limited; the "charges" rise as the amount borrowed increases; the United States and Britain have the heaviest voting power. Mr. Brown, in his well-reasoned answer to this criticism, points out that because other countries will produce raw materials for which there will be a heavy demand, we shall not be the world's sole source of needed goods. He quite properly urges a radical change in our present tariff policy to enable other countries to pay us in goods. His position in essence is that the safeguards in the Fund are adequate if soundly administered to protect the assets of the Fund, but that we must recognize that a creditor nation must ultimately accept payment in goods. The editors of *Fortune* (September, 1944) also flatly accept the necessity of the United States taking substantial risks and chide those who over-magnify this issue.

The success of the Fund will depend in large measure on the caliber of the administration and the whole-hearted, disinterested manner in which its members share the responsibility for making it work. If soundly administered and given an honest trial, it can do much to stabilize exchange rates and supply credit to meet temporary balance of payment needs. The lack of unanimity of support for the Fund naturally suggests the question of what are the alternatives. Of these, we shall here discuss the often proposed return to the international gold standard, the "key countries" approach, and the amendments suggested by the American Bankers Association.

There are many influential persons in the United States who look upon the restoration of the gold standard as the most practical basis for international monetary policy. Because of its historic position and the standing of its supporters, it is impossible to dismiss the proposal without due consideration. Dr. Edwin W. Kemmerer, Professor of International Finance of Princeton University, has, in a recent book, *Gold and the Gold Standard,* set forth effectively the case for gold and may fairly be selected as spokesman for the gold standard group. The advantages of the gold standard according to Dr. Kemmerer are that its essentials are easily understood, it possesses the confidence of the people, it calls for little political management, and it is an international standard. The last of these points he stresses as especially important. An effective gold standard automatically keeps exchange rates within a narrow range of parity. It also permits freedom in foreign exchange transactions.

Dr. Kemmerer proposes a gold standard. He would make the Board of Directors of the Central Bank in each nation its monetary authority, and would create a central bank of central banks, that is, an international bank. He insists that there should be gold convertibility, but would permit this convertibility to be in gold coin, gold bars, or gold drafts as best suits the needs of the various countries. Before going into the fundamental bases for opposition to the gold standard, we should make a brief analysis of gold production, gold distribution, and gold reserves. Our first discovery will be the fallacy of the popular notions that an international gold program is impracticable because the United States has all the world's monetary gold, and that the total supply of gold is inadequate as a basis for the monetary systems of tomorrow's world.

It is, of course, widely known that from 1934 until early 1941 gold flowed to our shores in a virtual "avalanche," and that from February, 1934 (following official revaluation), to December, 1940, our gold reserve increased more than $15 billion. But early in 1941 Lend-Lease practically put an end to gold importation; bookkeeping credits took the place of gold shipments. (*Federal Reserve Bulletin,* November, 1944, p. 1046.) Importation of gold was widely publicized, but there has not been equal publicity of the recent gold withdrawal. In the past two years our total gold stock has declined by $2 billion—from $22.7 to $20.7 billion—through exportation and earmarking. In addition to $14 billion of gold, foreign countries held $3 billion of dollar balances, making their total of gold and dollar exchange $17 billion. Thus the present distribution of gold, though by no means ideal, does not present an impossible situation.

Central gold reserves of foreign countries at the end of 1928 were $6.3 billion (at $20.67 per ounce); today they are $14 billion. Total gold reserves (foreign plus U.S.) which were $10 billion in 1928 are now $35 billion. Annual gold production reached approximately $1.4 billion in 1940 and 1941 and most of this flowed into the world's monetary stock. Revaluation in 1934 raised the dollar value of the existing stock and of the gold subsequently mined. Dehoarding and other sources helped to swell the total. These facts confirm our thesis that there is enough gold to form the basis for the world's monetary system and that its maldistribution is not an insuperable bar against reestablishment of the gold standard.

The explanation of the rejection of the gold standard must be sought elsewhere—in the present widespread and determined opposition of certain countries, notably England and the British Dominions. In 1925, Great Britain's return to gold with the exchange value of the pound at the prewar level proved to involve an over-valuation in terms of wages and prices that imposed on the British economy what has been described as the "straight-jacket of 1925-31." The depression of the 1930's was blamed on the gold standard, and its enforced abandonment in the international crisis of 1931 was hailed as a relief from its rigidity. Because of these experiences the British public, including the normally conservative bankers, are strongly opposed to a gold standard. Lord Keynes, in an address before the House of Lords a few days before leaving to participate in the Bretton Woods Conference, pledged his associates that he would continue his opposition to a gold standard. These views may be prejudiced, but in any event they reflect the sentiment of the British people. And their sentiment is shared by people in other lands and widely supported in the United States.

In the face of the British attitude and other anti-gold sentiment in the world, including that in the United States, the restoration of the gold standard is impracticable. It appears desirable, therefore, to see to what extent the merits of the gold standard can be incorporated into a program which avoids its objections and will be generally acceptable to the nations of the world. In large measure it seems to the writer that the program of Bretton Woods achieves these objectives. It will be noted that the parity of exchange of the various monetary units must be fixed in terms of gold or United States dollars. This amounts to making gold the index for establishing parities. The Fund will hold gold and deal in gold, and any country which so desires may retain gold as its monetary standard. On the other hand, there is more adequate machinery for adjusting the rates of exchange under this program than under an international gold standard. Thus the domestic economy does not necessarily have to adjust to the international standard if fundamental conditions within the country change. A member nation may be permitted by the Fund to change its rate of exchange rather than to undertake an adjustment of prices and wages within the country.

Discussion of the Bretton Woods Agreements centered principally around the proposed Fund. Organizations throughout the United States, leading bankers and economists, and officials of the Administration focused their attention upon the Fund, not only before the Bretton Woods Agreements Bill was introduced in the House and the Senate, but also throughout the hearings before the House and Senate Banking and Currency Committees and in the debates in the House and the Senate. The critics of the Fund, led by the Administrative Council of the American Bankers Association, and other associated banking groups, advocated enlarging the powers of the Bank and eliminating the Fund completely, thus having a single agency supplant the two separate ones proposed by the Bretton Woods Conference.

The principal objections to the Fund were that it does not have "effective provisions to safeguard it against misuse" and that liberal credit extension in the immediate postwar years will result in a repetition of the boom and collapse of 1919–20, when the United States continued to make intergovernmental loans and excessive private credits were extended to finance exports. The possibility of lax credit extension must be acknowledged but safeguards have been provided in the Fund as shown above in the analysis of Edward E. Brown, banker member of the American delegation at the Bretton Woods Conference. Mr. Brown's argument is persuasive.

After extended hearings and debates it became apparent that some amendment of the Bretton Woods Proposals was in order. While the leadership of the movement for a single agency was taken by the American Bankers Association and other associated banking groups there was, fortunately, not an alignment along the lines of economic or political blocks. Offsetting the official attitude of the American Bankers Association was the support of the Proposals by leading bankers, notably Edward E. Brown. The Research Committee of the Pennsylvania Bankers Association recommended adoption of the program without amendment but made suggestions for strengthening the administration of the two institutions when established. The

United States Chamber of Commerce favored deferment of the Fund until world trade expanded and proper commercial policies had been adopted. Economists were divided in their views.

Realizing the significance of the criticisms which had been made of the Fund but believing they could be met without drastic amendment of the Bretton Woods Proposals, the Research Committee of the Committee for Economic Development, under the chairmanship of Ralph Flanders, President of the Federal Reserve Bank of Boston, brought forward a compromise plan which was released in mid-April. The essential feature of this program was found in the first of the Committee's recommendations: "We recommend the approval of the International Bank for Reconstruction and Development and also recommend that at an appropriate time, which would not delay its approval, its powers be broadened to include the extension of general long-term or short-term loans for stabilization purposes." It was the Committee's further recommendation that after the Bank had been strengthened in this manner the plan for the Fund should be approved. Everyone agreed that the United States must share in world rehabilitation. Differences arose over the effectiveness of the proposed institutions, but these differences were sufficiently reconciled by the amendments to the original bill which were adopted by Congress in July, 1945, the vote in favor of the Act being almost unanimous in both houses.

The amendments of the original Bretton Woods plan which are now law include the authorization of long-term stabilization loans by the Bank and the limitation of the lending power of the Fund to short-term loans. The bill further restricts the Fund's operation by providing for a National Advisory Council of five for the purpose of determining whether the operations of the Fund (and the Bank) are consistent with the policies and interests of the United States. The problem of co-ordination of policies and the elimination of rivalry is solved by appointing a single person to represent the United States as governor of both the Bank and the Fund, he in turn to be advised by the Council. The effectiveness of this method of co-ordinating the activities of the Fund and the Bank will however be dependent upon the other nations of the world following a similar policy. It is to be hoped that other members of the United Nations will be in accord with the interpretation placed upon the Agreements by the United States.

## THE INTERNATIONAL BANK FOR RECONSTRUCTION AND DEVELOPMENT

A full-rounded program of international finance for the post-victory era must include means for increasing the volume and safety of long-term foreign investments. Nations which have felt the scourge of war need foreign loans for reconstruction. Far Eastern countries that are old in history and tradition but young economically can with advantage use capital in excess of their own capacity to produce and save.

For more than a century after gaining its independence, the United States was a borrower in the investment markets of the world, with the result that at the outbreak of World War I it was a heavy debtor on net balance. As a consequence of selling billions of dollars worth of food and munitions to our allies, we emerged from that conflict a creditor nation. When we changed from borrower to lender we found ourselves in a role for which we were not prepared. Lured by high interest rates, and stimulated to purchase securities by investment houses which enjoyed high selling commissions, the investors in this country in the years 1922–29 poured out American capital in the form of security purchases, direct investments, and short term funds to the amount of $7.7 billion. Though this was offset by an inflow from abroad of $3.3 billion, the net outflow was $4.3 billion.

Lenders paid little attention to the productive nature of these investments, or borrowers to the effect of heavy interest installments upon their balance of payments. The drastic decline in the price of primary goods in depression years made it impossible for the debtors to meet the demand for current imports and interest payments on the debts. Simultaneously with the fall in the value of exports, the possibility of added borrowing in the United States ended. The net outflow of American capital had fallen to less than $300 million in 1929. In the decade of the 1930's the return flow of American funds from abroad exceeded the outflow. The annual interest charges on foreign capital of the South American countries by 1930 were $250 million. Most of these countries relied heavily upon one or two export commodities to maintain their trade balance. Coffee, for example, constituted 71 per cent of the value of the exports of Brazil; Bolivia's exports were 77 per cent tin. Suspension of the gold standard and defaults on foreign loans followed as a matter of course.

The losses sustained by American investors in the 1930's discouraged foreign loans, but it is only fair to say that the real losses were not as large as is popularly believed, for many loans which were in default were ultimately paid in whole or in part. Even where the principal has not been recovered, consideration should be given to the higher interest rates which were collected and which, considering the investments as a whole, served as a partial offset for the loss of the principal of some of the loans. Obviously this did not help the individual investor unless he had a diversified portfolio.

Foreign investment is of special importance to the economy of the United States. In the first place, our country will be the principal source for loans now that the war has ended. Britain, historic creditor nation, is expected to be in a debtor position when account is taken of all her indebtedness to this country and of the billions of blocked sterling balances described in a subsequent section. We in the United States have a great pool of savings upon which we may draw in order to make loans abroad. In 1943 and 1944 the people of the United States saved approximately 27¢ out of every dollar of individual income in the form of savings deposits, war savings bonds, purchases of insurance and similar types of capital accumulation. If our future rate of saving even approximates the present volume it will make possible large foreign investments without hampering our own industrial development.

A second reason why foreign investment is of importance to us is that we are looking for export markets for our industries. While it is conceded that in the long run goods and services must balance goods and services, in the immediate postwar years we expect an excess of merchandise exports over imports. Nations devastated by war will require outside capital to build up their economies to the point where they can export enough to pay for the needed imports. We are currently exporting on an unprecedented scale, and we desire to maintain a high level of exports. To do so we shall have to give financial assistance to our potential customers until their own economies are in a position to export goods in exchange.

The principal forms of investment are loans and direct investment. The latter, which will chiefly take the form of ownership of subsidiary or controlled companies, has the advantage of not placing a burden upon the exchange market; it does not create a fixed charge which must be transferred each year regardless of economic conditions. In times of depression and low prices, such as the early 1930's, dividends would be nil; in prosperous years the larger earnings could be transferred without difficulty. Direct investment bids fair to increase in importance and needs little assistance by official agencies. There is also a large place, however, for foreign loans. Moreover, it is generally agreed that private investment abroad will not be adequate to meet the anticipated world need unless it is encouraged by governmental support. It is to assist this type of long-term international financing that the Bank proposed at Bretton Woods was designed.

A survey of the principal features of organization and operation of the Bank may give a background for an understanding of its purposes and its hoped-for services. The capital has been fixed at $10 billion, of which only 20 per cent will be paid at the outset; the remainder will be subject to call by the Bank only when required to meet obligations arising out of making or guaranteeing loans. Our quota is $3,175 million, which is more than double that of any other member nation.

With the head office located in the United States, agencies or branches may be established in other member nations. The administration of the Bank is separate from that of the Fund, but presumably the two will work in close cooperation since they were devised to complement one another.

Of the Bank's two general methods of making or facilitating loans, by direct lending out of its own funds or by guaranteeing loans made by private investors, it is contemplated that the latter will be its most important service. Private loans will be made through the usual investment channels and insured by the Bank in whole or in part. The American public is familiar with guaranteed loans made for home financing under the Federal Housing Administration and with V-loans made by the banks to finance war production. The Bank for Reconstruction and Development will apply the same principles to international loans. The borrower pays the commission which is, in effect, an insurance fee.

Loans made or guaranteed by the Bank must be for the purpose of specific projects of reconstruction or development, with the government or central bank of a member nation fully guaranteeing repayment of each loan unless it is itself the borrower. All projects must be approved by a competent loan committee which must include one representative of the member in whose territories the project will be located. The only restriction on interest rates and the schedule of repayment is that they must be reasonable.

Careful supervision and the limitation of advances or guarantees for specific projects should eliminate speculative loans. In time of stress the Bank more safely than private investors can give relief to the debtor by granting an extension of time. The endorsement of all loans by the member nation puts it on notice to consider how repayment of the loan would affect its balance of payments. The borrower as well as the lender is protected under the limitations placed upon loans. The Bank is not expected to supplant existing lending agencies, for it cannot make a direct loan until it has satisfied itself that the borrower would be unable to obtain the loan from private foreign investment agencies, on reasonable terms, with or without the guarantee of the Bank. Under this limitation its primary function will be to guarantee private loans.

For a decade the Export-Import Bank has served somewhat the same functions as will the International Bank. It is entirely owned by the United States Government and was authorized in 1934 to aid in financing and facilitating exports and imports. By the terms of the Export-Import Bank Act of 1945 (approved on the same date as the Bretton Woods Agreements Act), the capital of the Bank was enlarged and its lending authority increased. It is a going concern in contrast to the Bank for Reconstruction and Development which is still in the formative stage. Moreover, when both are fully functioning there is no reason why their operations will prove competitive.

### LIQUIDATION OF WAR-CREATED INTERNATIONAL INDEBTEDNESS

Our international financial program for the future must provide for the disposal of intergovernmental obligations arising out of the war. Settlement of Lend-Lease aid and adjustment of blocked sterling balances are the most significant problems of this type immediately before us. Reparations and intergovernmental debts plagued us for nearly two decades after World War I. We still have as a legacy therefrom the worthless I.O.U.s of our former allies and a punitive statute, the Johnson Act, which, however, has in effect been repealed insofar as it might apply to members of both the Fund and the Bank.

Near the close of the Versailles Conference in 1919, J. M. Keynes resigned as adviser to the British Treasury to write his prophetic book *The Economic Consequences of the Peace.* His warnings regarding the dire consequences of staggering reparation payments and huge inter-governmental war debts proved to be tragically accurate. The 1920's saw the breakdown of the original reparations which was the plan followed, as a retaliatory measure, by the French and Belgian occupation of the Ruhr. They witnessed the inauguration of the Dawes Plan, which fixed annual reparations payments but did so without limiting the time or total amount. After five years of operation, during which time Germany paid regularly and in full, the Dawes Plan was superseded by the Young Plan, which was intended as a definitive settlement of reparations. The Young Plan created the Bank for International Settlements to replace the Agent General of Reparation Payments as the administrative and transfer agency for reparations payments.

In that decade the allied and associated nations one by one signed agreements with the United States Treasury providing for the repayment of the money advanced by our government in 1917–19 to aid in the prosecution of the war. All agreed to repay the principal in full but obtained relief through reduction in interest rates, presumably adjusted to the differing capacities of the debtor nations. From the date when the several agreements were signed (1922–25) all stipulated payments were made promptly and completely until 1931. The same was true of German reparations from 1924 to 1931. From the international point of view, however, the indebtedness was not truly liquidated. Germany was the ultimate debtor; the United States was the principal net creditor. Reparations payments made to France and England were in substance transmitted to the United States in payment of semi-annual debt installments. At the same time private investors, chiefly in the United States, were lending to German municipalities and industrial enterprises more money than the German government paid out in settlement of reparations. The Dawes and Young plans each called also for international loans directly to the Reich. Germany was borrowing from Peter to pay Paul; in the role of Peter, United States investors acquired some sour loans. When in 1929 the flow of funds through private investment ceased, Germany by cutting prices increased her exports sufficiently to pay her 1930 installments. However, it was an unwelcome form of payment from the standpoint of the creditor nations. They would have preferred to cancel the debts rather than press for payment which would force Germany to search the markets of the world for outlets for her products to obtain foreign exchange with which to pay her debt installments.

In May, 1931, the Credit-Austalt of Austria crashed, after vainly trying to bolster the industrial system of a country that comprised only a fraction of the old Austria-Hungarian monarchy but included most of its manufacturing section. Austria's former customers were now citizens of independent states which sought to build up their own industries. The crisis spread rapidly to Germany, and it became apparent that her financial status had deteriorated to such a degree that she would be unable to make her mid-year reparations payments. In this emergency President Hoover proposed a one year moratorium on all intergovernmental debts to be effective immediately. For us this meant postponing the receipt of roughly a quarter of a billion dollars. France, whose net receipts (reparations less payments on war debts) were second in amount to our own, balked. She was aggrieved because her approval had not been obtained in advance of the announcement; she may also have foreseen that the definition of a moratorium as "insolvency for future delivery" would hold good with respect to further reparations payments. Ultimately she yielded, but the delay negated the good that might have been achieved by prompt action.

When the moratorium year was over the world's financial plight was worse than it had been in 1931 and the European nations gathered at Lausanne to seek a new settlement of the reparations issue. The "solution" that came out was a drastic reduction of the reparations, conditioned however upon a reduction of the War Debts. As net creditor we were asked to cancel a large proportion of our claims. But the American philosophy with respect to the debts had been succinctly summarized by President Coolidge in his statement, "They hired the money, didn't they?", and we persisted in adhering to the policy that there should be no official linking of the debts with reparations, manifestly an unrealistic attitude and one completely at variance with the Hoover Moratorium.

It was election year in the United States, and both candidates stood firmly for collection of the debts regardless of the reparations settle-

ment. On his way to Washington from Palo Alto where he had gone
to cast his vote, and immediately following the November election,
President Hoover invited the President-elect to a White House conference on the thorny debt question. The conference was held with
Mr. Roosevelt accompanied by Mr. Raymond Moley, but no solution
was found. Debt installments were due December 15 and President
Hoover apparently saw no alternative to insistence upon payment.
The British protested but boxed up $95 million in gold and shipped it
to us. The French boxed their gold also, but after a stormy all-night
session the Chamber refused to sanction its shipment. The Herriot
ministry fell, and the gold was dumped back into the vaults of the
Bank of France.

In the so-called Controlled-Inflation Act of May 12, 1933, we gave
the debtor nations the option of paying in silver at 50¢ per ounce
(approximately 50 per cent above silver's market price at the time).
Britain sent us a "token" payment of approximately $10 million, but
most of the debtors were no more interested in paying with silver than
with gold. Finland continued her relatively small payments until
attacked by Russia in 1940. As for the other countries, they appear to
have regarded Will Rogers' advice to the administration, that we send
them a cablegram "Pay up or default," as intended for their guidance.
They defaulted! In 1933 it might have been possible to get a settlement
that would have yielded some return to our treasury had a realistic
policy been followed, but our reply to the defaults was the passage of
the Johnson Act named for its sponsor, the late Senator Hiram Johnson
of California, in April, 1934. Under its terms it was unlawful for any
person to purchase bonds or securities of foreign governments which
were in default on their War Debt Settlements to the United States.

By 1939, the reinforcement of the Johnson Act by the provisions of
the Neutrality Act made necessary the cash-and-carry policy which we
followed in the early months of the recent war. From Cash and Carry
we gradually evolved to Lend-Lease, which was authorized March
11, 1941. By August, 1945, we had granted $41.2 billion of Lend-Lease
assistance to our associates. But since Lend-Lease was a program of
mutual aid we received through reverse Lend-Lease a measure
of assistance sufficient to make our net credit considerably less than the
above figure.

A fundamental difference between the loans of World War I and

Lend-Lease is the form of obligation created. Instead of a claim for money we will have a right to ask for payment in kind; this may mean the return of the planes, ships, tanks, etc., which we have supplied to our allies, although obviously much of the stock of war munitions will be virtually worthless. Some equipment may be sold in the countries in which it is physically located. Reverse Lend-Lease will cancel part of the obligation. Payment for Lend-Lease goods now overseas, which are subsequently sold to foreigners, will require extension of long term credit in some form. It is gratifying to know, however, that the nations will not be confronted with a great rubble of paper debts that will cause years of bickering and then end in repudiation. Dr. B. H. Beckhart, Professor of Banking at Columbia University, has advised that in the settlement of Lend-Lease aid we should accord "generous treatment," and with this we concur. It will be more realistic to close the books and remove from the exchange markets of the world the disturbing element of transfer of debt payments than to repeat our World War I experience.

Two pieces of unfinished business arising from the intergovernmental debts of World War I should be attended to early. We should both dispose of the debts and repeal the last vestiges of the Johnson Act. Though five years ago it was urged, with some reason, that we should hold the debts as a card to play at the peace table, today the only feasible solution is outright cancellation.

A second war-created international indebtedness which has provoked much discussion is blocked sterling balances. Huge purchases have been made by Britain in other members of the British Commonwealth, principally India and Egypt. Payment has been effected by an extension of credit in the form of balances in London to the credit of those nations. These balances are "blocked," i.e., the countries to which they belong do not have the right to draw them or spend them as they please. Because the amounts involved are large ($8 billion for India and $1 billion for Egypt), these blocked balances are held to be a threat to the functioning of the proposed International Monetary Fund. Certain American economists and bankers have proposed a huge loan from the United States to Britain, large enough to unfreeze these debts, as an essential step before exchange stabilization is undertaken. Edward E. Brown gives an excellent banker analysis of the blocked balance issue. Regarding such a loan as inexpedient he proposes the gradual repayment of these balances over a period of years through exports from Britain to the creditors. He anticipates that repatriation of English capital invested in these countries will help in repaying the debts. If the obligations are repaid slowly he sees no reason why the United Kingdom cannot "maintain a stable currency and settle its current international accounts promptly." It should not be too irksome for the countries holding the blocked balances to accept gradual repayment. The corollary that the countries will not have the right to spend freely in the markets of the world does not appear inequitable when account is taken of their war-created origin. Like the goods we have provided through Lend-Lease they have been used to fight a cruel enemy. Repayment in kind can readily be defended under these circumstances.

The fundamental thesis of this chapter has been that the financial program for tomorrow must be international in function and administration. In the mid-1930's after the fiasco of the London Conference of 1933, the crumbling of the League, the imposition of foreign exchange restrictions and the upsurge of nationalistic trade policies, advocacy of internationalism was described as a "triumph of hope over reality." Today UNRRA and the Bretton Woods provisions of the Fund and the Bank offer a possibility for international cooperation in the realm of finance. They deserve a fair trial. The slate should be wiped clean of the World War I debts and the Johnson Act which is associated with them. Lend-Lease because it provides for repaying advances in kind instead of money does not threaten us with such disturbing postwar balance-of-trade relations as did the debts which plagued us for a decade and a half after World War I. Liberal settlement of these war-created obligations on a realistic basis is urgent. An integrated financial program of this type can contribute toward achieving such larger objectives as expansion of international trade, the raising of the levels of employment and income in the member nations, and world peace. It is neither a panacea nor a final solution; it is rather a next step.

HOWARD H. PRESTON

# CHAPTER XII ♦

# *Cartels and Commodity Control Schemes*

CONTROVERSY rages at home and abroad over the question of what to do about cartels and commodity control schemes.

Cartels are strongly supported by British and European businessmen and governments; but while a few American businessmen seem to favor them the majority opinion of both business and government in the United States appears to be opposed. Nevertheless, commodity control schemes, which, as we shall see, have some of the characteristics of cartels, are looked upon with favor by officials of the United States Department of Agriculture, if not by other Americans. A clear understanding of the issues is essential to the formulation of sound public policy. Cartels and commodity control schemes have much in common: both are instruments of international trade policy, both are restrictive in nature and impose limitations on economic freedom, both may become weapons of economic warfare.

Webster defines a cartel as "a combination of separate firms to maintain prices; a pool," a definition which, while essentially accurate, is inadequate. A cartel, in the economic sense, is an *association* of *business concerns* which may and usually does restrict production, raise prices, divide up markets, set quotas, exchange patents, and endeavor by various means to "stabilize" an industry.

Cartels may be either national or international although the latter are most important to the problem of world peace. Formed by private business, the incentive is usually the ever-present urge of most industrialists to circumvent the uncertainties of full and free competition by curbing supply, to the enhancing of prices and profits. *Stabilization*, the avowed goal of the cartel, means the elimination of innovations which might disturb the market and have unhappy repercussions on the value of invested capital, and on the profits of the owners by

156

lowering the price of the product to consumers. Governments some-times are parties to cartels or give them official sanction, either because the governments are dominated by the industrialists, or because the men in control of government seek ends which cartels may further. Germany has long recognized cartels and used them as instruments of economic warfare, frequently participating in the management and, under Hitler, completely subjugating them to national policy. The British Government, yielding to the pressure of industrialists, has likewise been sympathetic to cartels, without going as far as Germany in actual participation.

Commodity control schemes differ from cartels, with which they are frequently confused, on several important counts. In contrast with cartels which largely deal in manufactured goods such as steel, dyes, chemicals, or services like transportation and communication, com-modity control schemes always center on raw materials or agricultural products such as coffee or rubber. Moreover, commodity control schemes are predominantly encouraged and participated in by govern-ments, without the aid of which, they would, indeed, be rendered largely ineffective. While the same goal of stabilization is usually pres-ent, the economic pressure for commodity control plans usually stems from farmers or miners rather than from industrialists. Frequently also the control may be the outgrowth or the attempted solution of an over-expansion in which the government may have been at fault in encouraging excessive production. Moreover, the leading nation in such a scheme usually has a strong advantage, if not a monopoly, in the commodities covered.

The important point is that both cartels and commodity control plans are monopolistic and restrictive in essence and may be used, as they actually have been, to wage economic warfare and to exploit consumers. They should, therefore, be viewed with suspicion and permitted to operate only under stringent supervision and where no other effective solution to a particular problem can be found. It must also be pointed out and emphasized that cartels and commodity control plans are closely akin to protective tariffs and other interferences by governments with the free course of international trade.

Though Germany is only one of a score of countries in which cartels have flourished, the German dyestuffs industry affords one of the best examples of the development of an international cartel. According to testimony given before the Temporary National Economic Committee of the Congress of the United States in 1940, there were, in 1912, "16 independent firms in Germany making coal-tar dyes, with more than 90 per cent of the output controlled by five large firms." By the outbreak of World War I, through various interlocking devices, these firms had been divided into two major groups, *Hochst-Cassella* and *Badische*. Seeking to meet competition more effectively, to pool purchases of raw materials, to protect each other in patents and licensing, to exchange certain products and jointly to establish foreign branch plants, these two groups succeeded in controlling raw material prices, reducing competition, cutting costs of production and selling, and even lowering prices. In 1916, all of the dyestuffs firms in Germany united to form the great *Interessengemeinschaft Farbenindustrie Aktiengesellschaft,* popularly called I. G. Farben or the dye cartel. By 1925, the organization had branched out into many other fields and had made cartel agreements in dozens of commodities with producers in every part of the globe not excluding the United States.

Despite the prohibitions against monopoly in the anti-trust laws, the United States has been influenced by the cartel movement in several ways. An international cartel might establish a branch factory in the United States; an American firm might enter into patent or license agreements with international cartels; American firms might organize an export association under the Webb-Pomerene Act, which has been on the United States statute books since 1918. Though the associations formed under the Webb-Pomerene Act have not, except in a few industries, been outstandingly effective, they have potentialities for restricting the free course of international trade and should therefore be recognized as part and parcel of the encumbrances of the past which may need overhauling. The very existence of this Act points up sharply the inconsistency between American foreign trade policy and that followed at home. Freedom of competition in the domestic market is the avowed goal of the antitrust laws; restriction, bordering on monopoly, characterizes our foreign trade legislation, as both the Webb-Pomerene Act and our protective tariffs testify.

As dangerous to economic freedom as cartels are commodity control schemes. We have noted in an earlier chapter the conclusion of an international wheat agreement by the governments of Argentina, Australia, Canada, Great Britain, and the United States in 1942. This plan savors so highly of the restrictive schemes of the past to control coffee, rubber, tin, and other commodities, that it does not augur well for the future. It must be recognized, however, in appraising such programs, that they are designed to correct conditions which have become critical national, if not international, problems. Most of them have been engineered by the governments of interested countries, a fact which places them in a somewhat different category from privately organized cartels although they have essentially the same economic effect on the market.

Experience with rubber affords a good illustration of how such schemes originate and operate. Before World War I, plantation rubber in British Malaya, Ceylon, and the Dutch East Indies had displaced wild rubber as the chief source of supply. Plantings had been so heavy that stocks of rubber were beginning to be excessive by the end of the war. By 1920, prices had fallen so low that plantation owners became deeply concerned and turned to government for aid. The Stevenson Plan, adopted by the British late in 1922, was essentially an effort to restrict production and raise prices and sought to achieve its goal by limiting exports. The argument made, that prices should be adequate to cover costs of production, was familiar to our own agricultural program. Though the plan was partially successful for a few years some of the prices sought were exhorbitant and the plan was weakened both by the unwillingness of the Dutch to participate and by the antagonism of the United States, the chief consumer of rubber. Not only was the plan protested, but more positive efforts were employed. A much larger use of reclaimed rubber cut the consumption of crude rubber enough to arouse the concern of rubber planters. In addition, American interests started rubber plantations of their own in areas not controlled by the British.

The British withdrew their support of the Stevenson Plan in 1928 and prices declined steadily until 1934, when the governments of France, the United Kingdom, India, the Netherlands, and Siam signed an agreement to regulate the production and export of rubber with

the object of reducing existing world stocks to a normal figure and adjusting in an orderly manner supply to demand and maintaining a fair and equitable price level which will be reasonably remunerative to efficient producers.

Recognition, unique in such schemes, was made of consumer interests in the provision for an advisory panel of three members. Judged by the effect on production and prices, this program succeeded in its objective until World War II disrupted it. By 1937 the price was over two and a half times that of 1933, though it fluctuated both before and after the former date. Both production and price rose steadily between 1938 and 1941. Since 1941 war conditions have dominated rubber production and distribution.

The American people may be expected to oppose cartels. Responding to a traditional sentiment against monopolistic practices and undisturbed by refinements of definition, they instinctively and correctly identify cartels with the genera of business practices condemned by our antitrust laws. At the same time, there is danger that they may cling to an equally repressive international obstacle to their own welfare, the protective tariff system. Actually, protective tariffs are one of the causes of cartels. Evidence in support of this statement may be gleaned from British experience since 1932 when the Import Duties Act marked the reversal of nearly a century of free trade. That British industry became widely cartelized is shown by Dr. Ben W. Lewis of the Oberlin College faculty of economics after a first-hand investigation. In a report published by the University of Chicago Press ("Prices and Production Controls in British Industry," Public Policy Pamphlet No. 25), he points out that

The essential condition making it possible for private industry to inaugurate effective schemes of control has been provided by the Import Duties Act of 1932 and the activities of the Import Duties Advisory Committee under the terms of the Act.

From the standpoint of the welfare of the United States, cartels and tariffs must be linked together. Just as tariffs frequently have given rise to cartels in the past, so the removal of tariffs may provide a competitive opportunity which will make cartels less effective if it does not destroy them. Moreover, if the United States proposes to negotiate with Great Britain and other nations for the elimination of cartels now the war is over, it is very certain that those nations will counter with a request that we reduce our high tariffs and repeal our Webb-Pomerene Act and other restrictive legislation.

Such an exchange of concessions is only fair and reasonable. If we want monopolistic practices removed from international trade, we must do our share to open up our markets to other nations. In so doing, we must be practical and recognize that protected American interests will shout loudly against the removal of the umbrella which we have held over them. Each industry should be studied carefully and the decision be reached on the basis not of the wishes of the industries but of the welfare of all American citizens and the peace of the world. For some industries, the decision may well be that a gradual reduction of tariffs over a period of years would be fair and would enable the industry and its employees to make necessary readjustments; for others it may be found that protection merely adds to the profits of a few and that the tariff could be removed without serious repercussions on the public. If it is found that protection serves chiefly as an instrument of economic warfare it will have to yield to the pressure for disarmament—to the requirements for a world at peace. In the final analysis, protective tariffs are essentially a disguised W.P.A. for business, a device to provide a few jobs in industries which could not stand on their own legs without government subsidy of some sort.

A possible solution to the cartel problem may be to establish an international antitrust division under the Economic and Social Council of the new peace organization of United Nations. Such a division should be empowered to find the facts on international monopolistic practices inimical to world peace and to make recommendations to the international court and the security council for appropriate action.

Our attitude toward commodity control schemes is not likely to follow so clear-cut a pattern. Attention has been called to our recent participation in a wheat scheme. The United States Department of Agriculture appears to look with favor upon such programs, no doubt because we are surplus producers of wheat and cotton. As much as fifty per cent of our cotton has been exported, and large tonnages of wheat have been marketed abroad. Moreover, our domestic policy has been to maintain prices on farm products regardless of world markets. The Government has extended liberal loans to farmers and has taken over substantial quantities of cotton and wheat. The Government is therefore in business and anxious to dispose of its holdings.

Under the existing law governing the disposal of surplus war commodities, the United States Government now encourages exporters to sell wheat and cotton abroad at whatever price they can get. If this price is below the artificially high price maintained by the Government in the United States, the difference is paid to the exporter by the Commodity Credit Corporation. The C.C.C. gets its money from the American taxpayers, who thus have to pay a double subsidy, first in the higher prices for wheat and cotton, and second, in taxes to reimburse the exporters of those commodities to foreign consumers. Here is another glorified W.P.A., this time for the farmers.

In other products such as bauxite, tin, and natural rubber, the United States is a large consumer with but little or no domestic production. (Artificial rubber has not yet demonstrated its ability to replace the natural product for most uses and it remains much too expensive.) These commodities have been controlled in the past by producer schemes without much, if any, representation by consumer nations. It will therefore be difficult for the United States to formulate and adhere to a policy of disavowal of all commodity control schemes on the same forthright basis as it may condemn cartels. While we are the chief sufferers of control schemes of others, we have our own problem children. A middle course may be forced upon us.

Such a course would be based on a recognition of the two problems involved and would seek a sound solution to both. The first of these derives from the commodity control schemes which have evolved as attempted solutions of the admittedly difficult problem of excessive production and falling prices. They attempt to mitigate the effect of unrestricted competition because such competition would work severe hardship on many producers. Governments which, like our own, have encouraged production by subsidies and other devices are reluctant to let competition take its course. Indeed, it has been politically impossible in the United States in recent years to do so. The second problem to be faced squarely is that of the danger in the commodity control scheme as a monopolistic device. Branding it for what it is does not necessarily mean that it has no place in world economy. We have many monopolistic industries in the United States, recognized as such and protected by the law. The procedure is to regulate them so as to prevent abuses. There is much to be said for both cartels and commodity schemes on the side of organization and administration. An ideal economy would be one in which commodities flowed smoothly and continuously from producers to consumers with a minimum of market distortions. At the same time the price structure should yield equitable terms to producers and distributors without gouging consumers. Cartels have developed skills in adjusting production to consumption and in orderly marketing. Their abuse or misuse as instruments to exploit the consumer should not cause us to ignore their possibilities for production and market planning. As a solution to the harassment of ever-recurring surpluses of natural products, or as a means to orderly distribution of scarce, strategic materials, it may well be that a modified form of international control is defensible. If so, the United States may be able to make a contribution to world peace by joining in such control on a new basis. Instead of limiting it to producing nations, we must strive for equal voice by consuming nations in its actual operation, thereby evolving a program of orderly production and distribution of "problem" crops and raw materials without encouraging economic warfare and exploitation of consumers. When we face the fact that the only likely alternative is not free competition but a continuation of chaos, it would seem to be the wiser course to investigate the possibilities for improvement inherent in experience with control.

The United States, with much at stake in finding a sound solution to these problems, has the powerful leverage of concessions which it may make in exchange for improved world trade conditions. Tariffs may be reduced, the Webb-Pomerene Act repealed, artificial price supports withdrawn, credits extended—all on the condition that cartels are eliminated, foreign tariffs removed, and full and equal representation on commodity control plans accorded to consumers as well as producers. Such questions should be considered, as they undoubtedly will be, at an international trade conference patterned on the Bretton Woods financial meeting. Once the United Nations security organization were set up, such problems as these would fall properly to an office of the Economic and Social Council of the new organization of United Nations. A raw materials bureau might well be established to deal with strategic natural economic commodities and international control schemes.

In conclusion, then, it is recommended that the policy of the United States be a realistic opposition to cartels and a limited participation in commodity control programs carefully supervised by the Economic and Social Council of the new United Nations organization for world peace. The people of America must be prepared to make radical concessions if they want to be sure of world peace. Cooperation is essential and cooperation is a two-way street.

NATHANAEL H. ENGLE

# CHAPTER XIII

# *International Communications*

FROM the beginning of modern history, international commerce has been closely linked with international politics, and foreign trade has flourished or languished as statesmen have aided or hindered means of transport and communication between nations. The events of the past few years likewise indicate that the development of postwar international transportation and communication will depend upon the kind of international political system which will follow the conclusion of hostilities.

Prior to 1939, excellent work had been done in getting nations to agree upon various types of control over international transportation and communication. Unfortunately, however, considerations of security, national prestige, and national welfare became progressively paramount in most nations, and international transportation and communication were not allowed to develop along logical economic lines. The lack of international cooperation prevented the even distribution of landing facilities and meteorological safeguards, a type of installation involving expenditures beyond the capacities of smaller countries. Likewise the national self-interest of the larger nations worked a hardship on small countries in the development of their merchant marine, and made possible the concentration of control of international communications in the hands of Great Britain and the United States. Commonly one thinks of communications and transport as being purely economic, but where they operate internationally they express national policies and it is impossible to separate their military, political, economic, and psychological ramifications. If the so-called Great Powers, ignoring this fact, resume their competition for air bases and zones of exclusion, and carry on cutthroat shipping-rate wars, the future of commercial aviation and international shipping will indeed be dark.

164

Before the war, international competition had become modernized and refined. The big nations, seeking international prestige and advantage, aided their carriers by liberal subsidies and their foreign trade by means of tariffs and other restrictive devices. Great Britain, for example, early started to subsidize her merchant marine, and made use of legislation and even naval force to restrict her competitors. At first, Britain tried to operate her international airlines without government aid, but subsidized competition forced her too to subsidize; later the depression forced increasing government investment, so that by the beginning of the recent war British Overseas Airways was a government monopoly. The British have always recognized the value of communications and transportation to any nation aspiring to create and maintain a great foreign trade. And although Britain built up her huge world-wide communications system by means of private enterprise she maintained close government supervision; and, at government suggestion, the system was unified by a great voluntary merger in which, because of depression losses, the government assumed an important role.

The United States, however, followed a different path in the development of its communications and transportation facilities. Shipping has received aid, it is true, but not to the extent provided by Great Britain, France, and Italy. The American Merchant Marine on the other hand has suffered because labor legislation has made it unable to compete with the low-cost foreign operator. In international aviation, the United States has followed the policy of a "chosen instrument" (public or private monopoly), by which it aids its one big foreign airline through mail subsidies, and when necessary, through State Department intervention. There has been, however, no government ownership or control over policies and methods of operation or extension of service.

United States international communications facilities have been developed by private enterprise on a competitive basis, the companies competing with each other as well as with foreign communications systems. Competition with foreign subsidized and often government-owned companies has been severe for American companies because political considerations have been more important than economic factors in the setting of policies. And, unfortunately, these political considerations have frequently served to prevent technological developments from being of the utmost benefit to mankind.

The number one problem at the close of this war, so far as the shipping industry is concerned, is undoubtedly the disposal of the tremendous surplus of ships in the possession of the United States. This country probably controls between fifty and fifty-five million dead weight tons of shipping at this time. When this figure is compared with the eleven million dead weight tons that made up the American Merchant Marine in 1939, one begins to realize the immensity of the problem; and when we discover that 2,200,000 tons were idle in 1939, the surplus appears even more formidable. Of this large tonnage, about one-tenth are vessels more than twenty years old, and thus ready for the scrap heap, while vessels purchased abroad, or taken over during the war, account for about one ton in thirty. The largest part of the fleet, however, consists of modern vessels built in the United States. More than one-half of these are Liberty ships, ten-thousand ton general cargo vessels with welded steel hulls, propelled by twenty-five hundred horse-power reciprocating steam engines, rated at eleven knots. These Liberties are good ships, basically sound, and have given excellent wartime performance. Less than five per cent have suffered serious fractures, a record which compares favorably with that of any other type of ship. Their weakness is an economic one and in the postwar competition they will often be found to be too big for many trades, too costly to operate, and too slow to compete with foreign ships.

In addition to the over-age vessels and the slow Liberties, there remain in the hands of the United States some twenty-two hundred vessels of twenty-four million tons capacity, a fast modern fleet twice the size of the prewar merchant marine. This fleet consists of high-speed tankers and swift, new, dry-cargo ships, all of them capable of taking and maintaining their place in the competitive postwar shipping world, a great contrast with the merchant fleet of 1939 of which more than one-half of the ships were obsolete, two-fifths comprised small vessels, and five-sixths were slow.

But equally important is the change that is taking place in the reallocation of tonnage throughout the world. The United States, which has been launching about three-fourths of the world's new ships, has become the world's greatest shipping nation. Out of this situation will come one of the momentous postwar economic problems. In 1939, the United Kingdom had twenty-six per cent of the world's ships. The United States was second with twelve per cent, followed in order by Japan, Norway, Germany, Italy, Netherlands, France, Greece, Sweden, Russia, and Denmark. At the end of 1945 the United States, as we have already noted, probably has fifty to fifty-five million dead weight tons; and the British merchant fleet though second is considerably reduced from its prewar level. The greatest sufferers have been the important prewar shipping nations of Norway, the Netherlands, France and Greece, and though somewhat less important Yugoslavia, Belgium, and Poland, all of which at the end of the war had only small fractions of their former tonnage available. Consequently, while the problem of the United States will be one of cutting down its wartime merchant fleet, the other nations will be looking for means of rebuilding theirs.

Clearly the principal source for the rehabilitation of these fleets lies in the excess tonnage of the United States. Whether we should sell our ships to foreigners to compete with our own merchant marine in the postwar period is at present a much debated question. Admiral Land, Chairman of the U.S. Maritime Commission, recommends that surplus American tonnage be sold to foreigners at a figure equal to their cost of construction. While some claim that foreign competition will be delayed by our refusing to supply foreign operators with American built ships, it should be obvious that we will have competition whether we sell ships or not. In addition, there is the important matter of good will. The United States is indeed morally bound to help the other United Nations, and in at least one case, that of Norway, is legally bound by agreement to assist that government in a program of replacement as soon as conditions permit. There may be other commitments that have not been published.

Great Britain's position as officially stated in a British White Paper (Cmd 6373, 1942) is

that Allied Governments who have made their merchant vessels available to the Minister of War Transport for the service of the common war effort should be enabled, in order to assist them in replacing in some measure tonnage lost, to purchase a proportion of the new vessels built by H. M. Government in the United Kingdom yards and second-hand vessels purchased by H. M. Government from foreign flags.

American commitments remain vague. Lend-lease applied to wartime needs, permitting the full utilization of British, Norwegian, and

Dutch officers and other crewmen, but does not touch postwar problems.

Transfers that will have postwar effect will require consideration soon, but how far the United States will go on these commitments is not clear. The American Merchant Marine Conference at its 1944 convention renewed its 1943 recommendation proposed originally by the United States Chamber of Commerce and concurred in by the Propeller Club of the United States. This resolution, which reflects the thinking of leading men of the shipping industry, urges the policies of maintaining a large American Merchant Marine, of expanding our trade routes, of selling new fast ships to private American companies and destroying others or selling the slow ships to foreign operators, of continuing an American shipbuilding program and the training of merchant marine personnel.

Since no mention is made in this resolution of the sale of fast ships to foreign operators, one may presume that it is deemed inadvisable by the American Merchant Marine industry and the United States Chamber of Commerce. However, if the demand for these ships on the part of foreign operators is sufficient to induce them to pay a reasonable price, it seems wise for the United States to sell them. Foreign countries, by using their natural resources and labor to make products other than ships, could then help to increase general world economic production and provide goods for international trade to the benefit of the shipping of all nations. At any rate the United States can hardly refuse to turn ships over to Great Britain since the agreement in the dark days of 1942 was that Britain would concentrate her shipbuilding industry on warships while the United States would build cargo ships.

A direct parallel with aviation equipment appears, for here too Britain agreed to concentrate on the fighter craft while the United States was to build cargo ships. In consequence the United States has accumulated a large supply of commercial aircraft suitable for international routes in the postwar period, while Britain has lost considerable commercial aviation opportunities. Though the problem of disposition of surplus aircraft does not at first sight seem to be as great as that of surplus ships, it is in reality every bit as serious. Probably the same moral obligations exist, for the United States has again profited from the war situation; indeed its advantage extends much beyond the ownership and control of the aircraft, as the United States Army Air Transport Command and the Navy Air Transport Service have far-flung networks covering the globe, giving service over many more miles than were covered by all of the international airlines together before the war. The air fields, communication systems, ground facilities, and the technically trained personnel now operating on these routes place the United States a long way in the lead.

The war did not have the same effect on other international communications. Some cable operations and radiotelegraph services to occupied areas and to enemy territory had to be suspended. Undoubtedly, many facilities have been developed by the armed forces, the details of which are a closely guarded secret.

Bernard Baruch, in a report on postwar problems, has placed international communications on a level with problems of international shipping and currency. The international telegraph, telephone, and radio are the great universal catalysts of trade and culture. The money taken in by the United States international communications companies is relatively insignificant, but the kind of business they do is extremely important, for upon their efficiency depends whether the United States will grow in the future, as Great Britain has in the past, and become the center of world information and trade.

Competition is the great concern of American companies which operate transport and communications systems today—foreign competition probably more so than that of the home front. The operators of the American Merchant Marine have solved the problem of competition among themselves largely by means of the shipping conference, a device which has even helped iron out competition with the foreign operators. However, shippers are now concerned whether they can compete with the low-cost foreign carrier, particularly the tramp ship operator. To help in this respect, the Merchant Marine Act of 1938 set up a parity payment program to offset the difference in cost of building and operating ships as between the United States and foreign shipping. A continuation of this policy seems advisable especially as under the provisions of the act, should the difference in cost of operation and the cost of building ships in the United States as compared with foreign countries disappear, the parity payments would automatically be dropped.

A significant step has already been taken by delegates of maritime unions from twelve different countries which met in London late in 1944 to draw up an international Seafarers' Charter. The charter calls for minimum wages for able-bodied seamen of $72 per month as well as for general improvement in working conditions on shipboard and maximum working hours. It calls for the creation of a manpower pool in each country in order to stabilize employment in the industry, for a minimum age of sixteen years for employment, and for minimum competence to gain certification. Such agreements would lessen the gap between American and foreign operating costs and eliminate some, at least, of the need for operating and construction differential subsidies for the American Merchant Marine.

In contrast, American airplane operators have long believed that they can operate on equal terms with any foreign competitor and come out ahead because of the higher quality of service, equipment, performance and efficiency of the American technician. There is deep concern however over the fact that the United States international communications (telegraph and radio) are divided among twelve different companies, while their greatest competitor, the British, have combined into one big company. Various suggestions for overcoming this difficulty have been offered, but in general a merger of the United States-owned companies is favored.

The leading proponent of this solution, James Lawrence Fly, chairman of the Federal Communications Commission from 1939 to November 1944, believes that a monopoly would best serve public interest in the international communications field. He wants all the cable companies, radio, telegraph, and telephone services, combined into one government-regulated, government-aided, but privately owned monopoly.

The other chief proponent of unification is the Navy, which demands mandatory unification of all United States international communication facilities in a completely new company. Under the Navy's plan the Government would take all required facilities by eminent domain, the payments to be handled by the Reconstruction Finance Corporation, and stock to be sold to the United States public. To assure Congress definite powers over it, the company would be organized under a national, rather than a state charter. The FCC would be given jurisdiction over the company's rates and practices only; high policy would be government-controlled, either by an advisory board of representatives of the State, Army, Navy, Commerce, and other departments, or by government-appointed directors, but both the State Department and Congress would approve final policy.

President Roosevelt assigned to the State Department the task of correlating the ideas of business, the Navy, FCC, and other interested government agencies, and an interdepartmental telecommunications committee on which Congress is represented was set up under an Assistant Secretary of State. Apparently this committee will favor something more conservative than the Navy proposal. As for Congress, Senators Wheeler and White of the Senate Interstate Commerce Committee indorse a strong system, but want Congress to make its own study and draft its own bill.

It has been found that communications do not serve the public best under competition. A single United States company in the international field would probably be stronger in dealing with a foreign government-owned or government-backed monopoly than would any one of several competing American companies. A unified service would permit managerial economies and incur fewer such expenses as the one thousand dollars per day cost of a cable ship. A better distribution of messages over the different systems would make possible more efficient use and better service. And finally, an American company interested only in international communication would be free to use the best technicians and the most modern equipment and solve its problems without outside influence.

The present lack of national policy stems at least in part from American opposition to monopoly. Not until 1936 did officials decide that competition between United States communications companies in the foreign field was not in the public interest. Since that time the Federal Communications Commission has chosen those whom it has wished to represent the United States. It is high time for the American people to demand that Congress take a definite stand and aid in building one strong United States communications company in the foreign field.

Another important problem to confront the peace conference is the form of control over international air navigation. The many plans which have been advanced can be reduced to five, ranging from the freest type of competition to the strictest monopoly:

1. Free, unregulated competition, controlled through bilateral agreements only;

2. Control through an international convention similar to the Convention of 1919;

3. Regulation by an International Aeronautical Commission;

4. Government regional monopolies; and

5. A United Nations monopoly.

In free unregulated competition each nation would decide whether it would have a "chosen instrument," or competition among its own carriers. After making its decision, it would negotiate bilateral agreements with other nations with which it wished to do business. This plan, the least regulated, internationally, would require minimum international cooperation, and would go hand in hand with an international policy of sovereignty of the air. But it would not lead to a healthy expansion of international commercial aviation because each nation would try to grow at the expense of others and the resulting cutthroat competition would hamper the economic development of all.

Control through an international convention, allowing free access to air space of all signatories by every other signatory, gives commercial aviation a better working basis than a series of bilateral agreements. Scheduled services under this plan are still left to the discretion of individual nations through bilateral agreements. This method of regulation is in force in the world at the present time under the Convention of 1919 and the Pan American Convention of 1928, and seems to be favored by many in the United States, notably L. W. Pogue, chairman of the Civil Aeronautics Board. It follows the modified principle of freedom of the air as previously discussed. In the absence of complete international accord, this plan is the one most likely to be used after the war, simply because it is already in effect and requires the least change.

The two suggestions calling for government monopolies have Great Britain as their principal backer. The British would prefer a United Nations monopoly comprising one international airline corporation owned and controlled by the principal commercial aviation interests of the leading nations of the world, which would entirely eliminate competition and nationalism in international aviation. The British people look upon the airplane as a political rather than an economic problem, and realize much better than we can the potentialities of aircraft as a weapon of destruction. They therefore approach the problem from its possible evil aspects, seeking the strongest safeguard through strict control over aircraft. Failing sufficient agreement among nations to set up a United Nations commercial airline, the British would like to see regional monopolies established, which the British Empire owing to its widespread territories would be in a position to dominate. This plan entails the dividing of the world into regions, each to be served by a commercial airline monopoly set up and controlled by the leading nation in that region. The plan has few backers outside of Great Britain, and has many weak points that need not be brought into this discussion. Neither monopoly plan has much backing in the United States, though Henry Wallace advocated a "globe girdling airway" to be operated by the air arm of the United Nations police force, trained especially for war, but utilized for commercial transport during times of peace. Few advocates of these plans have as yet been heard in Europe, but undoubtedly, with the end of the war, the nations lately under German control, having experienced the horrors of total war, will voice their view in favor of strong control over international aviation.

The remaining plan, that of an International Aeronautics Board or Commission, resembles that in force under the present Convention, but represents a step forward toward a freer commercial system. Such a Board could be patterned after the Civil Aeronautics Board of the United States, and the powers vested in it would be decided by the nations making up the international cooperating group. Governor Stassen of Minnesota, an American advocate of this plan, favors a world aeronautics board to license and regulate international flying, which is to be done by private companies, rather than by state-controlled or owned "chosen instruments." Certainly, safety matters and standardization of rules and equipment and operational procedure could and should be handled by such an international body, with a great deal of benefit to commercial aviation and to the world in general.

The degree of economic regulation is the heart of the problem. Some advocate a high degree of control over rates, practices, and competition, even to the extent of granting certificates of public convenience and necessity to operators in the international field. Probably a policy of regulated competition, such as our own regulatory body is following, would be the best for the public good as it would act as a spur to quality of service and to technological improvements. Many difficult problems remain to be solved, such as the membership of the Board, the method of their selection, and the extent of their powers. Certainly some form of international representation would have to be provided, but in a framework of complete international agreement as previously postulated, such problems are not insoluble. An international commission to regulate international air navigation would be desirable and would logically follow the establishment of an international political organization.

At the International Aviation Conference held in Chicago during November, 1944, various plans were advanced. The United States advocacy of an international regulatory body to control technological phases of the industry met with very little disagreement from the other delegates. The international organization was set up in two phases; a provisional body to become active upon acceptance of the Interim Agreement by 26 states and to give way to a permanent organization when 26 states have formally ratified the permanent convention. The primary tasks of the Interim Council are to study and distribute information on problems of international air traffic. The permanent Council is given a high degree of control over technical matters. It offers the world a wonderful opportunity to forge an international air network of true benefit to mankind. In order to keep up with the rapidly changing developments in aviation, the permanent Council has been given full power to adopt, amend or annul technical annexes to the Convention by a two-thirds vote. However, the United States opposed any attempt at economic regulation because of difficulties of administration and the fact that there would be no law to guide such a regulation.

The Australian-New Zealand proposal for an exclusive international airline to be owned and operated by all nations jointly was voted down early in the Conference. The British proposed strong economic regulation, similar to that provided by the United States law, which would allocate routes and amount of service as well as rates. The Canadian proposal which called for a regulatory board and regional commissions to set rates and allocate routes was clearly a compromise.

The novel part of the Canadian plan is the basis upon which the service would be allocated. Each nation could permit as many carriers as it wished to start operating from its own territory, the minimum service being one trip per week. The regional commission would allow additional service if the line could show an average pay load factor of 65 per cent or greater. Thus a Swedish line operating between Sweden and the United States could compete with an American line, and both could operate one round trip per week. If either or both could show a load factor over 65 per cent they would be allowed to put on two or possibly three round trips per week. Thus an incentive would be provided for better quality of service, safety, and reliability. Unfortunately the irreconcilable difference between Britain and America prevented the Chicago Conference from reaching full agreement on economic problems; but two documents were prepared which paved the way for much more complete agreement in the future. The transit agreement (known as the "two-freedoms agreement") opens up most of the world by allowing aircraft of signatory nations to fly and land for service and repair in the territory of any nation which has also signed this document (by February 20, 1945, thirty-three had signed). The "five-freedom" document included the right of transit and service landing, the right to carry property and passengers between the country of origin and any other country also signing. The fifth freedom over which so much controversy arose involved the carrying of persons and property between foreign countries. It is obvious that without that right, long distance airlines would not be practical without government subsidy. Strangely enough, no mention was made of the stand to be taken by any of the major aeronautical nations on this touchy subject of subsidies. By February 15, twenty-one nations had signed the "five-freedoms" agreement. The Chicago Conference at least added to our store of experience in international cooperation and brought to light some of the points of difference that can be expected to prevent cooperation.

Modern means of international communications and transportation make it impossible for any nation to draw within itself and ignore the rest of the world. It is more imperative than ever that the family of nations have friendly, political, social, and commercial relations. Without a political agreement sufficiently strong to prevent aggression we cannot expect the remarkable developments in modern communications to bring other than misery and ruin to mankind, as the events of the last five years in Europe have so terribly demonstrated. Moreover, science has merely begun to reveal the possibilities of the airplane which even now has shrunk the earth to the point where no place is more than fifty hours from any other.

International control over all technological matters such as safety at sea and in the air, signals, lights, and rules of procedure, is certainly a necessity and seems fairly easy of attainment. International economic control can be attained gradually as conditions become more settled at the close of the war. But all these things depend upon the formation of an international political organization capable of restraining aggression and maintaining the peace. It would seem that international control over shipping, air transportation, and communication, allowing for regulated competition, world-wide in all fields, would promote the greatest welfare of the human race.

GILBERT L. GIFFORD

## CHAPTER XIV

# *Labor*

LABOR has a great stake in a sound, constructive postwar international organization which will guarantee peace, full employment, and civil liberty. Trade unions can only flourish in a society which respects civil liberties, where freedom of association is permitted, and where labor is recognized as truly as much a by-product of the democratic system as political parties, employers' associations, religious denominations, and other social groups.

It is significant therefore that the World War of 1914–18 and the years immediately following witnessed a great growth in both the numbers and the influence of labor organizations. Membership grew in Great Britain, France, Germany, and the United States where trade unions had been relatively well established; they made their appearance elsewhere, particularly in Europe where the democratic revolutions overturned the autocracies of prewar days. In return for their support of the war the unions had asked for a voice in the peace negotiations and outstanding labor representatives from many countries gathered in Paris and assisted in formulating Part 13 of the Peace Treaty which established the International Labor Organization.

The workers insisted that economic factors had been largely responsible for the war and that if imperialism could be eliminated or lessened by raising labor standards throughout the world and by giving labor a voice in policy, substantial steps toward world peace would be made. Like their predecessors of the previous century, they believed that if the purchasing power of the workers were raised throughout the world industry would find expanding markets and thus avoid the periodical crises of so-called overproduction. Above all, they took their stand on the principle of social justice which alone could overcome the unrest which imperiled the peace and harmony of the world.

The International Labor Organization which was established in 1919 marked an outstanding step in the advance of labor, but it was not universally accepted and had to make its way despite opposition from certain influential quarters. Conservative and reactionary employers argued that society should trust to the law of supply and demand. Many of them opposed collective bargaining and claimed that the running of a business was the exclusive affair of the employer. Some critics alleged that conditions varied so greatly in different countries that the attempt to establish more uniform labor standards throughout the world was fantastic and that in any case labor legislation was primarily a matter for national action, since the nation and not the world constituted the more natural legislative and economic unit. And of course the defenders of national sovereignty looked with jaundiced eye upon any attempt to develop international institutions for the promotion of social welfare. Finally, those who believed in the class war, and these included the great revolutionary class in the Soviet Union and many communists and other extreme left-wing groups elsewhere, violently opposed the new organization on the ground that it represented a recognition of the capitalist system, and therefore merely tinkered with the surface of the economic problem.

In spite of these objections the International Labor Organization began its work. Under the distinguished leadership of the first director, M. Albert Thomas, the institution marked an increasingly significant development in international life. The annual conference was attended not merely by government representatives as had been the general custom in previous international conferences, but also by representatives of workers and employers. Moreover, conventions and recommendations might be adopted by ⅔ vote, thus marking a breach in the rule of unanimity; and delegates from member countries did not have to vote as a unit. The conference could not of course legislate directly for the member countries. What governments did undertake to do was to submit these conventions or recommendations to their respective legislative authorities for consideration, and if adopted to apply them in good faith.

The twenty-year period between the two world wars proved that the ILO had an important part to play in modern civilization. By 1939 it had adopted sixty-three conventions and fifty-six recommendations which covered many phases of modern economic life: the eight-hour day; hours of work in maritime occupations, in agriculture and in commerce, offices, and mines; a weekly rest for workers; abolition of night work for women and children and the prohibition of night work in bakeries; the protection of young people and women in industry; the provision of a six-week rest period before and after childbirth of working women; annual holidays with pay; the establishment of seamen's employment agencies on a non-profit basis; the prohibition of employment of young persons at sea. The recommendations included matters related to unemployment, labor inspection, vocational education, workers' compensation, hours of work in hospitals, hotels and theaters, unemployment in agriculture. The Office became the center of a remarkable amount of economic research. It published the *Encyclopedia of Industrial Hygiene,* made intensive studies of social insurance, weighed statistics of unemployment, vocational guidance, apprenticeship, and technical education. It cooperated with other international agencies, such as the Pan American conference on social security, and an international conference held in 1937 to draw up schemes for promoting immigration to South America. Its specialists advised national governments in Egypt, Turkey, Venezuela, and other countries of Latin America, and the governments of colonial areas in the Far East.

As it proceeded with its work the organization was driven to the conclusion that modern society could no longer afford to regard governmental policy as limited to emergency measures against unemployment and other social evils, and industrial legislation as "a sort of humanitarian excrescence on the economic conscience." Harold B. Butler, then Director of the Office, wrote in 1935 that the purely pro-

tective conception of social action is now giving way to a wider conception of social security and that the negative aim of guarding
workers against social risks and abuses "is being replaced by the
positive aim of affording him adequate opportunities both of achieving
a decent level of material comfort and of ensuring his individual development." Consequently the International Labor Conferences viewing
economic matters in the broader light of social policy and in the light
of the failure of the self-adjusting economic system had to take into
account the deeper and more fundamental questions upon which social
progress or reaction were seen to depend.

Between 1930 and 1940 the world economic depression and the
breakdown of the League of Nations precipitated a crisis which profoundly affected the ILO and the labor movement generally: the rise
of the dictatorships caused the workers from other countries to
challenge the right of fascist union members and of Soviet management
representatives to be accepted as representatives of either employees
or employers; the promulgation of communism by the Third International aroused the antagonism of the International Federation of
Trade Unions; and the American Federation of Labor refused for
a while to associate with either, though its later re-entry into the
IFTU, together with the adherence of the United States to the ILO
in 1934, helped in some measure to offset labor's losses.

The outbreak of war in 1939 had profound consequences for the
ILO and for the labor movement generally. The International Federa-
tion of Trade Unions moved its headquarters from Amsterdam to
London in 1940 but became a mere skeleton of its former self. The
Nazi conquests resulted in the destruction of the trade unions in
Belgium, Denmark, Holland, Norway, and the Balkan countries, and
today, apart from Switzerland and Sweden which still can boast of
free labor movements, Great Britain, the Dominions, and the United
States represent the only existing strongholds of the free trade union
movement. The Soviet Union has what might be called the administrative or state trade union organization. As Lewis Lorwin points out
in the March–June, 1944, issue of *World Economics,* the Soviet unions
"make collective agreements, take part in the fixing of wage rates,
adjudicate grievances, and carry on educational and recreational activities," but they operate within the collective ownership of the
USSR. Further, another type of trade union developing in Latin

America is what Lorwin calls the semi-political or semi-governmental type which functions "only insofar as it is permitted to do so and [is] supported by the governments of the respective countries." Although the trade unions of Great Britain appear ready to cooperate with the Soviet unions, the American Federation of Labor has steadfastly refused to participate in any international labor organization to which the Soviet unions may be admitted.

Thus we see a significant and perhaps ominous divergence of trade union organization and it would still appear to be an open question whether these great groups can be organized into an effective international labor organization. It is at this point that the International Labor Organization may play an invaluable role. For a generation it brought together workers and employers despite their divergent interests, and produced a remarkable degree of agreement between them. In the postwar world it may well be that the ILO will likewise become a meeting ground of the different trade union interests and provide them with wider tasks which may serve to harmonize attitudes that appear irreconcilable when viewed in a narrower light.

The question then naturally arises concerning the future of the ILO. First we must recall that the organization has suffered heavily as the result of the war, in that it has been unable to hold the annual conferences and the quarterly meetings of the governing body and has had to transfer its headquarters to Montreal, Canada, and to operate with a reduced staff. Nevertheless it has carried on a most important work and its large number of remarkable studies have formed the bases not only of two general conferences, one at Columbia University late in 1941 and the other at Philadelphia in 1944, but also of special regional conferences and of detailed policies looking toward postwar reconstruction.

The Conference at Columbia University took place at a time when the fortunes of the Allies were very low. To have held a conference at all was perhaps a remarkable act of faith, for despite difficulties of transportation and the military situation, over 200 members from 34 countries were in attendance. Even at that time, despite the overwhelming pressure of the war, the delegates realized the importance of anticipating the problems of the reconstruction period. They pledged themselves to continue the fight against the Axis powers whose philosophy spelled death to the government-employer-worker collaboration which characterized the ILO and to democracy within industry. The conference resolved that the ILO should help to translate into practice the principles of the Atlantic Charter, that the ILO should be represented at any peace or reconstruction conferences, that each member of the ILO should establish agencies to study the social and economic needs of the postwar world, that the Office should take necessary action to draft a scheme for regulating economic and social conditions in the merchant marine, and that it should prepare a plan for the establishment of a world textile office.

The later gathering at Philadelphia reaffirmed the fundamental principles on which the organization is based, emphasizing in particular that labor is not a commodity, that freedom of expression and of association are essential to sustain human progress, and that poverty anywhere constitutes a danger to prosperity everywhere. It affirmed the right of all human beings irrespective of race, creed, or sex to pursue their material wellbeing and their spiritual development in conditions of freedom and dignity, of economic security and equal opportunity. It affirmed the necessity of full employment and raised standards of living with all the measures of social security and protection for life and health of workers which such a policy entails. It passed seven recommendations providing among other things for income security, social security of the armed forces, and adequate medical services. It set forth in detail the general principles and methods of application which should implement policy in the transition period from war to peace. It urged that national employment services should be strengthened and that in view of the great damage done during the war to many countries and of the need of extensive repair national planning of public works should receive the full attention of national authorities. It passed no fewer than twenty-three resolutions which emphasized the importance of giving prominence to social objectives in the peace settlement and in the postwar period. The conference emphasized the necessity of keeping clearly in mind the social implications of economic policies undertaken in relief and rehabilitation, and the reestablishment of a satisfactory international monetary system particularly in internationally financed development works. It recognized the necessity of removing all officials identified with former totalitarian regimes in liberated countries, of reestablishing trade union organizations as soon as possible, of protecting the social insurance rights and satisfactorily adjusting the social claims of displaced persons.

The Philadelphia Conference also drew attention to the desirability of having the ILO consulted whenever international loans were to be made. In the past international investment has often been at the expense of the social welfare of the workers in the country receiving loans; the investment has not served to raise the standard of living of the people themselves however much profit it may have brought to the foreign investors. The organization urged the importance of assuring workers in the country to which capital goes that they shall not be exploited and of assuring workers from nations whence the capital comes that they shall not later be subjected to unfair competition from underpaid industries abroad.

In the period between the two wars special industrial conferences have been held, dealing with maritime, coal mining, and textile questions. The advantages of such specific conferences are obvious, for workers and employers can deal more intimately with the detailed problems which arise. Combined with the general conferences these specific conferences may do a great deal, and with this belief the ILO is laying plans for other conferences and for setting up joint committees in a number of industries.

The organization may also serve as an advisory body in drawing up labor treaties and supervising their enforcement. It can be used as an arbitration and conciliation agency in labor disputes of an international character. For example, in countries where a great deal of foreign capital is invested capital-labor disputes take on a far-reaching significance; they are not primarily intra-national questions which can be finally settled by the government of the country concerned, for they may involve the actual or alleged discrimination against the rights of foreigners. In order to take these matters out of the diplomatic field where they have in the past become badly tangled with power politics, it is suggested that an independent non-political body might serve a valuable purpose in acting as a disinterested arbitrator or conciliator.

The ILO has done extraordinarily fine work in holding its forces together even on a drastically reduced scale during the years since the outbreak of the war, but its representatives have emphasized that it faces a serious problem in the inadequacy of its finances, the complexity of the budget arrangements, and above all in the effects of wartime strain which have told upon those who has served the organization for the last twenty years. The future of the office as is well pointed out in a report prepared for the Philadelphia Conference will depend in no small measure on strengthening its ranks "by the early entry or reentry into its service of substantial numbers of men and women, young in outlook and, in a majority of cases, in years, who have the integrity, imagination, drive and technical grasp, for the challenge the age requires and who are inspired by the standards of disinterested public service to an international institution which Albert Thomas evoked among his collaborators." With the many thousands of young men and women highly trained in economics in our modern universities it should not be a matter of great difficulty to find those ready to undertake this task; those who have risked their lives on the field of battle and many others stand ready to serve the world in peacetime if they are given the opportunity. Once again we are driven to the conclusion that democracies stand on trial; they still must prove that they are ready to expend money in the building of conditions necessary to the establishment of genuine freedom; if they will devote to this but one-thousandth part of what they have spent in war they can achieve social security and personal welfare.

But it is not sufficient merely to wish in a vague and sentimental way for these ends. It is necessary also to will the means, and unless this is done the world will witness a bankruptcy of democratic purpose and achievement which will lead inevitably to the triumph of the Nazi method of solving the economic problem, i.e. providing employment by building up military power. This, however, is the road to dictatorship and war, and would make the losses in the recent struggle of wealth and human life not a sacrifice but a grim mockery.

DONALD H. MACKENZIE AND
LINDEN A. MANDER

## CHAPTER XV

# Relief and Rehabilitation

### I. RELIEF

CITIZENS of the United States may look back somewhat wistfully now upon the years from 1938 to 1941: years of crop surpluses in our country, years when lack of shipping space and our neutrality policy curtailed our agricultural exports and resulted in a glut of food, years of cheap and plentiful shoes, clothes, and tools. Those years led many Americans to feel that out of our great surpluses we could easily promise postwar relief to all the war-torn European peoples.

But what of the now liberated Europeans? With what wistfulness must they look back to prewar days, even if to less fortunate circumstances than ours! They have been under German domination for from three to five years, during which time many of them have been victims of looting, persecution, and brutality. According to official reports, during the year ending March 31, 1944, 12.9 million tons of food were moved into Germany from the occupied countries while 1.5 million tons were moved out of Germany into the occupied countries. This gives one index of the looting of food supplies, which was in addition to losses through lack of labor, lack of tools, destruction by war and deliberate destruction by guerrillas or by Germans to deprive the guerrillas of a means to existence. It is small wonder that these people are getting as little as one-quarter of what we consider the minimum essential diet. And now, in spite of our early promises, we find ourselves unable to help them as we should like. Even with the end of the war we shall not for some time be able to be of large-scale assistance, for lack of shipping space. Even after shipping has eased, we shall still be encountering difficulties.

The clothing shortage is acute. Imports of raw cotton have been cut off for over four years. Most of the other goods produced have

184

gone to the German army and the German civilian population. Blankets and heavy clothing of all sorts were gathered from all over Europe to supply the German army during the Russian campaign. Hence it is easy to believe that in liberated Europe almost as many people have died from exposure as from starvation. Fuel to relieve this distress has been scarce or unobtainable. Our official observers sum up the situation thus: "They need help in meeting the critical deficiencies in food, clothing, medicine, shelter, and transportation that have been caused by the retreating Germans and the ravages of occupation and war. They need help in returning to the homes from which they have been driven and in restoring their own production of the necessities of life."

As our forces have liberated occupied areas it has therefore been a part of military necessity, if nothing more, to relieve the distress of the people. Our first experience with military relief in the war was following the liberation of the western portions of North Africa. Because of previous preparation on the part of our government we had a civilian relief organization ready to assume the responsibility. For in December, 1942, President Roosevelt set up the Office of Foreign Relief and Rehabilitation Operations within the State Department, and in June, 1943, after preliminary conversations with other governments, the United States proposed an international relief organization, a proposal which resulted in the establishment on November 9, 1943, of the United Nations Relief and Rehabilitation Administration (hereinafter UNRRA). The Council of this body, made up of one representative from each of the forty-four United Nations, moved at once to set up a working machinery. The ideal was proposed that each uninvaded nation pledge one per cent of its national annual income for the year ended June 30, 1943, of which ninety per cent might be in agricultural or manufactured goods, and the other ten per cent in cash to cover the salaries of a trained staff and other operating expenses. A very large sum, $2,000,000,000, would thus be available, the share of the United States alone mounting to $1,350,000,000. It was understood, of course, that relief could not be given for any extended period of time to 100,000,000 people for such a sum; but fortunately this number of persons is not in need of relief. Many are still living on their own land and continuing to till the soil. In addition each national government which can afford to do so will finance its own relief, with whatever assistance it may need from UNRRA. France and Russia for example will take almost entire care of their own problems.

A Director General was provided for in the original agreement and was granted rather large powers. Ex-Governor Lehman of New York was named to the office and moved with characteristic energy in setting up an organization. He has succeeded thus far in obtaining the cooperation of the member governments. But it has been no easy task to cut across the customary bounds of national sovereignty; indeed we shall see later how many actual obstacles have been encountered by the UNRRA.

The central office of the agency is in Washington, D.C., but a European office has been set up in London with authority to make many independent decisions. A Balkan Mission-Cairo office was established, since the great bulk of war refugees from the European combat were in that area; and later a staff of twenty were sent to set up an office in Chungking. UNRRA representatives are also in Algiers, Casablanca, and Geneva. Missions have been sent to both contributing and receiving countries to arrange details of procurement and distribution. A training program was set up in May, 1944, on the campus of the University of Maryland to insure a steady supply of skilled personnel. Personnel recruited in North America receive a four weeks' intensive course for service overseas, including language study, UNRRA organization and policy, and field procedure. By September, 1944, UNRRA employees exceeded one thousand five hundred. The facilities of this program have been offered to and employed by the private relief organizations for the advancement of their work. Committees on various aspects of relief have been set up and have combined their work with that of the Inter-Allied Committee on Post-War Requirements, which has been working since September, 1941. We have thus for the first time a relatively complete picture of the requirements for the relief of suffering in this world, and the organization necessary to carry out policies has been decided upon. The question now is not whether we can make the sacrifices necessary to effectuate this relief but whether we are willing to do so.

*Food.* For the next few years the problem of supplying sufficient and appropriate food to the people of the world represents one of our chief tasks. We make the assumption here that we do intend to relieve the hungry, as indeed our leaders have promised, and consider only what it is necessary to do to fulfill our promises. Hardships will perforce be inequitably distributed for some time. Crops may be harvested in some liberated areas of Europe before sufficient transportation becomes available to handle all the food that is needed. This means that careful attention must be paid to what is actually shipped in the space that is available. Seeds may within a few months mean more in the way of available foodstuffs than an equivalent supply of food itself. Vitamins added to a grossly deficient diet may be of more value than a few added calories. Fortunately vitamins are available. Even if the supply became short it would do no harm to limit the superfluous vitamins which the people of the United States are consuming in such quantities, albeit without serious damage to the health of the population.

Though the staple grains are in good supply, the more expensive and protective foods are short. UNRRA has been unable to obtain adequate supplies of evaporated milk, edible fats, and animal proteins. When transportation becomes available the people of the United States will have to face the alternative of giving up rationing and eating more than their share of these foods, or of remaining on rationing in order that our allies and perhaps even the mothers and babies of our former enemies may receive help.

Here the true strength of UNRRA begins to appear. International cooperation in the production and marketing of wheat has been tried for a number of years though without complete success. Now a permanent subcommittee of the UNRRA has been set up to deal with the entire problem of supplying the materials judged to be needed. When a country like Australia suffers a drought which kills 2,000,000 sheep and seriously affects the wheat crop we are hard put to it to make up the deficiency. Such security as man can obtain for himself seems greatly enlarged when we know that a cooperating committee with influence in planning the cultivation of the greatest regions of the world is considering the results of such a catastrophe and taking steps to mitigate it.

The situation has been further aggravated by a food shortage in Bolivia, due in part to the restricted supply of Argentine wheat and flour, the scarcity of wheat and potatoes and beans in Paraguay; of meat in Uruguay and Chile, and of wheat in Brazil. Latin America is not the abundant source of foodstuffs that many people imagine:

rather it is a competitor for some of the world's present inadequate supply. In addition, floods and cyclones have caused "tremendous devastation on an almost nation-wide scale" in Mexico. An UNRRA mission of seven members headed by Dr. Edward Santos, ex-President of Columbia, undertook a tour to see how much Latin America could contribute to the relief and rehabilitation program, despite the unfavorable food conditions which confronted the several countries.

*Clothing.* After food, in the colder regions of the world, clothing becomes a primary concern. While ample stocks of wool and cotton are available the problem of fabrication of the raw material into cloth and then into garments appears almost insuperable. The machines of the United States and Great Britain were engaged in production for the war effort right up to V. J. day. By skillful encouragement it may be possible to get a large amount of the work done in the liberated countries themselves, even though the shortage of tools will make some of the work relatively crude. The United States has recently purchased $21,000,000 worth of United States wool to be fabricated in other United Nations plants; this should be only the beginning.

The people of the United States at first carried out a drive almost entirely through the churches of the land which contributed 15,000,000 pounds of used clothing. In addition the Red Cross, Russian Relief, China Relief, and other agencies did and are continuing to do splendid work. The United National Clothing Collection under the chairmanship of Henry J. Kaiser asked Americans to contribute 150,000,000 pounds of used and usable clothing, shoes and bedding. Participating were more than fifty voluntary war relief agencies, churches, schools, service clubs and other bodies. The success of the drive induced Canada and Australia to launch a similar appeal.

*Shelter.* Though the sheltering of the homeless people of Europe should properly be discussed under the subject of rehabilitation, two aspects of the problem cannot be dismissed here without mention. The first is the work of sheltering homeless refugees. We are already embarked on this project on a limited scale in the Near East where about 50,000 refugees from Greece and Yugoslavia were gathered. The work had previously been handled by the British but was taken over to UNRRA in recognition of the international organization set up to perform this task.

UNRRA has been too far-sighted to limit its plans to the supplying of food and primitive shelter and clothing. It is obvious that we will greatly gain by helping the people to help themselves. Hence the orders have gone out for tool kits of all kinds by the tens of thousands. These include, for example, carpenters', electricians', plumbers', masons', and blacksmiths' kits; seeds, fertilizers and farm tools; sewing machines; and even hundreds of locomotives.

*Health and Medical Care.* The health of the liberated people of Europe suffered greatly under the German regime, as indeed it was intended that it should. A definite policy of enslavement and undernutrition was in process of being carried out to portray as fact the fiction that there was a master race. By 1943 dysentery and poliomyelitis had increased over 100 per cent; diphtheria, spinal meningitis and scarlet fever over 200 per cent; and typhus, the scourge of war-torn populations, had increased over 650 per cent in regions where the disease is endemic. Malnutrition will leave a permanent mark on a part of the European population if we do not make it a primary concern to reverse the ailments caused by deficiency diseases. The situation raises the problem of who is going to render medical care to the world for the coming many years. Under the rule of the Germans a generation of young doctors has been lost from European medical schools and even in our own adjustment to war insufficient attention has been paid to the preparation of doctors. American medicine has come to occupy the top place in the profession in the entire world. We must be prepared to open our schools to more foreign students than ever in the past at the same time that the number of applicants of our own nationality will be the highest in history. We must also look forward to providing American medical men to other parts of the world, both for instruction and for the actual care of the wounded and sick. UNRRA is even now recruiting doctors in this country. It will be a real triumph if enough of them can be found to render even reasonably adequate care in areas where UNRRA is carrying on other types of relief work.

*Relocation of Displaced Nationals.* It is estimated that in Europe alone 20,000,000 persons have been dislocated by the tides of war. UNRRA has assumed that it is a right of a national of one of the United Nations to return to his former district as soon as the military report it safe for him to do so. On this basis large-scale operations are foreseen in handling the feeding, sheltering, and transportation of an enormous group of people. Very evident also is the need for preventing the dissemination of disease or if infected insect vectors of disease. It may be necessary to provide much larger sums than UNRRA is now receiving to meet this problem satisfactorily. Nevertheless the beginning has been made boldly, and we trust that this aspect of relief will not be hindered by political action and general callousness as it was so disgracefully and disastrously between 1919 and 1939. At least a beginning has been made in the arrangements completed between SHAEF and UNRRA in France, February 6, 1945, for teams of UNRRA workers to assist the military authorities in the care and movement of displaced persons.

*Far Eastern Relief.* Our aid to China has not measured up either to our hopes or to what this gallant ally deserves for its long and bitter war with the Japanese. We were unprepared to keep open the sea lanes at the beginning of the war and with the failure of the Burma Road supplies reached China in exasperatingly small quantities. Obviously no bulk foods of any kind could be delivered. UNRRA's activities for China were confined to planning—or to helpless contemplation of the requests which it received. However, these requests at least indicated the scale upon which we should be prepared to act. In comparison with all of Europe, where it is estimated 20,000,000 people have been dislocated, 40,000,000 people have been uprooted in China alone. Moreover, the transportation system of China has never been adequate and the relocation process must necessarily be of long duration.

We may place the relief of hunger in its proper perspective by examining a report in *Science Magazine* on the diet supplied Chinese soldiers during the war. The author, a Chinese scientist, states that new recruits were in a poorer physical state than soldiers maintained for a long time on a daily diet of:

> 2    lbs. rice
> 1/2 lb. leafy vegetables
> 1/3 oz. fat
> 1/3 oz. salt

The implication of this report is that the average civilian diet is even more alarmingly restricted.

In view of such evidences of the devastation which has been

wrought, we can readily understand the request for 1½ million tons of brown rice, 1.2 million tons of whole wheat flour, and 0.5 million tons of protective foods such as dried meat and dried milk. In addition to foods, large amounts of vitamins, seeds, fertilizer, and medical supplies are requested. In all, almost a billion dollars worth is requested of UNRRA, of which 45 per cent may be classified as material for direct relief, the remainder for rehabilitation. It should be pointed out that the Chinese Government, in keeping with the principle that each nation shall pay what it can, proposes to contribute about 63 per cent as compared with 37 per cent to be contributed by UNRRA. It is clear that we are not in a position to take care of these needs as yet and that we shall have no small task in helping China take her place among the democratic nations of the world. We can more easily supply the 3,256 experts in health, agriculture, industry, flood control and welfare service, and train the 400 Chinese experts requested, though the requests represents a larger drain upon the brains of our country than most people will realize. Furthermore, not even estimates have yet appeared of what relief will be required for Burma, Siam, Korea, the Malay States, the Dutch East Indies and the Philippines. However at the first meeting of the Committee of the Far East Council held in Lapstone, near Sydney, Australia, from February 15–20, 1945, comprehensive plans concerning relief food to China were discussed. The possibility of stepping up new production, the prevention of epidemics in liberated countries, and the acquisition of sufficient shipping facilities were also discussed at this meeting.

*Difficulties of UNRRA.* It is not an easy matter to estimate how far politics has been entering into the problem of relief and rehabilitation. From the limited evidence available it would appear that UNRRA suffers from several disadvantages. The Combined Resources Board in Washington, comprising representatives of the United States, Britain, and Canada have kept in their own hands the power of deciding what nations shall be helped first. The shipping difficulty referred to above has provided a serious handicap, and political differences between the Soviet Union and the other Allies are alleged by several critics to be resulting in a situation where food has become a political weapon and humanitarian conditions have been subordinate to diplomatic jockeying and possibly class hatreds. Director General Lehman announced at the beginning of 1945 that UNRRA could feed and clothe Poland and Czechoslovakia immediately if the Soviet Union would consent, though he added that the relations with Russia generally were most cordial. UNRRA for some time had a staff in Italy waiting to disperse the $50,000,000 of special relief voted by the UNRRA Council at Montreal in September, 1944; its work here has been handicapped by lack of shipping. However, in February of 1945 a beginning was made on a limited basis, including the dispatch of ships with food supplies and the planning of medical and welfare work.

It was not until August, 1945, that UNRRA began operations on an established scale. It has now given "full-fledged" aid to Greece, large-scale assistance to Yugoslavia, and a certain amount to Czechoslovakia and Poland. The Soviet Union has asked $700 million and China $900 million for relief which will be closely geared to reconstruction plans. Hundreds of teams of UNRRA workers have helped displaced peoples. The recent monthly reports reveal a program truly amazing in the scope and variety of its operations. Hundreds of physicians, welfare officers, highly trained technicians in transportation, machinery, veterinary science, etc.; thousands of tractors and trucks; livestock rehabilitation; anti-epidemic supplies, mobile canteens, DDT to spray malaria-infected areas of Greece—these and other items indicate that the relief organization has got under way despite mistakes and frequent heartbreaking delays due to the obstruction of national red tape and prestige and the complexities of recruiting and training an international civil service. Unfortunately, during the last few months the food situation in Europe has grown worse, and in truth, what may be the greatest battle of the war lies ahead—the battle against the winter of 1946. The European economy is disrupted, and transportation is totally inadequate. President Truman has warned us: "If we let Europe go cold and hungry, we may lose some of the foundations of order on which the hope of world-wide peace must rest." And O.W.I. has announced: "Thousands of persons will starve to death in Europe this winter, unless help can be rushed from outside."

The success of UNRRA is therefore essential for humanitarian reasons—hundreds of thousands of lives are at stake. And a great political issue is also at stake. Will the European peoples be driven to look back to the days of Nazi rule as a time when at least they had more food than they now have following a victory of the democracies?

If so, we shall have won only the preliminary phase of the recent war—the shooting—and lost all the rest.

Without question, UNRRA must have more funds. Congress is currently asked to vote a new contribution of $1,350,000,000 and authorize the $550,000,000 balance of our original contribution (a total sum equal to less than two weeks of our war expenditure!). Unless the United States and other members of the United Nations act promptly, we and they will be guilty of having made great promises to the peoples who resisted Nazi oppression, and then betrayed them when it came to deeds. A Gallup poll taken in the spring of 1945 showed that 79 per cent of American citizens were ready to eat a fifth less food, and a later poll taken by the *Woman's Home Companion* showed that an even larger percentage of American housewives were willing to continue rationing in order that Europe's food needs might be met.

That the United States can afford the small individual sacrifices required to help save Europe from starvation the following examples given by Americans United for World Organization will show:

Half the sugar America uses in soft drinks and other luxury products would give every resident of France about 26 pounds of sugar a year. . . . A pint of milk a month given up by each American would provide enough milk for millions of babies, young children and mothers in Europe for the last part of this year. . . . An egg a week from each American would mean 100 a year for everyone in France, Holland, Belgium, and Norway. . . . Three ounces of meat a week from each American would meet two-thirds of Europe's needs.

Finally, it is imperative that UNRRA succeed for another reason. The United Nations Charter was signed at San Francisco several months ago, but it will be a long time before it becomes a truly functioning agency. The Bank and the Fund provided by the Bretton Woods Agreement will in all probability not come into operation before 1948. But UNRRA is in operation. It gives the greatest evidence of the United Nations in action, and at the level of humanity's greatest daily need—food, clothing and shelter. If it fails it will indicate that the victorious Allies have yet to prove that they are not bankrupt in statesmenship and humanity and are superior to the Axis in much more than strength of arms.

## II. Rehabilitation

Difficult as are the problems of relief, they appear relatively easy in comparison with the problems posed by rehabilitation. (In fact, our international agencies have hardly begun the consideration of the latter.) We must recognize that UNRRA is a temporary agency and that as Director Lehman himself has stated: "UNRRA is not the agency for the economic reconstruction of the world. The United Nations have recognized that first things must come first and that relief and rehabilitation are among these first things. UNRRA is not devoted to planning for the general economic welfare of the postwar world. It is designed to plan, coordinate, administer or arrange for the administration of measures of relief for victims of war and to facilitate such rehabilitation as is necessary for the adequate provision of relief." But though we must perforce agree with this statement, it does not make clear the scope of the agency. It is well that we recognize its limitations before we embark on a survey of what rehabilitation needs to accomplish.

*Movements of Population.* Following the initial period of relief in Europe, the civilian populations will still face many trying problems. Not only will they take up life in devastated areas but they will be without certainty of property ownership within those areas. In many cases the Nazis have deliberately destroyed the records and sought to transplant populations in accordance with their plans for world domination. Properties have changed hands inequitably under the pressures of war to the advantage of Nazi sympathizers, and restoration after the war will in all probability be complicated by mutual charges of Nazi collaboration among contestants for title. These problems will have to be met by courts of the nations concerned. We cannot hope to be of much assistance in such cases.

On the other hand, we cannot hope to escape involvement. We plan to supply agricultural equipment, on whatever scale possible, to get food production under way at the earliest possible time. We will inevitably be faced with choices. To what extent in our support of agricultural production shall we recognize occupation as presumptive ownership at the risk of extending a tenure which in many cases will in justice ultimately be challenged? Little as we may like it we shall have to make judgments in such cases, and we shall need to exercise our utmost skill if we are to avoid contributing to war-breeding civil conflicts.

The general problem of national minorities has been dealt with in our chapter on that subject. But here we call attention to an interesting aspect of this problem in the fact that technology can now render the tropics not only habitable but pleasantly so. The variety and productivity of tropical areas may offer a real inducement to some Europeans who are now settled on unproductive lands in numbers greater than their type of agriculture will support. Experience warns us however that the unplanned migration of a few such persons into countries like Brazil will not be successful—they will finally settle in the cities rather than in the jungles whose cultivation science has now made a next great human project. Only carefully planned and well-supported enterprises are likely to succeed, and they will not be worthwhile unless carried out on a large scale. Migrant groups must include their share of the highly skilled workers and professional people, who ordinarily are not inclined to migrate, if they are to be transplanted successfully; or such elements must be supplied by some special authority. Here again an agency operating on humanitarian principles, one which had a large trained staff and was financially supported by all the leading governments of the world, would have to assume responsibility. This would indeed be rehabilitation!

*Physical Rehabilitation.* We may turn now to a consideration of what physical facilities are available to the European peoples. Areas which have been fought over present a picture of utter devastation. Because masonry served largely for prewar building, large areas are now buried in rubble. The process of building must be from the ground up. Industry has been brought to a standstill by destruction of plants, and agriculture is inefficient for want of tools and particularly of power-driven equipment. Luckily the armies moved so rapidly through parts of France, Belgium, and Italy that the greater part of the land itself escaped devastation. Even so, what source of credit can the people draw upon? Here are some fundamental problems, the solution of which may very well change the economic face of Europe. During the occupation the Germans nationalized much of the heavy industry and many of the physical resources of France. To whom do these now belong? Though it is true that for the most part the French or the Belgians or the Greeks or the Czechs must settle these questions themselves, we enter the picture when we plan to provide such things as machine tools or agricultural implements. We must determine to whom we are supplying such materials and recognize, in the light of experience, that we are probably giving rather than selling or lending a large proportion of them. Such giving, however, will be merely nominal, for it will be a necessary contribution to the rehabilitation of the world in our own interest. But since it would surely be our intention to help the mass of the people rather than industrialists or entrepreneurs, we face the problem of how and to whom we are to send permanent equipment and structural materials of all kinds. Let us hope that there will be a modicum of humanitarianism in our planning.

Let us hope also that we shall be able to recognize that humanitarianism is in this case but another name for the beginning of a long-range social enterprise. For an effective program of relief and rehabilitation must lead toward sound policies of reconstruction. We shall miss a splendid opportunity if we do not take advantage of the chances created in the postwar period to build better than we have done in the past. Particularly does this truth apply to certain economically backward areas, such as Southeastern Europe, which we may analyze as an example of what will be required if victory is to bring more than a mere resumption of poverty due to inefficient agriculture and poor economic organization.

In this region small cultivators and hired laborers have received little more than two or three dollars a week. The people are land-hungry, for the farms are too small to be well cultivated. In many sections the scattered strip system continues in operation; there are few if any sound marketing organizations, and peasants have not learned to grade and pack their products in the best way. They have had little or no agricultural training; their livestock is poor in quality and gives very little in the way of meat and milk products. Poor seed and fertilization of the soil mean scanty crops. Above all, the low level of general education (as shown by Yates and Wariner in their excellent book, *Food and Farming in Post-War Europe;* Oxford Press, 1940) makes it impossible to give technical training to pupils who come straight from elementary schools; "their minds are so unformed that they cannot grasp the subject matter put before them."

In the light of these considerations, it is clear that if Eastern and

Southeastern Europe are to enjoy the substance of victory, they must have an economic revolution and not only a military triumph over the Axis powers. This revolution must comprise a consolidation of the farm strip system; a development of cooperative processing and marketing; better transportation so that goods may be exchanged more readily; irrigation in order to promote efficiency in grain growing; breaking the big estates in Hungary; draining the marshes in Poland; improving the grassland in Yugoslavia, Bulgaria, and Greece; overcoming climatic defects by irrigation, perhaps through a Danube Valley Authority (the possibilities of which have been discussed by many people); a program of regrouping and rebuilding houses; introducing small machinery such as water pumps, fruit presses, milk coolers, and small motor plows; providing better seeds and manures; improving cattle in order to increase their yield of milk and butter fat.

But agricultural measures alone, in the opinion of the two authors cited, will not be sufficient. The standard of living in East and Southeastern Europe can be raised only by a measure of industrialization. The agricultural improvements which have been suggested will necessitate a great deal of capital investment, but so also will the establishment of small industries which can be suited to local needs, such as making shoes and cereal by-products, fruit canning, or paper making. These measures will create the necessity of international markets for small countries which must be in a position to repay the interest and capital on loans that will have been made to them. This possibility in turn depends upon international tariff agreements. It becomes clear that relief must lead to rehabilitation which in turn must lead to reconstruction, but that reconstruction cannot take place without its being geared into the wider European and still wider world economic system. Finally the world cannot be organized for economic welfare as long as it remains in a state of political anarchy and as long as national passions and the danger of total war remains a constant threat to mankind.

ARTHUR W. MARTIN<br>
RICHARD G. TYLER

# CHAPTER XVI

## *The Promotion of Physical and Social Welfare*

THE World War of 1914–18 caused the spread of disease in many lands; the destruction of normal life, the break-down of communications, the interruption of medical training by reason of the loss of medical schools and hospitals and the lowered vitality due to the interruption of food supplies brought into sharp relief the need of more effective international cooperation. The catastrophic dislocation which followed the war brought evils of frightful magnitude culminating in famines and epidemics of a continent-wide nature. Millions of people perished and the situation was so grave that despite theories of national sovereignty immediate international action had to be taken if disaster were not to overtake large portions of the world.

The generation preceding World War II witnessed a remarkable advance in the national public health services of many nations. The comprehensive activities of the League of Nations Health Organization and the Rockefeller Foundation in the field of world health, the growth in the number of hospitals, the development of administrative measures against the transmission of disease, the increasing attention to nutrition and housing, the provision of funds to promote research and disease control, and the joint planning by the professional health personnel of many national organizations bore witness to a new outlook. In addition, the public was becoming more health conscious and educational campaigns were producing gratifying results.

These developments show clearly that in order to promote the health of mankind institutions at all levels—international, national, state and local, governmental and non-governmental—are required. Only by carefully safeguarding the health defenses of mankind will modern civilization avoid a disastrous breakdown. In my *Foundations of Modern World Society* (Stanford University Press, 1941) I ventured the judgment that the world might well have to choose between indulging its political emotions and cooperating to promote the physical welfare of all peoples, for even then it was apparent that the war threatened to do well nigh irreparable damage to modern life both by reason of the destruction wrought and by the heightened nationalism which tends to blind people to the real problems which confront them. Events since that time have shown all too clearly how terrible a price modern war exacts in terms of physical and social health. It is true that the war hastened many remarkable developments in medicine and stimulated research to an extraordinary degree. One is grateful that these advances saved the lives of many thousands of soldiers, sailors and airmen in combat duty, lessened the number of deaths of civilians subjected to air bombardment, and through the application of recent discoveries in nutrition and other branches of medicine enabled Great Britain and other countries to maintain a reasonable standard of health despite the shortage of shipping and other means of communication.

But these advantages have been more than offset by the widespread suffering caused in all lands, particularly in those subjected to invasion and air attack. Even in the United States we experienced a serious shortage of doctors, dentists, and nurses; social disease and delinquency appear to be increasing; housing difficulties are causing grave social problems; and everywhere the tension created by war has produced serious nervous strain. Our situation, however, cannot for one moment compare with that of Europe or China where destruction on an unprecedented scale and the uprooting of millions of people created physical and social problems which will leave their enduring mark upon the rising generation. Universities, schools and hospitals have been amongst the heaviest sufferers; medical training has been interrupted and in some countries has virtually ceased; and the social services rendered by central and local governments have been discontinued. After the First World War many millions of people died of epidemics while malaria and other diseases reduced the vitality of people in many areas of the world. The much greater disruption and destruction which have taken place in the late war render imperative a great amount of international cooperation if we are to prevent a disastrous spread of disease from one country to another.

Fortunately the world is better organized than it was a generation ago to meet this immediate challenge. The Health Section of the League of Nations despite its shrunken staff has carried out important studies on malnutrition and its effects upon European countries so that the authorities in charge of postwar food relief may be better able to distribute supplies where they are most needed. The magnitude and importance of this task may be appreciated if one considers the difficulties of obtaining accurate information and the extensive collaboration required with the relief and rehabilitation authorities of the United Nations. The health section has been making studies of the epidemic danger; its staff "having the benefit of long-standing archives and of twenty years' experience in gaging the significance of epidemic events" has collected information on the main communicable diseases occurring in Europe, which it has sent regularly to all health administrations. In this way it has assisted in allaying exaggerated fears and has helped national and international organizations to concentrate upon those diseases which constitute the most real and immediate menaces to public health.

International cooperation has also made notable contributions in Central and South American. Much of this medical work has arisen out of the needs of the war, since in order to produce the materials required the thousands of workers have had to be given adequate medical care. To this end the United States has signed health and sanitation agreements with at least seventeen other American republics, and the Rockefeller Foundation has made substantial grants for public health education and for training nurses. A Congressional grant has facilitated the interchange of prominent medical specialists, and schools of tropical medicine in various parts of the countries to the south of us have expanded their research work. Brazil's special agency which cooperates with the Institute of Inter-American Affairs in employing many hundreds of United States and Brazilian doctors, sanitation engineers, and other specialists provides a pattern for similar health work being carried out in other countries. New hospitals, health centres, nursing schools and dispensaries have been established and food programs have been initiated by several governments. A chain of malaria control posts running for more than two thousand miles along the Amazon River and its tributaries has been built and a unique fleet of floating dispensaries is being operated.

In the South Pacific the health problem is also forcing an increasing amount of international cooperation. In 1928, thanks to the initiative of Dr. S. M. Lambert, and of the Rockefeller Foundation, the governments in charge of several colonies contributed toward the establishment of a central medical school at Fiji. Recently, the Legislative Council of Fiji approved in principle the expansion of the work of the central medical college and is now negotiating with other governments and especially with the Colonial Welfare and Development Committee in London to raise some five million dollars in order to provide a central directory, a general teaching and research hospital, an enlarged medical and nurses training school and other medical and health services. If these hopes are realized we should witness the establishment of a significant international medical centre capable of carrying out an efficient health program for the many scattered islands of the South Pacific.

Much more needs to be done, however, if the world is to give effective expression to the four freedoms and the principles of the Atlantic Charter. First and foremost, the people of the United Nations must realize the necessity of spending sufficient money to establish adequate public health organizations, local, national, and international. Professor C-E. A. Winslow of the Yale Medical School, an outstanding authority on international health problems, sets forth the following requirements for the nations of the world (*Citizens for a New World,* published by the National Council for the Social Studies):

1. Sanitation of the environment.
2. Control of community infections.
3. Education of the individual in the principles of personal hygiene.
4. Organization of medical and nursing services for the early diagnosis and preventive treatment of disease.
5. The provision of a standard of living adequate for the maintenance of health.

Dr. Winslow well remarks that "no democratic world order can be built on a foundation of starving and disease-ridden peoples." The grants-in-aid which the United Nations will need to make to countries which do not as yet enjoy a minimum standard of health safe for the rest of the world must however be regarded as only temporary in nature, for such grants cannot be unduly prolonged without producing undesirable effects. Ultimately, we must have a closely knit international order in which the health agencies of the United Nations will

202 IF MEN WANT PEACE

cooperate as intimately with national authorities as the national agencies now cooperate with state and local bodies.

That this ideal is realizable can be seen from the work already accomplished by the first inter-American conference on social security held at Santiago, Chile, in September, 1942, where about one hundred delegates from all parts of the Americas gathered to consider methods of promoting the social and economic security of workers and their families. These delegates comprised outstanding officials in all fields of social work—people with years of practical experience in labor, agriculture, social insurance, medicine, and other branches. The Conference adopted a comprehensive declaration of social and economic security and fourteen resolutions designed to initiate a many-sided program. In order to provide continuity of effect the conference established the Permanent Inter-American Committee on Social Security to comprise one regular member and at least one substitute member from each country represented at the conference and representatives from the International Labor Office, the Pan American Union, and the Pan American Sanitary Bureau.

We must make allowance for the inevitable gap between aspiration and achievement; nevertheless, this conference may well mark a vital turning point in the social history of the American continent. It shows how erroneous is the belief of those who claim that a country should first set its house in order and then progressively enter into wider international relations. The truth is, this conference like the world opium, labor, and other conferences has set standards beyond those now existing in many of the member countries and has provided the possibility of technical collaboration which would not have existed if the countries had been content to develop their social institutions in the atmosphere of sovereign exclusiveness.

Few more serious menaces to social and physical welfare have appeared in the last few decades than that furnished by opium and other dangerous drugs which have wrecked the lives of hundreds of thousands of addicts. It is an astounding fact that until recently four-fifths of the drugs produced in the world found their way into illicit channels and only one-fifth was used for medical and scientific purposes. The League of Nations Opium Organization which came into existence in 1920 undertook its work in three successive phases: (1) the only partially successful attempt to control the traffic itself; (2)

limiting the amount of manufacture; (3) controlling the production of the raw materials—the poppy in the case of opium and cacao in the case of heroin—which was under consideration at the outbreak of the late war. It was able drastically to reduce the illicit traffic and build up a world organization to deal intelligently with the drug question. Indeed, it was in the field of narcotics that international government reached its highest point in the pre-1939 period. Yet many evils remain.

With the remarkable development in modern chemistry we must expect that many drugs will be produced which, if not carefully controlled, will be used by evil exploiters to harm the health of mankind. Constant vigil including close cooperation between the medical and police authorities of all countries will be necessary if the discoveries of science are to be a benefit and not a curse.

Already the Opium Section of the League has taken several steps to prevent the release of dangerous drugs into illicit channels at the end of the war when many new centers of manufacture find themselves loaded with excessive supplies because of the diminution of demand for drugs which had been used in the war. The Section has established branch offices in Washington, D.C., so as to maintain better communications with governments outside of Europe and in this way to keep the statistical information as to output and need of drugs as accurate as possible. It is examining methods of improving national and international systems in order to make control more effective and is giving particular attention to methods of strengthening control in colonies and more backward areas. We may be thankful that the Opium Section, limited though it is in funds and personnel, is carrying on its work, for it may enable the world to organize with sufficient rapidity in the years ahead in the field of drug control and thus prevent a repetition of the chaotic and harmful conditions which prevailed after 1920.

The development of communications has enabled other exploiters to profiteer from human weakness, for the traffic in women and children known as the white slave traffic has spread over an increasingly wider area with the coming of modern shipping and other forms of travel. Space does not permit a description of the many activities in this field undertaken by the League of Nations, including the establishment of committees to inquire into the white slave traffic in the Far East, and to investigate similar conditions in Europe. Such activities are promising, but because of the terrible dislocation and the hunger and disease occasioned by the war we must expect that this evil will be intensified for many years to come; and the social agencies of various countries will undoubtedly have to cooperate with the reestablished international organizations to protect, as far as possible, those whom misfortune will have placed in a peculiarly vulnerable position.

Relatively few people, in all probability, know of the international efforts which have been made to promote child welfare and to protect children against exploitation and injury by detention and imprisonment, to insure an adequate legal age for marriage, and to minimize the misfortunes that come as a result of the status of illegitimacy. Because legal systems and social customs vary considerably from one country to another, the League officials have had to make detailed studies and collect information which have proved to be of great value in the formation of a more adequate policy of public responsibility toward children. The Child Welfare Committee of the League undertook a study of the laws "relating to the age of marriage and consent" and were able to persuade several governments to raise the legal age of marriage. It also examined the legal status of illegitimacy of children; and what the Committee found concerning the treatment of children and young people imprisoned for crime led it to "recommend the abolition of detention of minors as punitive measures," and to "substitute character training and education as corrective measures." The Acting Secretary-General of the League points out in his 1942–43 report that such work will have to be resumed. "As a result of the war, problems affecting women, mothers, children have become more important and the interest taken in those problems has become more widespread."

Many people may be surprised to know that slavery still persists in parts of the world and that several millions of people still do not enjoy the legal freedom which is ours. Despite the humanitarian advances of the century preceding World War I many grave problems still remained and a League of Nations Committee found that a recrudescence of slavery had taken place during the years of hostilities. After considerable effort the 1926 Assembly approved the Slavery Convention which marked a distinct step forward despite some disappointing omissions from the convention itself. A temporary (and later permanent) slavery committee was appointed to continue investigations and make recommendations, but many obstacles masquerading under the name of national sovereignty have hindered the work of the League. Special attention has been directed against forced labor which in some colonial territories has amounted to a more or less disguised form of slavery, and the 1926 Slavery Convention established the general principle that compulsory forced labor might be exacted only for public purposes. The International Labor Organization passed the 1930 and 1936 conventions to lessen the evil and presented to the 1944 International Labor Conference a report and a number of recommendations on minimum standards of social policy in dependent territories. These refer to the international steps desirable or necessary to promote the welfare of native peoples in the matters of the prohibition of slavery, of traffic in opium, of forced and compulsory labor, of the safeguarding of the recruiting of workers, and of the supervision of their contacts of employment, as well as the precautions to be taken in the employment of children and young people. Special measures are recommended for women—general education, vocational training, protection against special forms of employment. The principles which should be observed in paying wages, administering land policies, improving health and housing conditions and social security arrangements are also set forth.

Another evidence of international progress under the League of Nations is found in the field of crime and punishment. During the course of the nineteenth and twentieth centuries, at first slowly but with accelerated speed in recent years, the conviction grew in the minds of the experts that effective scientific work in improving prison conditions could best be served by international cooperation. After 1920 the International Penal and Prison Commission organized several international congresses and published a regular periodical giving information concerning penal legislation and reforms throughout the world as well as certain standard sets of penal rules to be observed by various countries. But unfortunately the League of Nations did not take as energetic action in these matters as it did in that of narcotics, the protection of women and children, and the suppression of counterfeiting currency. The need of effective cooperation nonetheless remained very great, and will increase.

A conference held at Cambridge, November 14, 1941, established an

International Commission for Penal Reconstruction and Development which, it is anticipated, will have much to do for "the political up-heavals of recent years have caused a catastrophic denial of criminal justice" and have widely extended "the zone of penal deterioration." Without the closest international cooperation the tide of violence and criminality must surely mount in the years following the cruel world struggle which destroyed the normal restraints of civilized life in the major part of the European continent. The restoration of individual, local, community, and nationwide social health will require the con-certed efforts of all countries. The task will be too heavy for nations acting independently.

Space does not permit the enumeration of the scores of international private organizations which exist to promote the welfare or lessen the sufferings of human beings. The mere list itself would be imposing, and one may gain some idea of the interdependence of nations from the fact that in the decade before World War II more than four hundred international conferences and congresses of a social, cultural, and scientific nature were held. Add to this the many activities of such organizations as Russian and other War Relief agencies, Red Cross, World Students' Federation, the World Council of Churches, and a host of others which are engaged in humanitarian work of various kinds and one receives the impression that if only the world political structure could be put on a rational basis nations would enjoy unprecedented opportunities for fully realizing the advantages which accrue from mutual help.

If people were adequately informed by the press of the amount of international effort which is required to maintain civilized life they would realize that uninterrupted intercourse between the peoples of the world is of overwhelming importance and that the history of civiliza-tion itself has been a history of this intercourse. In cultural and scien-tific matters nations have advanced through the stimulus provided by trade, commerce, and the exchange of ideas. In the moral and spiritual realm the same truth holds good; nations are peculiarly dependent upon one another; no country can guarantee the continuance of social justice within its own borders if it ignores injustices which flourish abroad. To take but one example, Christians in one land cannot witness persecutions elsewhere and remain unaffected. "They cannot, without denying their Christianity, ignore the suffering and starvation of peoples outside their own borders, nor can they sit by unmoved and watch the imprisonment of Protestants and Catholics by the totalitarian rulers. Even if those who profess the same faith are indifferent to the sufferings of those in other lands, the latter in their misery and starvation cannot remain unaffected by this indifference. What Christians do or suffer in one land constitutes a matter of vital importance to those in other lands." This moral problem affects all classes and professions of people; it is not confined to religious and intellectual groups. Merely to hold vague convictions on the question of promoting the welfare of human society will do little without a stern determination to translate ideas into action. It is a terrible commentary upon the distorted character of modern civilization that in the years which followed the First World War less than ten million dollars annually were spent on the League of Nations while several thousands of millions of dollars were spent upon preparations for war. Such a grotesque disproportion could have but one outcome, for individuals and communities get what they pay for.

To the objection that nations will be unable to afford to establish the many services referred to in the present chapter one example should be sufficient answer. The Beveridge plan providing for unemployment, disability, retirement, widows and guardians, maternity, marriage and funeral benefits, together with assistance pensions of various kinds, children's allowances and health rehabilitation services was estimated by its author to cost approximately seven hundred million pounds in 1945, rising to eight hundred and fifty-eight million pounds in 1965. The latter sum amounts to less than five billion dollars, that is, about one-twentieth of the peak annual war costs of the United States and but a relatively small percentage of Britain's annual war effort. If countries can be organized to fight against external enemies and during the struggle can increase their national income by better organization and more united effort there is no reason why, short of indifference to the implications of democracy, the free peoples should not achieve the goal of security from the cradle to the grave. If they do not do this they will confess to bankruptcy of their own ideals and moreover will miss a magnificent opportunity of wedding social security to the program of full employment after the war.

We hear much of finding jobs for all and the necessity of maintaining full employment if economic disaster is to be averted and victory truly won. Surely there could be no more promising time for boldly conceiving comprehensive and long-range policies of social and cultural improvement. All countries will require more doctors, nurses, psychiatrists, social workers, administrators, hospitals and clinics if national health is to be improved. The list could be extended almost indefinitely to include adequate plans for adult education, scholarships for less privileged but intellectually brilliant students, interchange of scholars of all kinds on an international scale, provisions for hundreds of anthropologists, educators, missionaries, doctors, and administrators for service in colonial and other backward areas. Here are but a few of the possible openings for highly trained professional people. Jobs await thousands upon thousands of people if we have the imagination to provide them. No idle dreaming here. There are innumerable highly practical and necessary things to be done.

To the skeptic one must reply with energy and some impatience that surely the condition of the world at present shows that where there is no vision the people perish. If the democracies cannot match their magnificent efforts in war with equally striking feats of statesmanship in peace, if they cannot see the implications of their own welfare but prefer to indulge unreflective national political emotions they may have done little more than to have sacrificed on a funeral pyre precious human lives in their devotion to a national ideal which will have become but little more than an idol.

LINDEN A. MANDER

# PART FOUR: The Cultural Basis of World Order

# CHAPTER XVII

## *Some Psychological Postulates for Peace*

THE reasons men give for fighting wars have obviously very little to do with the causes of war, since wars keep on but their slogans wear out and give way to new slogans.

When a war is finished, its reasons become unimportant and are forgotten; but its causes may be argued for generations. The trouble with the question: What causes wars? is that there are so many answers rather than so few. Every specialist tends to find the causes within his own field. Every war has its history, its economics, its social changes, its medicine, its readjustment of populations, its diplomacy. Every war has a multitude of explanations, and it is not possible for all the explanations to be correct. The full cause of any social event includes the whole history of society up to that point.

We should mean by the word "cause" that particular one of the recurring antecedents which is subject to our own control. We can, for instance, do nothing whatever about climate, even though we make up our minds that certain wars could not have taken place without certain climatic conditions. Nor can wars be looked on as caused by human nature, though it is obvious that they would not be fought unless human nature included the behavior necessary for combat. Wars are not caused by human nature because there is nothing we can do about human nature. In looking for causes we must look for conditions that we can, by taking thought, control.

What will in this chapter be suggested as one of the chief causes of war is open to considerable criticism in this very respect. We do not know just what we can do about it. But it is suggested by the writer because it is his conviction that something can be done about it, and that something must be done about it if future wars are to be avoided.

Wars, like forest fires, have two distinct kinds of causes. Any particular fire may have been set by a particular match in the hand of a particular man, or may have spread from a very definite and special campfire neglected by a specific camping party on a specific morning. To avoid forest fires it is well to avoid such incidents and to control them as well as we can. But there are conditions in the forest, conditions of low humidity and temperature, conditions prevailing in the nature of the forest underbrush, which render the forest subject to fires. When the forest tinder is dry, any match, any campfire, any lightning stroke, may result in the destruction of the forest. When the forest cover is moist, it would be impossible for a force of a hundred men with torches to burn an extensive area.

Are there like conditions that make the nations prone to war? If there are, it is more proper to ask for the causes of belligerency than for the causes of wars. If human beings can ever set controls over belligerency, it will not be necessary to set up elaborate machinery for arbitration, or for policing.

There is one widespread notion of the causes of belligerency that a psychologist must regard as silly and mistaken. This is the belief that nations are prone to war when they are driven by hunger or need. But hungry men are not belligerent. It is hard to interest them in glory or in conquest, or even in revolt. They will listen attentively only to talk of food. And they will not exert themselves particularly even to get food. Outside the walls of a Chinese city there encamped, according to one account, some two hundred thousand starving peasants. Into the city, which was on a trade route, came large shipments of grain on their way to a more distant market. The starving thousands died quietly without violence. During the great Irish famine, families lost members by starvation though the proprietor's share of the potato crop was in the cabin untouched. During the Russian famine starving folk lined the banks of the Volga, occasionally in the presence of a red soldier who was adequate to guard a storehouse of grain which was government property. The French Revolution, often misunderstood because of Marie Antoinette's famous "Why don't they eat cake?", was a revolution of the best fed peasants in Europe. They were not hungry. They were full of the fighting energy that only food and freedom from want can give.

Hitler himself made extensive use of the effect of reduced diet in controlling the populations overrun by the German conquest. Their ration allowances tended to be fixed below those of Germany and food was the lure used to get subject peoples to cooperate in the making of munitions, or in assisting the German control.

Belligerency has an origin very different from hunger. But it takes more than ample food to make a nation belligerent. The normal effect of a hearty meal on a man is like the effect of an ample meal on an animal. The effect is in general quieting. Aldermanic stomachs are not symptoms of belligerency.

But while an economy of plenty is one of the conditions of belligerency, it is only one feature of the situation that makes nations ripe for war. There are other more important and more complex determiners.

When a nation or a tribe has been settled in an area for many generations, one of the common consequences is a gradual improvement in the efficiency of the cultural devices for living and livelihood. If the culture is pastoral, the arts of breeding and increase improve. Skills and handicrafts improve. Fewer and fewer individuals are required (proportionally) to furnish goods and food to which habit has accustomed the group. The span of life may increase. Specialization and the division of labor increases and becomes more fixed.

In our own culture we have seen an enormous acceleration of these tendencies. Technological advances have enabled three men and machines to do the work of two hundred in the wheat field. The assembly line turns out machines in one-twentieth the number of man-hours that would have been required a generation ago. More sinister even, the advance of medicine and of the standard of living has raised the average span of life since colonial days from a figure in the upper twenties to well along in the sixties. Millions of sixty-year-olds are occupying jobs that would, in a less fortunate combination of sanitation and adequate food and housing, be open to the oncoming generation.

It is in this oncoming generation that the second requirement of belligerency lies. But the requirement is not simply an oncoming generation. Not even large numbers in the oncoming generation are sufficient. Something more is needed. That additional determiner of belligerency, to state it in full, lies in the existence of a large body of youth for whom the culture can easily provide food and shelter but for whom there are open no adult roles. These youth provide the man power, the energy, the enthusiasm for conquest, invasion, political revolution, adventure, colonization.

Sociologists and psychologists are only beginning to pay attention to the importance that the role of individuals plays in directing the lives of persons and peoples. We have been accustomed to notice only certain conspicuous cases in which friends play up to roles which are slightly out of contact with the realities about them. Two generations ago the phrase "doesn't know his place" was used of a man who had taken a role a step above his origins. The insane hospital shelters patients whose roles are highly divergent from their circumstances. The bulk of children's toys are properties for the enjoyment of temporary roles. The trappings of a scout, a soldier, a policeman, a fireman, a nurse, a sailor, encourage small boys and girls to the passing behavior appropriate to the role.

What we have not realized is that a man's conception of his role is even more effective in making bankers behave like bankers, plumbers behave like plumbers, big shots behave like big shots, failures behave like failures, soldiers fight like soldiers, than are the roles of children or the insane effective in producing the behavior that we tolerate in them. A man's notion of what he is, the verbal phrases that he accepts as applying to himself, are the guide of his life.

When a wife says to her husband, "Remember you are the boy's father," she is attempting to recall to him his role, and thus guide his actions into channels of paternal function.

It is highly probable (and the reader will do well to note at this point that the writer is no historian) that careful historical examination of the records would show that the necessary condition of belligerency has always been a plentiful younger generation in an efficient and well-fed people, which is growing up to manhood to face a life in which the traditional roles of adults are jealously held by adults. We may ourselves, particularly those of us who are high school or college teachers, recall recent years in which large numbers of boys and girls graduated from school and found no possible opportunity to be what they had trained to be and expected to be. College teachers felt as though they had helped to coach a few hundred young people for parts in a play, only to find that there would be but fifty places in the cast.

Not only was the older generation occupying the trades and professions toward which youth is steered by education, tradition, example and the whole impact of the movies and radio—the older generation was actively organizing to keep the oncoming generation definitely out of the activity. Memberships in many of the tighter unions come very high, and waiting periods are long. Mr. Kettering's advice to young engineers to start working at the machine bench and learn their profession from the ground up was splendid advice, but it could seldom be followed before the war. Young college graduates were not wanted in machinists' unions. In general, the attempts of the schools to train youth for vocations were severely frowned upon, and the schools were compelled to limit themselves to teaching vague handicrafts which were not in demand in industry.

But it is not the unions that set up the most effective barriers to membership. In order to enter medical practice the average boy must have approximately $10,000 in support during his training, and spend four years in college, four years in a medical school, and two years in an internship which pays him bare subsistence. There is good reason to suspect that the requirement of four years of college work to precede entrance to the medical school was placed there by the medical profession not in order to produce better doctors. At the law school of my own university the length of "pre-law" training has recently been upped from two to three years. It takes great credulity to believe that this is done in order to make better lawyers. Neither law schools nor medical schools have shown any great interest in what studies are carried on during the pre-law or pre-medical waiting period.

In any people a large body of youth brought up in the tradition, well fed, energetic, and with no available roles, no available part in the social drama, *nothing to be,* furnishes the actual material out of which belligerency can be made. The existence of such a body of unoccupied youth is the necessary condition of war or the necessary condition of revolution. They are the underbrush that makes the forest inflammable.

It was exactly such a body of youth without prospective adult careers that Mussolini used, first to seize control of the state and later to enter upon a war of conquest. He offered Italian youth, who were in large numbers at a loss for a role, the elemental role of Roman legionnaire, with all the childish but extremely effective trappings of uniforms, parades, song, and titles. Boys who joined his movement no longer had to search for excuses when asked, "What are you? What do you do?" Mussolini made the world realize that boys who at twelve are playing enthusiastically with wooden rifles and wooden swords can, at sixteen, have military rifles placed in their hands and be made deadly instruments for acquiring power.

The same thing happened in Germany. Even before the First World War Germany had reached a state of technological efficiency that made a large portion of its youth unnecessary. Much of the ready anti-Semitism that Hitler succeeded in conjuring up was based on competition for roles, particularly in the professions and in retail trade. In 1912 the crop of young doctors of philosophy from the German universities far overran the available careers. In one pill factory at Essen there were employed four hundred Ph.D.'s in chemistry—not that there was any need for so many highly trained chemists, for most of the jobs could be performed after a short apprenticeship in a factory. The point was that young chemists could still think of themselves as chemists and be thought of as chemists by their friends, though many of them were in reality only factory operatives on routine tasks.

To this body of youth not wanted by the adult world Hitler offered enough to interest nearly every able-bodied young man, and many young women. They were not only given uniforms, authority, titles, but before them was a prospect of governing Europe and the world. So firmly ingrained are many of these ambitious roles in German youth that their unreality and their impossibility will need to be driven in with all the means at our disposal. And even then we shall have to deal with a generation that has missed the normal period in which ambitions and interests are formed, presumably a generation of black cynicism and bitter frustration.

In America it is the tradition to regard a man as having many rights as against public control. It is the right of American college students to fail in a college course, for instance. In Hitler Germany no student had that right. This value of independence makes most Americans view with aversion the Russian control of the detailed behavior of Russian citizens, the control of speech and writing, of assembly, of the expression of opinion in act as well as in speech, of careers. But in justice to our relations with Russia it should be recognized that in prewar Russia there were places for youth and there was no large body of well-fed young men with no prospect of meaningful occupation. Prewar Russia was fully occupied in the development of Russian resources. Not until

1937, when the threat of a German invasion was fully realized, did the Russian state turn its effective controls of behavior and opinion to a preparation for a defensive war. It is our good fortune that the victory will be followed by a resumption of this preoccupation with internal development. Prewar Russia was not belligerent in the sense in which Germany and Italy were belligerent.

What has here been described as the conditions of belligerency is, of course, not the whole story. Something more than the pressure of a new generation on a static structure of occupation is required. That something more lies in the possession of a military tradition. Military roles must be part of the literature and song of a nation. In Germany, Hitler could not have created these out of whole cloth. He could only cultivate intensely what already had familiar expression in German tradition.

Herein lay the great difference in belligerency between Germany and the United States, or between Germany and Great Britain. In all three countries modern industry, modern science, modern medicine, had contributed to produce an order in which children kept turning up in great numbers, but in which the older generation had the parts of the play in their control. Children were not needed in industry, but they kept coming. The unions were doing the best they could to keep them out of the trades. The professional associations did their best at the same task. But in both Britain and the United States the military tradition was rather remote. Soldiers had little prestige. War was of so little interest that almost no attention was paid to the march of events that was leading inevitably to war. Both countries were caught almost totally unprepared and only the fact that Germany had many necessary tasks preliminary to a full attack on England, and a fortunate idiocy in the high command that led to taking on Russia— only these facts saved the day.

The thesis of this chapter is therefore twofold: (1) that belligerency is limited to nations or peoples with a large proportion of well nourished youth for whom there are no available places in the occupational structure of the group, and (2) that there must be woven into the tradition of the nation or people a familiarity with the notion of war and with the military roles, and a high valuation put upon such roles.

Italy appeared to embark on conquest without the military tradition that is here asserted to be one of the conditions of belligerency. Italy is then an apparent exception. The lack of the military tradition can be granted. It was necessary for Mussolini to go back to the old Roman conquests to find the roles that he urged upon his people and that started his younger generation playing at being Roman legionnaires. This tradition was not a live one in Italy, and we may contend here that Italy went to war without belligerency—a contention which is sustained by the sequel. Italy alone represented no danger to world peace and only succeeded in playing an important part in the world war because of the German entanglement. Italian soldiers alone were a threat neither in Greece nor in Africa.

Returning to the general thesis of this chapter, we observe that if it is correct certain of its implications must be taken into account by anyone who is working toward world peace. One of these has to do with the popular misconception that it will be essential for the Allies to take over the German and Japanese educational systems, and to send to those countries teachers who will instill in the oncoming generation notions opposed to war.

If we applied this program of pacifist education to ourselves, it might have a disastrous success. It could result in depriving us of any power of defense against aggression. Education for pacificism had a powerful influence in delaying the British and the American war efforts. If we now undertake it after the war, it will not insure peace but only an easy defeat by any warlike aggressor.

In Germany such a program would be a certain failure. The reason a program of education by American teachers in Germany would fail is that it would be remarkably easy to turn the belligerency of the German people to resistance directed against the foreign teachers and the alien ideas presented in the schools under American auspices. Attempts have been made before this by a conqueror to control the thought of subjects, and such attempts succeeded only when they were carried out by ruthless means—by means which our gentle planners would not contemplate. German patriotism could go underground, and if there were enough recruitable and unoccupied youth it would gain formidable strength within six months of the beginning of the program. The Nazis tried this in Belgium, in Holland, in Denmark, in Norway.

If we cannot teach the Germans to be peaceful, to give up their notions of a German destiny to rule, how can Germans be led to a pacific national program and philosophy?

The answer is that the teacher must be actual events—events which Germans will interpret in their own way to mean the renunciation of conquest. The records of the fluctuation of public opinion in the United States during the last four years prove that it is not speeches that influence public opinion, but events. When the British were in retreat from Dunkirk, isolationist opinion in the United States dropped to a new low. Opinion was not responding to arguments and propaganda, but to the prospect of a British defeat, which obviously was, to Americans, not a tolerable prospect. It will be events and not word formulas that will associate conquest and ruin in the minds of Germans. It will be events which prove the recent war effort so definitely a catastrophe for the aggressors, which make it so clear that the day of world conquest by one nation is over, that both Germans and Japanese will develop a new philosophy of life to fit the realities. It was a belief in the superiority of German genius, German military tradition, and a mistaken contempt for the rest of us that enabled Hitler to get German support for the conquest of the world. It will be only a conviction that the world reacts strongly and successfully against such programs that will teach an improvement in national manners. This must become a German idea.

The active measures to prevent war should include modern methods of gauging public opinion and modern methods of propaganda. There was undoubtedly a time when the war party in Germany—Hitler, in short—had only a minority support. Its opponents could have been strengthened by any slight encouragement from France, Britain, or the United States. Only after having been established in power could Hitler demand and get a $500,000,000 annual budget for propaganda. Our eventual emergency provisions for insuring peace should include both adequate information about popular movements abroad, and an arm of the government empowered to do something about what is discovered, though whether the latter could be managed by a democracy in which foreign policy becomes a target for politics is, of course, questionable.

None of these proposed emergency controls gets at what we may call the fundamental belligerency of a nation. That would require that the nations of the world solve the problem of the new generation.

Until we discover ways and means of providing meaningful and desirable roles for youth, and succeed in devising an education that will lead them to accept the roles that are available, the world will continue to be thoroughly inflammable, and ready for the casual match that will start a new conflagration. A forest service may use posters, issue regulations, establish patrols, to minimize the effect of casual fires started in an inflammable forest. But until new methods of forestry which clear the forest of underbrush or interlace it with fire lanes are devised, the forest will be subject to the danger of catastrophe.

EDWIN R. GUTHRIE

## CHAPTER XVIII

# *Education*

DURING World War II thoughtful persons the world over changed their estimate of what education must accomplish if we mean to build a sound world order. They also developed a new respect for the obstacles it must overcome. Their disillusion in itself justifies a certain sober hopefulness.

What we find is a curious contradiction. On the one hand, the world has grown closer physically because of the remarkable development of communications; on the other, cultural differences have persisted and, in some cases, grown deeper. More than that, within the major cultures many disintegrating forces have been at work. The explanation must be sought in the intellectual history of the world during the last three or four hundred years.

In the Middle Ages, Europe possessed a cultural unity. The Catholic faith bound Christian believers into a spiritual fellowship, despite the local nature of feudal and town life, and Latin, the language of the scholars, enabled educated men of different lands to converse with one another. The other major world cultures—Chinese, Moslem, Indian, Central American, etc.—although each was pretty much isolated from the rest formed fairly homogeneous units.

With the rise of the modern age both the breakdown of the medieval

European unity and the isolation of the non-European cultures proceeded apace. In Europe the rise of nationalism and of national
languages and the decline of Latin made for increased difficulty in
intellectual communication between peoples. The Reformation led to
division within Christianity. The rise of the middle classes, especially
after the eighteenth century, tended further to promote division, since
those interested in trade and commerce concentrated attention more
on material values than on universal culture. National systems of education grew up which promoted an intensified national patriotism by
giving greater attention to national history and relatively neglecting the
European heritage.

The imperial expansion of Europe from the seventeenth to the
twentieth century led to the dominance of the Western powers throughout the world and has had, particularly in recent years, tremendous
disintegrating effects upon the native cultures and civilizations in
Asia, America, Africa, and the Pacific. The power of the West swept
all before it, and though the Chinese might regard us as barbarians they
could not remain indifferent to the remarkable achievements of our
material civilization, which indeed threatened the whole basis of their
traditional life.

The breakdown of the accepted scales of values, both those derived
from European civilization and those derived from other cultures, has
in an age of increasingly bitter international power politics led to
great and in many cases excessive national self-consciousness and to a
decline of the critical spirit, of tolerance, and of objective inquiry into
truth.

Before 1914, several agencies attempted to stem the divisive forces,
and many bodies, such as international law associations, scientific units,
and religious groups, reached across national boundaries.

But men of good will failed to see how deep the cultural problems
really went. All the efforts of religious groups, philanthropic foundations, scholars, the statesmen who sponsored the Peace Conferences,
and so on, brought nothing but the pathetic "too little and too late"
to pit against the tide of World War I.

The interwar period saw redoubled efforts again fail to strike with
anything like the necessary force at the tough roots of intercultural
separatism. The League Committee on Intellectual Cooperation and
many private agencies stimulated the exchange of students and leaders,

international meetings, translations and needed new publications, the revision of textbooks and curricula, and the use of the moving picture and radio for international education. Governments began to see the need of cultural cooperation, following the earlier example of the French Foreign Ministry's *Alliance Francaise.* The good neighbor policy in the western hemisphere modified the earlier pattern significantly toward a more equal two-way cultural exchange between nations of unequal wealth and power. Several semi-public agencies, such as the Rockefeller Foundation, the Carnegie Endowments, and the American Council of Learned Societies carried on important work. They helped to rebuild the universities and schools of Europe shattered by the ravages of war, and they provided libraries, scientific and other technical equipment, and financial assistance to enable scholars to resume their labors. They encouraged the study of foreign languages, especially in the United States where relations with South America and the Far East gave an extraordinary impetus to the study of Spanish and the Far Eastern languages. Many societies for the scientific study of international relations, such as the British Royal Institute of International Affairs, the American Council on Foreign Relations, the Foreign Policy Association, to name but a few, published many scholarly works; and in the universities and high schools remarkable development of social studies took place. People became more aware of the problems of international relations. Yet at the same time the great force of education was divided against itself. Just as deliberately as some nations evolved toward cultural compatibility with their neighbors, others, without being wholly to blame, were trying the opposite course. The revolt against reason and even against civilization itself was reflected in many writings in Europe where scholars argued for race or nation or class and rejected the idea of a European let alone a world culture.

Today we can see that the efforts which looked hopeful in the 1930's were still too weak to strike at the roots of the problem; we can well suspect that we need not only more copious energies but a shrewder penetration as well. We are prepared to discover that beyond the more tangible objectives of restoring schools, libraries, and laboratories, of arranging conferences, study abroad, and educational programs of all sorts, we must deal with objectives of a subtler sort. We have given all too little attention to what makes one people feel cooperatively disposed toward another; what makes a culture evolve into a harmonious relationship with another. We are like an industrialist who has worked out fine machinery, assembly plans, and so on, yet still to his consternation finds the whole personnel at loggerheads with one another.

This analogy brings to the surface a very important question. Who are the "we" who ought to expand and deepen the scope of our educational efforts? Certainly not the school and college people alone, nor least of all government alone. We are rather all the men and women and young people who will be endeavoring to build toward a better world. No regimentation need be feared so long as voluntary groups themselves take the initiative with the necessary understanding and without falling into cross purposes. The aim of such discussion as the present book is precisely to contribute toward the hammering out of ends and means on which the harmonious, voluntary cooperation of groups depends.

Let us explore in what sense international organization needs the help of education, and then, reciprocally, what sort of organization is really called for to serve the needs of education.

Numerous writers on postwar planning have argued, and very cogently, that some problems of a cooperative world society require an international organization equipped with a police force. But whatever the specific form of an international organization, its success will depend on the support of education in two ways. First, education must so surround it with loyalty that it can weather the unavoidable minor storms. And second, education must help to protect it against major conflict, if this can possibly be done. For such tempests as burst upon France in 1789, on the United States in 1861, and on the world in 1914 and 1939, would strain any political organization to the breaking point.

The matter of loyalty to the new organization we can all concede to be one of the promotional problems calling for effective projects of education. The strategy would be to make the most of the rising idea that good government should minister to the needs of men—the idea of "the social-service state." At the same time, the lesson of the war should be dramatized and brought home that the nation state can not provide today for the basic human need of security—the idea that "self-interest does not equal national sovereignty."

Even more important therefore than the restricted problem of education for loyalty to an international organization is that of providing social conditions in which the organization will not be strained and broken; and here again we must rely heavily on education. Within each nation, in some concrete form that attaches firmly to local traditions, a public opinion must be developed that will refuse to tolerate conditions that can be exploited by egocentric dictators and that stimulate egocentric national ambitions, with attendant distrust of and unwarranted notions of racial differences. Unless we promote this social understanding in the minds of the entire community, small selfish minorities, profiting by general indifference as in interwar Germany, Italy and Japan, will again have the opportunity to carry on a fanatical miseducation of the younger generation. In short, education must play a large part in overcoming economic injustices.

But education for all the purposes we have reviewed needs the support of world-wide organization, almost as much as international government needs the support of education. The need in this case calls for organization of both official and unofficial sorts.

Unofficial organizations, with little or no centralized power, could possibly carry on all the long-range educational programs. The horizon of cultural education can be broadened to the necessary intercultural view through local initiative, publications, and such meetings as the East-West Philosophers' Conference held at the University of Hawaii in the summer months of 1939. Unofficial institutions like the Institute of International Education can promote the needed interchange of students and educators, and stimulate the needed scholarship aid. Similar conferences and institutions can spread technological information and training, and bring about the extension and equalization of the opportunity to go to school, to read books, and to share all the other benefits of education in its widest and fullest sense.

An interesting example is the *Bibliographical Guide to Comparative Literature and Cultural Relations* now in preparation by the Committee on Comparative Literature of the National Council of Teachers of English under the sponsorship of the American College Association and the American Library Association. The *Guide* will cover four fields: (1) world literature in English translation; (2) historical and critical material bearing on foreign impacts on English and American literature; (3) historical materials which reveal the debt of American

literature and culture to foreign heritages; (4) the relation of literature to the other arts, and the history of ideas, religion, folklore,
anthropology, and general cultural movements which are international
in scope. Able contributors from American and Canadian colleges,
from public libraries and museums, and from various agencies of the
United States Government are now busily engaged in shaping this
composite body of materials.

In all these matters our advance thus far has been greatly accelerated
by the assistance of national governments. An indication of the potential benefits is furnished by the successes of the League Committee on
Intellectual Cooperation and of the Scandinavian countries in the
matter of textbook revision. While private organizations could have
promoted some voluntary exchange between nations, the official organizations did far more than the private could have done.

Above all let us not fall into the fallacy of regarding our own culture as the standard for others. The right is not always on the side
of the highly technological culture. Our civilization often proves
relatively inexpert and crude in matters of appreciation of beauty, or
in the capacity for contemplation. On the intellectual side, our potential
wisdom often remains ineffectual because its elements exist only in
the form of partial insights and conflicting guides to action. For
example, the fields of economics, history, and anthropology have
led to decidedly different views of human nature. Until these views are
thought through in the light of their modifying effect on one another,
we shall have only a disorderly sort of practical wisdom and a social
structure in which the enlightened groups of specialists are out of
touch and out of tune one with the other. But learning makes only
one modest contribution to the cultures of the human race. The
present inharmonious state of intercultural relations, both within single
nations like our own and between the great geographical regions,
needs the careful attention of men of good will, just as much as does
the more restricted situation among the fields of knowledge.

The immediate task confronting education in the postwar world,
that of restoring the lines of communication between the cultural
forces of the nations, will be one of unparalleled magnitude, since the
intellectual divisions have become so deep and national hatreds so
strong. We will have to rebuild the institutions of learning in countries
which have been overrun by the Axis powers and have seen their

buildings, libraries, and equipment destroyed, their scholars scattered or imprisoned or shot, and their intellectual development checked at all levels of human growth. Fortunately even during the war the unity of scholars has not been entirely broken. The American universities and colleges have done splendid work in providing openings for refugee professors and teachers, and some public institutions, such as the Carnegie Endowment, the Rockefeller Foundation, and the American Council of Learned Societies, have been preparing plans for assistance to foreign countries. The American government has provided scholarships for many Chinese students and has facilitated the visit of several Chinese professors to this country. British students of medicine have continued their training here. The list might be extended did space permit.

The occupied countries will need much assistance in the form of grants to enable them to build their schools and universities. They will need to restock with books and all other equipment which goes with modern educational research and teaching. For unless the smaller countries can be assisted in restoring as quickly as possible their cultural life, civilization will be the poorer and a return to a wholesome creative life will be rendered the more difficult.

In this connection it is appropriate to note that in 1942 several governments decided to form the Conference of Allied Ministers of Education to which ten European Powers (some of them governments in exile) sent representatives and eight non-European countries sent observers. The European countries have been drawing up plans to obtain "rudimentary supplies such as desks, pens, pencils, paper, slates and books." Higher institutions of learning will require libraries and scientific and laboratory equipment. In order to support these undertakings some countries will require financial assistance.

The Conference has set up a number of commissions, among which the Commission on Basic Scholastic Equipment has been making estimates of the school materials that will be required and the methods by which the needs can be met. The Commission on Scientific and Laboratory Equipment has listed approximately ten thousand items which will be needed for the reconstruction of scientific education. It is considering ways and means of preventing the European countries from again becoming dependent upon German apparatus and consequently upon German technical services and industries. The Books and Periodicals Commission has been drawing up projects for obtaining books from British and other libraries and for launching a great public book drive which it is hoped will bring in a million volumes. A book pool comprising copies of some two thousand of the best books published in England since 1939 and of nearly four hundred British periodicals has been housed in London under the supervision of an inter-Allied Book Center Committee. The American Library Association and other United States organizations are undertaking a similar service.

The Commission on Films and Visual Aids is assisting European officials in preparing for increased use of radio and motion pictures in their postwar schools. Above all the ministers of education at the conference in London have been giving prolonged attention to the problem of teaching personnel. According to a Department of State bulletin of November 19, 1944, Czechs, Poles, and other nationals "in very limited numbers from the armed services have been receiving higher education in Britain; interned Polish soldiers in Switzerland have also been receiving university training." The smaller European countries are determined not to send students to Germany for postgraduate study; the higher institutions of Britain and the United States will have a remarkable opportunity to attract the type of student who has hitherto sought advanced training elsewhere.

In the totalitarian countries the problem of education will demand serious and prolonged consideration. The victorious United Nations must avoid any attempt to re-educate these people. We repeat that only the Germans can re-educate the new Germany. Only the Japanese can re-educate the new Japan. The task will not be easy, for these countries have been indoctrinated for many years, and the liberals who have been in hiding will face formidable obstacles. There will be a grave shortage of teachers and other educators. There will be the task of weeding out those who are active supporters of the military regimes. Some help will be required from abroad—not in the form of sending in a high commissioner of education or an educational army of occupation, for such a step, as we point out in our chapter on the psychology of peace, would promote resistance and resentment—but rather by a series of informed discussions with foreign experts in small conferences with little publicity. Japan and Germany will both have to plan short concentrated courses for new teachers. They will have to make use of special techniques, such as school broadcasts and films in order to overcome the teacher shortage. They will require millions of inexpensive school books, some of which are already being prepared in the United States by German refugee scholars for use in postwar Germany.

They will have to transform the Youth Movement and, in the case of Germany, re-direct its energies along the lines of the Weimar period. Especially will adult education be important. This education will not consist merely of listening to lectures and participating in discussions on "cultural" subjects. It must come also from participation in local committees, parent-teacher associations, trade union groups, etc. The task of re-developing personal responsibility will not be easy, but it will be a necessary one. Throughout all these efforts, as a group of anti-Nazis have written (*The Next Germany,* Penguin Book Series), international personal contacts will be required, for nothing will be more disastrous than a boycott of German science and teaching such as took place at the end of the First World War. The same truth will hold for Japan. Liberal scholarship, there as elsewhere, will be largely dependent upon the spirit with which the scholars and teachers of the United Nations receive the scholars and teachers of the defeated powers.

Above all, the victorious countries must realize that education takes place in a total situation and that the world will witness a grotesque mockery if those who win the war in order to promote freedom should once again betray their victory by failing to establish a world organization and by degenerating into a miserable condition of power politics with all the disastrous consequences which that situation will bring in an age of total war. It simply will not do for us to preach peace to other peoples and for ourselves to continue to prepare for war. If we expect the defeated enemy powers to resurrect education for a liberal society, we must do a better job of organizing the world for that society than at present we show signs of doing. We must live up to our plighted word, and show by actions that the Atlantic Charter, the Four Freedoms, and the idea of a United Nations have been proclaimed as serious objectives not as propaganda to be cynically thrown overboard when the shooting ceased.

By the time this book is published a United Nations conference to establish an international educational and cultural organization will have met in London. The conference will prepare a constitution for what will serve as one of the "specialized agencies" provided for in the United Nations Charter to work with the Social and Economic Council. Among its responsibilities the new organization is expected to promote international interchange in the fields of science, education, the arts, and the social sciences.

The tentative draft of the charter, which might be likened in a sense to the tentative United Nations Charter as conceived at Dumbarton Oaks, is the product of the combined work of our State Department and the American educational, labor, and civic leaders who are interested in developing a permanent agency and is to serve as a basis of discussion at the November sessions.

Under the charter there would be a conference meeting periodically to determine the general policy and by two-thirds majority vote submit to member nations agreements on educational and cultural programs, to receive and consider reports, to elect the executive board and admit new members. The executive board would comprise fifteen persons of outstanding reputation in the field of education, in the arts, the humanities, and the sciences, each member to serve for three years and not be immediately eligible for reelection. The secretariat should be under a director general and the staff should be responsible only to the organization. Provision is made for national commissions which shall be cooperating bodies within the member states for the purpose of bringing together the national viewpoints and harmonizing them in the most effective manner.

This conference on education will, it is hoped, provide the machinery whereby the solemn promises of educational cooperation written into the San Francisco Charter may become effective. It is too early to say what will be the outcome, but two general observations may be made. First, that the United States delegation does not include a scientist; and this omission is serious because the atomic bomb has revolutionized international relations. We have witnessed the grave disabilities under which the San Francisco Conference labored in that it was made up primarily of political and legal representatives; the representatives of the forces which are most transforming modern life were conspicuous by their absence. It is to be hoped that when the educational cultural organization is established ample provision will be made for the encouragement of international efforts to make the world vividly conscious of the implications of the atomic age.

The second comment concerns the necessity of having adequate facilities to train a sufficient number of international civil servants, a policy which will become more urgent if and as the United Nations becomes firmly established. Here the national commissions or cooperating bodies could be of particular help in devising ways within the member states of training young men and women for the varied careers which a properly functioning world society could offer.

HOWARD LEE NOSTRAND

## CHAPTER XIX

# *Arts and Letters*

"GIVE me the right word and the right accent," wrote Joseph Conrad, "and I will move the world." And whoever has read one of Conrad's tales will know that the right word is fidelity and the right accent the accent with which each "one of us" sustains the rest of us against "the tremendous disdain of those Dark Powers whose real terrors, always on the verge of triumph, are perpetually foiled by the steadfastness of men."

Today perhaps more than ever in human history it is necessary to move the world. Some have said that religion is the only adequate mover of the world and that art in comparison is often content to move only a handful of initiates, or in extreme cases its makers alone. It must indeed be admitted that the esthetic coteries which flourished between the two world wars produced nothing to compare with the *Ballad of Chevy Chase* that moved even Sir Philip Sidney's heart like a trumpet. Though many of their creations were subtle or bold and need not be despised for their eccentric forms and strange revelations, their general tendency was to atomize rather than integrate man and his world. In this they were doubtless expressive of something that was going on in every department of human thought and activity.

And the total consequence is something we must remedy if we would live.

It is not surprising, then, that Dorothy Thompson among others calls for a return to eloquence and declares that "actually art has never been so divorced from the life of the masses of the people as in the last generation. Poets have written poems for other poets, painters have painted pictures for other painters—and the dealers—and the art of the people has been swing adaptations of great musical themes—and the comics and the movies." (*Saturday Review of Literature,* Dec. 2, 1944, p. 9.) Miss Thompson adds that even the so-called radicals in art have not really been radical. They have feared the mighty line, and she offers a scripture from Walt Whitman in reproof. But she does not include from the mighty Walt my favorite among his manifestos for the artist:

This is what you shall do: Love the earth and the sun and the animals, despise riches, give alms to everyone that asks, stand up for the stupid and crazy, devote your income and labor to others, hate tyrants, argue not concerning God, have patience and indulgence toward the people, take off your hat to nothing known or unknown, or to any man or number of men—go freely with powerful uneducated persons, and with the young, and with mothers of families—re-examine all you have been told in school or church or in any book, and dismiss whatever insults your own soul; and your very flesh shall be a great poem. . . .

The totalitarians who decry democracy indict it particularly for its failures in faith and enthusiasm, for its incapacity to make its very flesh a great poem, or a great cause or great nation. By now the totalitarians are doubtless surprised at democracy's dedications of the flesh as well as of the spirit, but their miscalculation is intelligible in the light of democracy's comparative loss of the old moving words and accents. For democracy in its recent phase has suffered from its successes, it has become preoccupied with defending rather than extending itself throughout its own society or to the other societies of the earth. Nothing is dead that men will die for, but democracy must enter its next phase before it can recover its old self-confidence and affirmation. And its next phase can be neither partial nor local. "By God," said Walt Whitman again, "I will not have anything except what everybody else can have on the same terms!" Democracy will have recovered this spirit when it no longer finds anything amusing in such expressions as "globaloney" or anything fantastic in the theme of "milk for Hottentots" except the fact that Hottentots still lack milk. And democratic art will have returned to its full vitality when it has rediscovered along with Ernest Hemingway the full import of that wonderful passage from John Donne: "No man is an island, entire of itself; every man is a piece of the continent, a part of the man; if a clod be washed away by the sea, Europe is the lesser, as well as if a Promontorie were, as well as if a mannor of the friends of thine owne were; every man's death diminishes me, because I am involved in mankind; and therefore never send to know for whom the bell tolls. It tolls for thee."

Democracy is moving into its supernational phase, or nothing; and democratic art is necessarily in the same case. "The state of society," to apply Emerson's phrase to the interwar years, "is one in which the members have suffered amputation from the trunk, and strut about so many walking monsters—a good finger, a neck, a stomach, an elbow, but never a man." What was once a universe tends to become a multiverse with no nexus but that of artistic form, and a merely esthetic order has never attracted the mass of hungry, breeding, fighting, working, dying, sensual men. Art for art's sake or for the connoisseur's sake is aristocratic, class-conscious, tribal, personal; and it is profoundly ironic that the arts of democratic peoples as they have approached their crisis have grown esoteric in their purer forms as they have grown commercial in their more popular.

Fascism prides itself on its success in centering all its energies in a single aim, the glorification of the state, but that success has involved the destruction of the individual. Democracy, which seeks to serve society and the individual equally, has a harder task. Alexander Meiklejohn once discussed this task under the title *Democracy and Excellence,* and presented it as the problem of reconciling popular liberties and a high standard of values. He pointed out a conflict between the mediocrity of the average and the necessity of the ideal; and warned us that democracy must avoid both dead-levelling in its quest for justice and the creation of special privilege in its quest for quality. The compromise, though a necessary and a lofty one, does not like fuehrer-worship produce an immediate and simple focus for all the energies of a people.

But though the task of democracy is complex its passion can be simple. No expression was ever more single in its emotion than the Gettysburg Address or the Sermon on the Mount. The quality of these great utterances was no doubt due to their universality, to their importance to every man. At this very moment, as on those two earlier occasions, the democratic passion is stirring the hearts of men the world over, in the very midst of their intellectual and political confusion. There is not the slightest ambiguity about what it is that moves them, though there is chaos in their attempts at its realization. What they want from art, as from religion, is not the reflection of the contradictions of their minds but the strong symbol of the singleness of their hearts.

We are in the midst of one of the greatest crises in human history. We can resolve it or we can be destroyed by it. We will be destroyed by it, we who in our sanguine moments consider our course but just begun, if we fail to think and feel greatly about it. Everywhere men are longing to understand and to believe. As for the understanding, that is probably available. But it is not communicated. Though there are conceivably scores of plans for a better world any one of which would work a vast improvement on the world we have, none of them will be realized unless belief galvanizes understanding. Belief is the energy without which the motor does no work.

Perhaps this will prove to be the final message of one of the greatest literary voices of the last century, that of Leo Tolstoy. And there may be a special significance in the eagerness with which our generation has returned to his account of a crisis like our own. For it is not the intellectual complexity of *War and Peace* but rather its repetitive hammerstroke insistence on the power of a faith in the heart of a folk that fascinates us in our need. In the midst of a daily and hourly clamor of circumstance and before the outcome is clear, here we have a complete analysis of a similar historical cataclysm, helping us to look over the ramparts of the moment and understand that the sequel will depend less upon strategies and leaders than upon the total quality of the causes and peoples that are embattled. This is a challenge to each of us as an individual, for it assures us that we, not Hitler or Stalin or Churchill, are the final disposers; and the fact should both make us rigorous self-critics and save us from the sense of personal futility which is likely to be the effect upon us of large events. What we are will make the future just as what we have been has made the present, and we need despair only if we despair of the total history of mankind. Not many of us are likely to make the choice of cosmic despair; the rest of us can pluck up our hearts and call it a day.

Consider, as an example of this sort of illumination—an illumination no more dependent upon a vast historical range than on a mighty art— Tolstoy's treatment of the Battle of Borodino. The Battle of Borodino, declares Tolstoy, was not won because Napolean made certain decisions and gave certain commands, nor was it lost because Napoleon had a cold in the head. Indeed, it is impossible, it is meaningless to say that it was either won or lost, thus taking it as an isolated event. A battle is a part of a campaign and a campaign a part of history. Borodino was won by the French in that the Russians withdrew and the French marched into Moscow; it was won by the Russians in that the French went into Moscow a hungry and exhausted lot and immediately became a mob of pillagers rather than an army. The battle was won or lost not because Napoleon made decisions and gave orders, but because the French were what they were and the Russians what they were; because the entire complex of antecedent factors focussed in this event and a vast complex of subsequent events flowed out of it. The present exists only as an instant between the past and the future from which this so-called present takes its meaning. The Russian people cannot be beaten until their love of Mother Russia is beaten, and a love streaming out of the past into the future cannot be destroyed in a battle at Borodino.

Tolstoy takes some eleven hundred pages to say all this because as an artist he has to say it in terms of the individual and mass living that makes his idea not a statement but a representation that is more emotionally recognized than logically grasped.

Perhaps some great historical novelist of the future will similarly make us understand that Singapore was not lost because Sir So-and-So failed to give the right orders or was too busy at a party at the Rafles Hotel to be tending to business at the climactic moment. Singapore fell because the command and tradition of the British colonial armies were what they were, and they were what they were because of nineteenth century British Imperialism; and nineteenth century British Imperialism was in turn the product of a modern international capital-ism which throve on the exploitation of dark-skinned backward peoples; and that system was made possible by the developments of science in the seventeenth century and its application in the eighteenth. It would be a bit nonsensical to say that Singapore fell because Galileo discovered the law of falling bodies, but no more nonsensical than to say that it fell because some identifiable Englishman failed to ingratiate the British with the Siamese or failed to get the big guns reversed in time. And besides, it may turn out that the fall of Singapore waked the British up to winning the war or quite as importantly the peace. It may lead us to a complete readjustment of relationships between white and dark skinned peoples, to a recognition that freedom and justice are indivisible. The good is a part of the bad, the bad a part of the good, and a lynching in Georgia or an act of injustice to a Chinese coolie are part of the moral fabric that will clothe or expose you or me.

It is of course not necessary that great art shall devote itself to the illumination of history; it is only necessary that it shall somehow devote itself to the illumination of man's relation to man and to the world in which all men live. Each of us has a relation to Napoleon and to the shadow of a leaf, and either relation is available to art. But the art that will move us and thus the world must put the shadow of the leaf into a pattern of meaning that can be extended indefinitely without being falsified. Neither a Wordsworth nor a Cézanne is indifferent to the shadow of a leaf, and neither fails to make it a part of his vision of total truth.

It is in this sense that art can be a tremendously powerful instrument in the making and keeping of the better world we hope for. Now as always it is at work.

Often its scope is limited enough. It may only be a story by Ernie Pyle about an American tank that stalled at a street crossing in France while its crew scrambled out under withering fire and ran to join Ernie in the inadequate shelter of a doorway—one of ten thousand such incidents but the only one in which some millions of Americans participate, to the good of their souls, through the imaginative notation of a modest war correspondent. It may be only a word picture on the air, in the voice of Ed Murrow, of a burst of shell fire on the Tunisian front—and again some millions of Americans have felt the beauty and terror of that blending of heroism and insanity which is war. It may be only a glimpse in a movie of the ground crew at an

air base counting the bombers that come back from a raid—and more
millions will be able to fill in thereafter the human content of that
monotonous phrase in the communiques, "Three-seven-ten of our
planes failed to return." It may be only a popular song about the biggest
aspidistra in the world, sung by Gracie Field through a loud speaker
to the great British fleet riding at anchor—and the British Empire has
suddenly become not a color on the map, but a listening, breathing,
cheering organism.

The possibilities are limitless and the need enormous. We are told,
for instance, that the concept of international democracy is remote and
pallid, that it cannot compete with such national consciousness as is
made vivid by "Deutschland Uber Alles" or "Britannia Rules the
Waves" or "The Star Spangled Banner." And up till now this caveat
is doubtless true. But Wordsworth, writing in 1800, said that the
symbols of poetry need be limited to the images of nature only until
the objects of science should become so familiar to men that they
too were a part of a universal language. Whoever has read Carl
Sandberg's *Smoke and Steel* or looked at the paintings of Diego de
Rivera or listened to the cacophanies of modern music knows that
the transition has taken place and that art can every hour stake out
hitherto unclaimed territories for the human spirit. The concept of
international democracy is now as familiar to men as the machines
that Tom Benton puts into his paintings or the auto horns that Vachel
Lindsay hears on the Santa Fe Trail. The sheer necessity to human
survival of inter-racial and international cooperation can be and will
be made as intimate and moving as a tribal chant, just as the great
mountains which were ugly and terrifying to Addison became sub-
lime to Coleridge and Shelley. The power of Wendell Willkie's *One
World* was less in its data, much of which can doubtless be contro-
verted, than in its vision; and the book won a response that was like
the lifting of a curtain on a long vista of men's hopes and desires.
Perhaps we are not yet ready to put a United Nations Anthem along-
side "The Star Spangled Banner," but we may be more nearly ready
than skeptics suppose. Perhaps we shall not for some time be in the
mood to recall that a German can be as supernational as Kepler or
Carl Schurz, or to recognize that a Japanese American can be as loyal
as any other American in a foxhole; but the time will come when
"krauts" will be an inadequate designation for all Germans and when

"ship 'em out" will no longer seem a satisfactory disposition of the Japanese in America. It would be salutary for us all if we should tune in some evening and hear a radio drama, perhaps by Norman Corwin, on the return of a wounded Japanese-American veteran to a community which had not yet taken down its hoarding, "No Japs wanted here!" Amelioration can come both by direct human contact and by its equivalent in art, often more effectively by the latter because of its dramatization of meaning than by the former. And all the little meanings accumulate into one great meaning; an Ernie Pyle and a Tolstoy alike help us transcend the barriers of self within which meaning perpetually grows stale and false.

Those who have in their hands the remaking of our shattered world will therefore do well to give heed to a means as powerful as any at their disposal. The poverty and obscurity to which we have too often consigned artists during their lives is a dubious blessing to them and no credit at all to us. But more serious than the personal discouragement, which so many artists have magnificently transcended, is the world's loss. Fortunately, progress has already been made and is even now being accelerated. Under such diverse economies as the Russian and the American, for example, the artist has latterly received increasing support. In Russia, as is well known, the artist rates high in the scale of recognition and reward, and though he may sometimes be embarrassed by the official auspices he has nevertheless attained a status that has freed him from many other impediments. In America, partly through governmental provision and partly through the activities of the great foundations, the arts, particularly in their broader social aspects, have been receiving a long overdue attention. Though we may lament the demise of the federal arts projects of the 1930's and wonder why so vigorous an arts program should flourish in poverty but not in plenty, we continue to have an impressive number of grants-in-aid for the study of the arts from such institutions as the Carnegie and Rockefeller Foundations, while the Guggenheim and other fellowships have encouraged the work of many individual artists. But such instances, though the list could be considerably expanded, are obviously but a start in the right direction.

Whatever international organization succeeds the League of Nations may well take over such a commission as the Institut International de Cooperation Intellectuelle and include in its activities the promotion of new works of art as well as the care and dissemination of the old: the replanning and restoration of destroyed cities in the light of modern technology and functional design; the international support of folk arts such as those which Russia has so carefully cherished among her minorities; the identifying and making generally known not only of such great works of art as have received the Nobel awards but also of many lesser but significant creations which now too often escape attention entirely or await the discovery of later generations. And such beginnings in art cooperation in the Americas as have been made under the Cultural-Cooperation Program of our State Department (see Publication 2137, Department of State, 1944) are capable of indefinite extension and of analogous development elsewhere.

The international exchange of works of art through such means as the trading of exhibits; the dissemination abroad of national music by recordings and radio or much better by artists in person—artists less coerced by commercial auspices than those who are now our musical ambassadors; the creation wherever possible in different language areas of something like bureaus or guilds of translators and the financial support of a great increase in distribution of works of literature in translation; the multi-lingual publication of new books or magazines such as that of a popular monthly which already advertises simultaneous editions in English, Spanish, Portuguese, Swedish, Arabic, and Chinese; the multiplication of international and inter-racial groupings and cultural activities such as may be observed in the "International House" on many an American campus or in choral and dramatic organizations in many of our cities; the increase in international understanding such as arises from the crossing of national art boundaries by persons like Pearl Buck and Lin Yutang; the elimination of racial boundaries such as occurs when a Marion Anderson sings German lieder or a Paul Robeson becomes the ultimate Othello:—these and many other beginnings of cultural inter-communication indicate practical lines of development. The first necessity is to establish the feasibility and value of such enterprises, and that is being done; the next step will depend upon the creation of a world society in which the energies of men will not be so totally subsumed in the preparation of destruction that the arts can only perish with their makers.

Avoiding such a completion of calamity we shall continue to find a chief aid to international, or inter-racial, or inter-factional understanding in the right word and the right accent. Though the specific subject of an artistic expression may be factional or bellicose—though it may sing songs of vengeance and hatred, or shelter a chosen people behind walls of sanctimony reared against the Philistines, or preciously embroider the decay of classes and nations, or make gorgeous the banners of vandalism—it will in the last analysis do none of these things. There is something in a bona fide work of art which transcends these superficial manifestations, which sends the listener or beholder away with a conviction of the fellowship of men. Even the pageantry of a Nazi rally in the Sports Palace escaped its immediate intentions and became a symbol of human rather than of merely Nazi power. Dedicate it to mischief how you will, art's final effect will still be the communication of understanding. The right word and the right accent are a broader and a deeper language than that of economics or politics, for art is a universal language. The uncoerced artist is intelligible alike to Germans and Frenchmen and Japanese, to capitalists and communists, to Protestants and Catholics and Jews. Nationalities are crystallized out of generations or centuries of belligerency; economic systems have been achieved in sweat and blood and are prone to defend themselves with the same; religious groups have the eternal task of liberating their essential religion from sectarian trivialities. But artists are only accidentally Germans or communists or Jews. An artist is an individual temperament appealing to a multitude of other individual temperaments who, insofar as they appreciate art, must come out from behind their institutional barriers.

There are, of course, great patriotic songs like "The Marseillaise" and great folk arts like the Jewish religious music, but the greatness in them is that which transcends their special origins, is that which speaks for love of homeland and of culture and is therefore universal. They are great for the very reason that the "Horst Wessel Song" is not.

If you are an artist, and I read your book or look at your painting, what I learn is especially how you *feel* about things, how *you* feel about things. True, your feeling may be a reflection of the feelings of a great many others; but it must also be freely and sincerely yours or it is not a part of art. Whatever is in your book or painting by pressure or command is false, and I will find it out, if not at once then presently, if not by myself then with the aid of my fellows. Ultimately we take your measure, and what we reject of you is proportional to the amount of common humanity you have sacrificed to being a German or a capitalist or a Presbyterian. For art escapes these classifications; from the artist and his appreciator in the moment of communication the whole world drops away. I forget whether you are ancient Greek, or medieval, or modern; I forget whether you are black or white; I forget whether your ancestor signed the Declaration of Independence or was hanged on a sour apple tree during a rebellion. All I am aware of is that I am participating in your vision, that I have by some miracle got out of my own consciousness into yours, and that I can never be quite the same person I was before. Above all I know that I do not want to fight with you about anything. If I do want to fight with you it can only be that you have missed the right word and the right accent and have talked to me in the language of a Jew or a Gentile rather than in the universal language of art. It's either thus, or it's that I am a bad listener, with no ear for anything but national or sectarian jargon. Each of us lives largely in a very private house, the house of the separate personality. The noisiest of us tell each other little about its inner appointments. The least noisy artist tells most. He tells most because he is able to create the symbols which are the only language that can shape and communicate these hidden half-realizations.

There can be no real understanding between individuals, races, peoples, until the humanity that is too essential to be named Nordic or Semite, Protestant or Catholic, conservative or radical—until that unlabeled but universal humanity is somehow revealed. If I had believed all that was told me about our enemies in World War I, I should have been certain that there were no such persons as Germans —there were only Huns; but I had read poetry by Goethe and heard music by Beethoven—I knew better than the propagandists. If I believed all that some Protestants tell me about Catholics and some Catholics about Protestants I should find Christianity divided between idolators and blasphemers; but I have read *The Divine Comedy* and *Paradise Lost,* and I know better. If I believed all that some of the communists say about the bourgeois or some of the bourgeois about the communists I should have to choose between blood-suckers by nature and bomb-throwers by wicked and deliberate choice; but I have seen the paintings of Cézanne and heard the music of Shostakovitch, and I know better.

In spite of all the propaganda, and the statistics, and the White Books and Red Books, in spite of the wars and rumors of wars I know better. I know that as long as any race, or sect, or political or economic group can produce an artist whose work moves me, that race or sect or group includes men who are my brothers.

In the peace that has come the dangers, as compared with those which followed World War I, are as ten to one in number and intensity. Not only are the problems vastly more complicated but the peoples concerned are more varied, more skeptical, more desperate, and more eager. Because they are varied they must find a common language, and I do not mean English or Esperanto; because they are skeptical they must be convinced in their hearts before they are convinced in their heads; because they are desperate they must speak to each other in accents that acknowledge and return their common sense of profound urgency; because they are eager they must be rewarded by the hope that good will as well as cold reason are engaged in their behalf.

Of course we all know that hell is paved with good intentions. No brave new world will ever be generated from the sentiments and emotions alone, or even from that emotive expression of human values which is art; but neither is it likely to be generated without them. We shall have to think hard about the geographic, the economic, the political, the technological, the psychological factors that must enter into the making of a stable peace in a better world. We shall fail, nevertheless, if we do not find the right words and the right accents that move the world.

JOSEPH B. HARRISON

## CHAPTER XX

# Science and Technology

ACCORDING to some historians of whom Arnold J. Toynbee is typical phenomena like World War II are due in part to basic social disequilibria, the result of the breakdown of sympathy and contact between the masses of the people and their leaders. The most overt evidence of this breakdown is the "exploitation" to which throughout recorded history large numbers of the population have been subjected, and of which physical and economic slavery are but extreme examples. Paradoxically it seems that civilization itself—the appearance of a more complex way of living with its social, political, religious, artistic, literary, and scientific developments—is possible only if a portion of the population have the requisite leisure. Thus a vicious circle results: a civilization exists as the result of the very exploitation that produces the social inequalities, class conflicts, and wars which themselves menace the civilization's existence.

The importance of science in the postwar world is twofold. (1) It should continue even more than in the past to provide an outlet for man's intellectual and aesthetic powers. (2) It seems to provide a means whereby natural forces may be increasingly harnessed to human needs. Science makes it possible to provide food, clothing, and shelter for all and still leave sufficient leisure to allow everyone to share in maintaining and enjoying the advantages which civilization gives, thus avoiding the disequilibria that have destroyed it in the past. We are in a position as never before to take advantage of a wealth of new developments, since at practically no point along the technological front are noteworthy discoveries lacking.

The engineer, for instance, is discovering the basis for increased mechanical precision, higher velocities, greater strength, greater size and increased electronic control in all that he handles. All along the line he has been dealing in superlatives. In the construction field, for example, he has been making higher buildings, longer bridges, and larger dams than ever before. For several millennia the Pyramid of Cheops at Giza was the largest pile of masonry in the world. Now the Grand Coulee Dam in Washington contains considerably more cubic yards of material. These massive structures are not built to satisfy individual or professional pride, but are an expression of large-scale communal action which requires that things be done on a more extensive scale than previously. Collective bargaining by group action in the field of labor relations is but the latest expression of large-scale operation and mass production. The individual tends to be lost in the group and must depend on it for his protection, his advancement, and the means of his self-expression.

Another manifestation of this tendency is seen in the development of increasingly rapid means of transportation. The turbine-driven ship, the streamlined train, and the transport plane are progressively annihilating both space and time. The jet propulsion which has been developed for fighting planes has actually accomplished in transportation the hitherto only dreamed-of feat of exceeding the speed of sound and has opened up unpredictable non-military vistas.

Finally, there are the innumerable aids to more comfortable living that the engineer is providing. The highly mechanized home of the future receives ample publicity on every hand.

The impact of chemistry upon technological development and progress has been largely in the control of chemical reactions, which makes possible the prediction and forecasting of new compounds and new substances that may be of tremendous importance in industry and commerce.* This so-called tailoring of molecules is exemplified in the dehydration of castor oil and the fractionating of fish oils for use as drying oils. If these semi-synthetic drying oils have permanently taken the place of tung oil in varnish production, future imports of the latter product from China will be reduced. Chemical treatment of soya bean oil has likewise made it usable in paints in place of linseed oil, thus making us less dependent upon imports from South America.

The success attained in the conversion of ethyl alcohol into butadiene for use in synthetic rubber is another outstanding example of the replacement of an imported product such as natural rubber. It is believed that 50 per cent of our rubber requirement will be met by raw materials produced close to the point of manufacture. Alcohol may be obtained from surplus grain, from sugar wastes, from synthesis of coal, lime and electricity, or from petroleum refinery gases. Furthermore, the synthetic rubber may be modified during its manufacture to fit special requirements for which natural rubber was never fully satisfactory. Thus both the domestic sources and the added properties of synthetic rubber make it unlikely that imports of natural rubber will ever again have the same importance as in the past.

The new drying oils and synthetic rubber point toward an unmistakable trend in our public life—our ability to convert our resources into our requirements, and thus to provide a solid basis for maintaining

* These paragraphs on chemistry were supplied by Henry K. Benson, Professor of Chemistry.

or increasing our standard of living. Special fuels through chemical processes may come as at present from petroleum or as rapidly as economic conditions prepare the way from other minerals or from annually renewable vegetation and farm crops. Our light metals came originally from imported ores or from special brines. Magnesium now comes in part from sea water and in part from domestic minerals. Aluminum, it is believed, will be made from clay deposits present in great abundance. To what extent the annual production of 300,000 tons of plastics and 2,000,000 tons of light metals will displace the 100,000,000 tons of iron and steel the future alone will decide. We do know that they will add immeasurably to the diversity and attractions of life as well as give a more independent and secure basis to our national economy. It is this underlying support that chemical technology has contributed to human well-being that must be taken into account in shaping future policies.

In agriculture, nutrition, sanitation, and medicine, discoveries have been equally striking. More efficient strains of domestic plants and animals, improved methods of crop rotation and fertilization, and the scientific management of fisheries are increasing the food supply, actual and potential, to previously unheard of levels. The new chemical DDT (dichlor-diphenyl-trichloroethane) has measurably advanced man's success in his contest with injurious insects in somewhat the same way that sulpha drugs and penicillin have advanced his control over bacterial growths in his own body. Increased knowledge of disease prevention and cure has so lengthened the span of life that for parts of the United States the life expectancy at birth increased from 38 years for men and 40.5 years for women in 1850 to 59 years for white males and 63 years for females in 1930. One result of these discoveries is that portions of the earth like the tropics may be found capable of supporting much larger populations than previously. There is no denying that despite anything that science can do, the world will eventually become "filled up" with people and man will have to learn to live in a balanced rather than in an expanding economy. Meanwhile, however, pending a more adequate realization of just how this is to be done, science seems to offer a respite of another generation or so.

The suggestion, sometimes made, that science is in some way peculiarly responsible for World War II, must be unequivocally rejected. The idea that science, through its perfection of submarines, airplanes, robot and other bombs, tanks, and *panzer* divisions, made the Hitlerian aggression possible, cannot be sustained. Hitler's penetration to Stalingrad and Egypt is matched by Napoleon's march to Moscow and Rome's extension of its power to the Euphrates and is dwarfed by Alexander's expedition from Pella to the Indus, and Jengis Khan's from Karakorum to the Crimea. Stories of German atrocity do not exceed those told of the Mongols and Assyrians. The economic effects of World War I and probably of World War II will not be qualitatively greater, though they may extend over a larger area than those say of the Thirty Years War in Germany. War is a socio-political phenomenon based on the social, political, and economic techniques of civilization itself and so far has not been profoundly modified by modern science. If science helps in the attack, it aids likewise in the defense, and war remains the great tragedy of man arrayed against his brother.

The postwar problem is (1) how shall science and technology be organized to assure their maximum contribution, and (2) how shall society use this contribution for the spiritual and material welfare of humanity.

### THE ORGANIZATION OF SCIENCE AND TECHNOLOGY

Science, like many other forms of human activity, has a dual nature —the practical and the aesthetic—and neither can flourish under coercion. Both must be kept in mind in planning a free and adequate society: science, on the one hand, as one of the most potentially useful of human activities, on the other hand as existing along with music, art, and literature, as one of the most powerful approaches to the appreciation of the beautiful. And there is a third reason for the continuance of absolutely untrammeled scientific research. With all the organization in the world, there is no surety that an adequate substitute will be found for first-class minds free to range as they will. Technology itself requires the continuance of unrestricted research if its supply of new ideas is to be unimpaired at its scource!

Moreover, scientists must remain free not only to do their research but to announce their findings once they have been made. The temptation of government to interfere with the free speech and the free movements of scientists must be resisted. The prostitution of German anthropology to Nazi myth should serve as a permanent warning of what must not happen again. Finally, schemes for central-izing and expediting the publication of scientific papers and books must be most critically examined lest they conceal within their streamlined efficiency the germs of censorship and suppression. The present chaotic methods of publication have the advantage that they do result in a nearly free press for the promulgation of scientific writing.

But no argument for permanent anarchy and chaos can stand. Not only must science continue among us as a free artistic enterprise, but it must also be harnessed and organized so that a greater portion of its mighty potential can be released to enable man to assume as rapidly as may be the place in nature to which his capabilities would seem to entitle him.

First, as pointed out by Bernal (The Social Function of Science, 1939, p. 265), the most efficient studies are made by cooperating groups aided by such laboratory, secretarial, and library assistance as they may require. The universities may well take warning that the day of the single scientist, or a single pair of scientists, working in isolation is passing. The day of the cooperating group, its members constantly checking and re-checking each other's findings, is at hand.

The advance must be all along the line. Some groups must be push-ing out into the unknown at as many as possible of the likely looking points. Other groups must be involved in integrating previous findings and preparing constantly more adequate reviews and summaries and syntheses, else science like some vast invertebrate animal breaks into pieces and the various parts wander off their own separate ways. Finally, pending the introduction of an adequate international lan-guage, there must be prepared and published translations of important scientific books that appear in other languages.

Perhaps the colleges, universities, and museums will remain as centers of undirected research while the industrial and governmental laboratories and experiment stations carry on the planned programs. Perhaps the ideal will prevail that no scientist shall completely give up his own initiative, and that, while he is occupying a niche in a larger whole, he will be allowed and expected to devote a modicum of effort to studies of his own choosing. There is no real incongruity between directed and undirected scientific activity. Both are necessary for an adequate society.

## SCIENCE AND WORLD POLITICAL ORGANIZATION

Science, concerned as it is with abstract ideas, is by its very nature not confined to national boundaries. Throughout the modern period it has remained a unifying centrifugal force at a time when other factors were making for international disunity. Galileo received his first intimation as to how a telescope might be constructed from the Dutch lens maker, and the later history of science is replete with scientific developments that have depended for their advance on information passing across international lines. In the seventeenth and eighteenth centuries even though their respective governments were frequently at war, the scientists of Paris and London remained in correspondence, interchanging and benefiting from each other's ideas. During the nineteenth and early twentieth centuries the importance of international cooperation in science and technology grew apace, and even between 1930 and 1939 when the world was witnessing a mounting arms race and headlong preparations for war more than four hundred international scientific congresses were held or announced—striking evidence of the extent to which scientific interests transcend national boundaries. In the very midst of World War II the United States government went to considerable expense to obtain and duplicate enemy scientific journals for use by its own people.

Science would, therefore, benefit by a world organization that would prevent periodic lapses into chaos. While war perhaps stimulates applied science studies that have a direct bearing on defensive and offensive measures, in almost every other respect it serves as a deterrent. Work on the installation of the lens of the 200-inch telescope on Mt. Palomar, California, was immediately suspended as a result of outbreak of war between the United States and Japan. Trained workers are taken out of more basic researches and younger persons are kept by military and war work from entering upon a scientific career. In the battle areas themselves, laboratories, libraries, and museums are destroyed and scientists killed or impoverished.

Furthermore, war itself is becoming increasingly a matter of scientific technique. Unless there is established a sound international political order capable of preventing war and rendering preparation for it unnecessary, postwar governments will place ever tighter restrictions upon the interchange of scientific ideas. Already in the 1930's, the

Nazis and Fascists were preventing their representatives from attending certain technical conferences, and it is obvious that governments will be reluctant to share the inventions of their nationals with those of other countries if they have reason to fear that such interchange will help to build up the military power of a potential opponent. A strong case might be made for the claim that, if power politics rules unchecked after this war, not only will international trade give place to increasing autarchy but the free international interchange of ideas, already beginning to be limited, will progressively diminish to the general impoverishment of the world.

All of these deterrents to scientific study would be avoided if an adequate international policy could be established. On the positive side, moreover, an international order would make it possible for geological, meteorological, biological, anthropological, and social studies to be carried on all over the world without regard to the international boundaries that in the decade before World War II were becoming an increasing hindrance to the movement of investigators.

A most important scientific effect of an adequate international order would be in disease control and the conservation of high-seas fisheries and other resources. Animal and plant diseases would be quarantined for their own sake, and not as an indirect means of restricting trade. Fisheries, like those of the North Sea and the whale fisheries of the Antarctic, could be regulated for the general welfare without interference by one or two nations, such as Japan's recent refusal to ratify an adequate whaling treaty, which rendered futile any intelligent effort to preserve this important resource.

Actual examples of international cooperation in the execution of policies dictated by scientific discovery may be found in the international public health quarantine measures and exchange of information that has long been maintained. More recently migratory locust control in Africa has involved a degree of international collaboration that is indicative of what is extremely desirable in this field (Ubarov, "The Locust Plague," *Jour. Econ. Ent.* XXXVII, 1944, pp. 93–99.) The possibilities are legion.

On the other hand, if we choose war and preparation for war as the normal modes of national existence, the increasing technological nature of modern conflict will force men and women everywhere into a hopeless armaments race. With ordinary goods, there is a limit beyond which production cannot go. Men can wear only so many shoes, eat only so much bread, use only so many houses or motor cars. But if one nation produces fifty thousand planes, its rival will try to produce twice that number, and so on in endless competition. Man, instead of being the master of his machines, will become their slave until our civilization becomes exhausted and a new Caesarism possesses us.

### THE SOCIAL USES OF SCIENCE AND TECHNOLOGY

The choices that lie open to society in the matter of its use of science and technology are rather fearful ones. A passive attitude would seem to mean that the twentieth century will repeat the experience of the nineteenth. The new discoveries, the new sources of power and wealth in industry, in medicine, in the utilization of natural resources, will continue to fall into the hands of the few who will come thereby to live off the labor of others. Are we to permit, for example, the suppression of labor-saving patents by large corporations or unions in favor of less efficient methods whose chief merit is that they bring the stockholders higher dividends or insure the maintenance of a particular labor leadership? Can we tolerate famine in India in the presence of modern methods of food production and distribution? Can we allow continued malnutrition and insufficient medical and dental care in the face of technical facilities for achieving the contrary? Can we afford unregulated population increase with its resulting wars and lowered standards of living in the face of the sociological and medical possibilities of its adequate control? If such practices are to be continued, there would be perpetuated the old disequilibria referred to in the opening paragraphs of this chapter.

On the other hand, the adequate development and use of science and technology may lead to a solution of these and other problems. Leisure and the good things of life may become widely distributed, exploitation and class struggle disappear, and man attain a new level of civilization and culture, though one of our group, Professor Frederick K. Kirsten, suggests that we must learn to lead simpler lives if we would reap the full benefit of the increased leisure that science and technology seem to promise us, and that the demand for an endless succession of new manufactured goods before the old are worn out is scarcely a manifestation of culture.

There are at least three things the scientist can do to promote the proper use of science and technology. (1) He can cultivate himself as a member of society, making as sure as possible that the quality of his general citizenship is as good as his specialization in science. He will thus be in a position to know what the social and political forces are that would employ the scientific and technological discoveries with which he is familiar. (2) He can help to assure by teaching, by lecturing, and by writing, that the non-scientist citizen is kept informed as to what science is and what it can and cannot do in the promotion of human welfare. The citizen will then come to know what to expect of his leaders and representatives in getting from science what he is entitled to receive. (3) He can be ready to cooperate closely with those in authority whenever his special knowledge may appear to be of service in solving the problem at hand. In this way the deliberation concerning intricate technical matters will not always be left exclusively to untrained persons.

The most significant fact that emerges from any general consideration of the social relations of science and technology is the emphasis that it lays on the extreme desirability of a corresponding development in the understanding and manipulation of human nature itself. Science gives man increasing control of his environment, more rapid communications, better houses, more food, better health, longer life—all for what? Is it simply to enable the age-old struggle for power over one's fellows to be fought out on a larger and larger stage? Or is it the function of science to suggest that with sufficient knowledge man can control his own essential happiness as well as he manipulates the superficies of his surroundings?

*Author's note:* While these pages were being prepared for the press and while World War II itself was becoming history, the United States presented the world with atomic energy. Like many other inventions such as the telescope, which is said to have been used to spy out the enemy before it was used in astronomy, the new discovery has been turned to the destruction of men before it has been applied to the enlightenment of their minds or the improvement of their condition. Nevertheless, such ultimate goods as an immense increase in potentially constructive power on the one hand and a further penetration of the nature of the universe on the other are ours for the asking. (It is even quite soberly suggested that hereafter such an interesting project as an observatory on the moon need not necessarily be left to comic supplement fantasy.) Perhaps this event is a technological advance comparable only with man's first control of fire!

Meanwhile, the destructive possibilities of atomic energy are such that one must reconsider the observation made earlier in this chapter that science builds up the defense in military situations as rapidly as the attack. A group of scientists who have been leaders in atomic research have recently declared that they can foresee no practicable technological defense against the atomic bomb. It is too soon, of course, to do more than speculate upon the military future of atomic energy when employed by both parties to a conflict. But, if it does turn out that this force provides such a powerful offense that science has no answer except the discovery of ever more potent sources of energy, we run the danger of plunging into a new armaments race which will make the two billions spent on the "Manhattan Project" seem small change but one which by its very monstrousness will give progressively less assurance that we and ours will not be destroyed. The alternative is more urgent but surely essentially the same as it was before atomic power was introduced—the elimination of war from human affairs and the institution of such international controls as will direct the development of new energies to constructive channels.

Good will and social intelligence cease to be the idealist's hope or the utopian's dream and become the minimum essentials of the realist's program for survival.

MELVILLE H. HATCH, WITH THE
COLLABORATION OF HENRY K. BENSON,
FREDERICK KURT KIRSTEN, ARTHUR W.
MARTIN, AND RICHARD G. TYLER

# CHAPTER XXI

# *Religion*

*What doth the Lord require of thee, but to do justly, and to love mercy, and to walk humbly with thy God?*—Micah 6:8

THE basic assumption made by the writers of the foregoing chapters may differ in detail but in general they agree with the fundamental ethical principles of our Judeo-Christian heritage.

(1) First and foremost is the renunciation of any arrogance on the part of the democratic victor-nations. More than that, the recognition that their failure to help solve the fundamental political and economic difficulties of the world was partly responsible for creating conditions favorable to the rise of fascism. Individual writers, not to mention readers, may make more or less of this, but it is there. The recent war was not simply a conflict between the children of light on the one hand and the black legions of the devil on the other. We all share, in varying degrees, the responsibility and guilt.

This contention is fundamental in prophetic religion's approach to any human problem. The moment we make a motes-and-beams division of guilt, we lose the perspective we must have to see clearly. But even more, we sever the bond that unites us with our fellows—the bond of common failure, our common need of wisdom and forgiveness. The "war guilt" clause of the last peace sowed the spiritual seeds of Hitler's "master race" propaganda. Our arrogance vitalized the seeds of fascism's super-arrogance. A common "conviction of sin," whether or not it be in the words of Paul, "All have sinned and come short of the glory of God," is essential.

As has been illustrated in another chapter, there is no difference in kind, only in degree, between Hitler's racism and the racism which beats Jews on the streets of Boston, would keep Negroes "in their place" in Texas, or organizes a "Don't Let the Japs Back" movement in Seattle. All are equally odious to our religious tradition: indeed, if more odium attaches to one than the other, it should properly attach to the hypocrisy of "Christian" nations whose faith calls for brotherhood but whose working motto is "white supremacy." As Shridharani tells us in his *Warning to the West,* we western peoples must choose between treating the peoples of the east as friends and fellow-citizens of this planet, and destroying ourselves in a futile attempt to dominate them.

(2) The assumption that cooperation between men and nations is better than strife springs directly from our Hebrew-Christian religious tradition, though it is found also in many other faiths. It is opposed to the "might is right" theory, the "law of tooth and fang" theory, or to the Nazi glorification of force. It is an assumption denounced as "effeminate" by Hitler. Indeed, one philosopher, Erich Kahler, reviewing the lessons of history, says that the "central issue of our time" is whether we believe there is one human race with a common destiny, or whether we believe only in a multiplicity of races and nations, warring against one another in a meaningless conflict. (*Man the Measure,* 1943, Ch. I.)

(3) A related assumption is that the strong have a duty to the weak, a "trusteeship" of their power, an obligation to develop less developed nations and colonies. This "trusteeship" is like any lofty spiritual conception, readily perverted into a top-lofty hypocrisy: a "trustee" easily persuades himself that it is his "duty" to keep power in his own hands for the "good" of the weaker party. Even parents find it hard to believe their children ever grow up, though it is their intention that they should help them to do so. And when nations, or natural resources, are wards of other nations or economic interest groups, it

is almost inevitable that abuses creep in. This question of trusteeship is the basic one when we consider colonies or "backward" peoples today. But however guilty western nations have been of exploitation, the fact remains that their religious heritage condemns exploitations and reminds them that "trusteeship" implies self-reliance and equality. This is a goal totally different from the fascist aim of master and slave races. If we do not always understand this clearly, the Nazis did, for they said the notion of trusteeship is "effeminate" and must be rooted out of the conscience of mankind.

(4) The aim of a peace settlement with the defeated Axis, as discussed in this book, is one of reform and rehabilitation rather than revenge. Here again is a corollary of the religious faith that men are, in essence, brothers, and that the end of all socio-political arrangements is the creation or re-creation of brotherly relationships between men. Conversely, a peace which is vengeful, or which fails to give an orderly and scheduled progress toward an international order resting on mutual respect and cooperation, must fail. At the same time the spiritual rehabilitation of Germany, for example, cannot come without genuine contrition and penance.

(5) A basic peace aim in the foregoing pages is that we shall have a world order in which each man, and each culture, shall be free to develop unique contributions toward the common store. This is but an application of the religious principle, that every individual is a unique gift of God, that his personality must be free to develop and grow, and that his talents are properly used only in the service of all mankind. The Kingdom of God is not a Prussianized or Americanized uniformity, but a unity of infinite variety; a cooperative enterprise of free souls; a world-culture drawing upon the resources and traditions of nation-cultures and region-cultures.

(6) Implicit if not always explicit in the foregoing chapters is the principle that persons are ends not means, and that political, economic, and educational machinery is means and not an end. Thus, when it is said that peace must be kept "flexible," it is meant that changing human needs may order and re-order its provisions. Again, even though the reader disagree with the particular arrangements herein set forth— let us say economic—we trust he will accept the underlying premise that persons must come before profits, and the welfare of all ahead of the advantage of the few.

(7) A corollary of the above is the assumption that government, national or international, must be made responsible to the people. Some governments will be more responsible or more easily made so than others. But no government will be acceptable if it violates this fundamental spiritual requirement, which is rooted in a faith that freedom means the individual citizen's ability to control his own destiny.

We have here assumed rather than proved that the ethical principles of brotherhood and cooperation are the core of our religious heritage. We do not think it necessary to go into elaborate proof that this is indeed the case.

For the conscience of mankind is proof enough. Eastern observers looking at our Western culture comment over and over how strange we are, calling ourselves "Christian" and yet not practicing what Christianity preaches. Secular idealists within our culture are at once critical of our existing churches and respectful of the prophets whose ethical insights and moral indignation they share. Young people again and again advance as the reason for not being interested in religion, that church people don't live weekdays by what they confess on Sundays, and that our pulpits fail to light up the real problems of our day with the insight religion ought to give.

Any discussion of existing religions as bases of collaboration must take account of these criticisms of our own churches. We cannot, unfortunately, assume that existing religion, as it is preached now, will do much toward providing the spiritual bases for a new world order. The churches of today are potentially powerful but actually doubtful allies in the struggle for that order. As the well known minister, Dr. Ernest F. Tittle, has remarked, "The churches are not the ark of salvation today, but themselves need to be saved."

First of all, the world's religions must make up their minds whether they have as their mission to bring the power and wisdom of God to man's aid in building a new world, or whether their mission is to save man out of a world which must, essentially, be given up as a bad job. Until this decision is unequivocally made, religion must be an equivocal force. This does not mean that religion need so far lose its perspective as to identify any particular social order, actual or proposed, with The Kingdom of God. But it does mean (1) that the churches shall give men ethical power and insight to create a better social order and

(2) that our awareness of the imperfection of any such order shall not thwart our attempts to improve what we have.

As matters stand, the balance seems to be in favor of an "other-worldly" religion, or, what is worse, a religion that is silent before the basic evils of the world. The fastest-growing sects today are the emotional, fundamentalist sects which frankly say the world is doomed. It is likely that these are growing, among other reasons, as a reaction of despair among men facing a new age. But even if one dismisses these churches as a symptom of spiritual funk, the average American church is not providing very effective leadership and has much less vitality in evidence than they.

If it is a Catholic Church, it has the advantage of a well-thought-out social program sharply challenging the motivation and goal of capitalist economy and a world of irresponsible nationalism; a program, however, whose underlying purpose and whose day-to-day political decisions are warped because the church itself, in vindication of its temporal claims, must, first of all, preserve itself and, most of all, reassert its ancient "right" to tell the state what it should and should not do.

If it is a Protestant Church, its membership is used to a gospel of individualism which supports a dog-eat-dog capitalist economy; and its aim is the personal salvation of souls, usually by an emotional experience; or if it serves meat less strong, it interprets religion in personal terms of "Christian living," and "sin" in terms of petty moralism. Protestant churches have far-sighted national leadership, but this leadership has few roots in the local congregation. (The Federal Council of Churches' 1942 Conference on a Just and Durable Peace at Delaware, Ohio, was as much concerned about how to get its findings down to the local churches as it was about the findings themselves!)

If it is a Jewish community it is paralyzed by fear of Anti-Semitism, of "what the Gentiles may say" when social or political issues demand solution or an unequivocal stand. The social idealism of Judaism and the actual experience of oppression naturally impel Jews toward progressive if unpopular causes. The stifling of what is a normal reaction of the offspring of the prophets and the partners of mankind's underdogs is one of the tragedies of contemporary Jewish life.

The average church, then, is more follower than leader on the great questions of our day. Though it has made challenge to the fundamental problems of our economy, it is itself often the greatest offender when it comes to narrow racial feeling. Its gospel is individual rather than social, exclusive rather than inclusive—a situation which deserves a special paragraph or two.

If the churches must decide whether or not they think it their job to bring spiritual help to the building of a better society on this earth, they must make an even more difficult decision: will they continue to insist that their particular way of salvation is the *only* way, or will they take the view that all men are seeking the same goal by different routes?

This question is fundamental, because no spiritual foundation for a world order can be grounded in intolerance and exclusivism. In the past each religion and each sect of each religion has claimed exclusive possession of the truth, and accordingly been contemptuously intolerant of others. The amazing missionary effort of the West has been based upon the assumption that the East must be saved from its paganism.

Fortunately, the laymen of various churches have not so exclusive an attitude as the clergy whose business it is to defend their particular doctrine and institution. And intelligent church leaders, laymen and clergy also, are able to see over the fences. Indeed a Laymen's Commission some ten years ago made the astonishing recommendation that the religions of the world should consult with one another on common objectives, and work toward common goals, rather than try to convert one another.

An outstanding member of this commission, Harvard's William Ernest Hocking, went even further in a pioneer work called *Living Religions and a World Faith,* pointing out that in today's "one world" even the great world religions have become, really, provincial. For the first time in history it is possible for a man to know enough about all the world to think in terms of a common humanity, instead of his own race, nation, or religion; to ask the question, "Can we have a world economy or a world political organization?" Dr. Hocking contends, however, that a true world faith will take account of men's immediate loyalties; it will be grounded upon living religions, not upon a synthetic common faith; each religion in its own tongue and doctrine stating common truths. Thus, if we need religious endorsement of the ideal of world peace, Judaism will rally its followers according to their tradition; Mohammedans will discover that Mohammed was a prophet of world peace also; while Hinduism will draw forth the same prophecy from its manifold scriptures. If people can be led to see the common content of particular cultural inheritances, each so precious to its owners, and not to insist that none is of value but their own, then a new day will dawn. These particular forms are not "non-essentials." They are rather the infinitely varied vessels in which are stored the great common ideals of justice, brotherhood and peace.

Meanwhile, there is work a-plenty right here in America, and here also are very encouraging beginnings. Within individual churches, we should recognize that top national leadership is frequently far ahead of the local church when it comes to attitudes and works of cooperation. The Methodists, for example, have been conducting nation-wide campaigns to make their people understand the need of an international organization to keep the peace.

Among churches, nationally and locally as well, there is already a high degree of cooperation. In 1937, hundreds of delegates from Protestant churches everywhere met in a World Conference on Church, Community, and State, in Oxford, England, and found themselves in fundamental agreement upon the spiritual problems of our time. (Findings obtainable from Universal Christian Council, 297 Fourth Ave., New York City.) This conference climaxed a collaboration which grew through several decades, and it has been followed by other conferences and by collaboration among world church leaders which is very much alive today. Indeed, the fellowship of Christian churches in every land continued unbroken by war, the only fellowship which so continued. Such conference and fellowship are preparing a common, intelligent approach to the world's problems by churches of all denominations of every nation.

In 1942 the Federal Council of Churches held a conference at Delaware, Ohio, where they clarified the spiritual foundations of a just and durable peace and translated these into specific political, cultural and economic terms. Locally and nationally also the various denominations have been working together to meet problems created by the war. They have helped refugees, relocated Japanese, established churches and other services for war workers, and ministered to the armed forces on a cooperative basis.

Among faiths, we must mention the splendid work of the National Conference of Christians and Jews in educating Americans to mutual understanding of Protestants, Catholics, and Jews. More lately, we have had the promising beginnings of a program of intercultural education, which seeks to develop understanding of our many religious and national and racial elements at the school-age level, when attitudes are being formed.

Do the existing faiths as a whole provide the dynamic need? We can not command the knowledge required to give a complete answer. Certain faiths obviously do not: the nationalist faiths, for example, of Japan and Germany. But those faiths seem to be only pathological extremes of the destructive nationalism shared by every people. Here in the United States we have, too, a nationalism which would endorse an American imperialism cloaked in self-righteousness.

But on the other hand, if the faith of the authors of the present work is correct—and so far as we can verify it, we believe it is—then all men and all nations have a better side. This, we think, can be strengthened by pointing out that the goals of brotherhood and international cooperation neither oppose nor repudiate particular religious or national traditions, but rather fulfill them. An American becomes a better American when he joins hands with Prussians, Frenchmen, and Japanese to build a world order in which the welfare of each is promoted. A Jew becomes a better Jew when he stands with the Christian and the Buddhist for the brotherhood of man.

We look, then, not for a renunciation of religions in general, nor for the creation of some entirely new religion which can provide the foundation for a world society. Such a foundation already exists in the common convictions and insights of existing religions. Those religions, institutionally speaking, cry aloud for reform and redirection, in many cases. But that reform will come not from outsiders so much as from those who work within, as supporters. It will be persons like the late William Temple—Archbishop of Canterbury, teacher, social reformer, and spiritual leader, symbol of a Church of England and a common Christianity made aware of men's spiritual and material needs, of a church reunited with all the people leading them toward a better world—and not the bitter atheists, who will swing our churches in the right direction.

JOSIAH R. BARTLETT
ARTHUR ZUCKERMAN

# CHAPTER XXII

## *Nationalism*

WITHIN the present-day system of international relations the center of man's loyalty is his own sovereign nation. To it he gives allegiance. It provides the symbols which call forth his deepest emotions. The national flag, national heroes, national customs, and national holidays are constantly before him. Five hundred years ago Europeans lived in feudal societies; they had a local but also a religious view of life and did not react emotionally to the ideal of the nation. In those days religious heresy and not treason was the great sin, and infidelity to one's feudal lord constituted the greatest political crime. Today, loyalty to the nation has outstripped loyalty to other associations. To refuse to salute the flag, or to express opposition to the national constitution creates more resentment than non-church going and disbelief in the holy scriptures.

National patriotism is stimulated at every turn. The national anthem is played at public gatherings; school children salute the flag; newspapers stir up national emotions; radio programs contain national music and dramatization of national history; the churches pray for the nation. A heightened national self-consciousness forms part of the atmosphere in which men live, and during war intensified patriotic fervor makes people still more aware of themselves as Americans, English, Dutch, Germans, or Italians. Here lies a contradiction of modern life which must be resolved before human beings can once more enjoy wholesomeness and stability.

As early as 1862 Lord Acton wrote that the theory of nationality "is a retrograde step in history." He lamented that nationality does not aim either at liberty or at prosperity and prophesied that its course would be "marked with material as well as moral ruin." He feared that nationality would be so jealous as to sacrifice all other associations

258

and that it would forcibly impose a fictitious unity which, in the long run, would be disastrous. Indeed, he seems to have foreseen something of what has since been realized in the totalitarian state. The French philosopher Renouvier later also criticized the idea of nationality as "mischievous" and "historically false." He believed that given a just government there was no special claim for nationalities to lead a separate existence; where different groups had lived together for long periods of time and had developed close economic and social ties, the principle of nationality should be subordinated to the larger question of the common interest of all groups.

The forebodings of these writers have been realized in recent years. We have seen the evils of unbridled nationalism. In 1920 the rights of small nations were given unprecedented expression, but after twenty years many of these peoples showed so little real unity that they had to be held together by force and by the oppression of dictatorships. Nationalism took on a darker hue. It became intolerant of minorities; overstepped the legitimate sphere of government; suppressed political parties, trade unions, Jews, Communists, international associations of various kinds, and attempted to make the individual merely a citizen. The modern highly emotional over-self-conscious nation suffers from deep-seated doubt, and attempts, by propaganda and symbolism, to conceal its own inner disharmony and disquietude. It is also in conflict with the modern machine age, since present-day economic life demands a larger stage than present-day nations can provide. And increasingly, political power has proved its impotency as an economic instrument; despite its great navy, Great Britain could not collect reparations from Germany, nor did the Japanese conquest of Manchuria appreciably strengthen Japan's economic life. We need not review here what has been surveyed often enough: the inability of modern nations to guarantee their own health and general standards of social life and intellectual welfare.

What should be emphasized, however, are the philosophic or spiritual consequences of unrestrained nationalism and of nationalism in a politically anarchical world. Political passion, writes Julien Benda, today affects more and more people until scarcely a person exists who is unaffected by "class, racial, and national passion." Indeed, nations increasingly differentiate themselves as moral entities, and patriotism becomes "the assertion of one form of mind against the other." Nazi

Germany, as we have seen, boasted its cultural mission; Italy spoke of its Fascist values; France has been the "bearer of civilization." Ours is the "age of intellectual organization of political hatreds," and passions are carefully cultivated and built up and provided with nourishing theories. "The present age is essentially the age of politics" which distorts and sacrifices so many precious values of life and tends to reduce literature, philosophy, and art to slavery in its service.

Whereas the church in the Middle Ages set its seal of approval on patriotism as an "extension of human love and not as a limitation of it," the modern age glorifies patriotism *because* of its exclusiveness and its claim to undivided loyalty. Moreover, nations heighten their own importance by despising others, and, according to Professor G. M. Stratton, this national self-consciousness has grown so unbalanced as to become in a large measure a delusion, making it impossible for the large body of citizens to examine the international situation with fairness and justice.

What is this thing called a nation which has supplanted practically every other thing in modern political life? What is its unifying principle? Why this unparalleled devotion to a particular human institution? The question may well be asked, for nationalism, in attempting to make itself a sovereign entity, has disregarded profoundly important aspects of human life.

We must recall that nationalism and nationality are in many respects of recent origin. In the Middle Ages, European peoples fought over religious, feudal, and civic issues. There were Florentines and Paduans but no Italians ready to fight for all Italy. In what is now Germany, many people had an intense civic pride but not an extensive German loyalty. The fact of the relatively recent development of this overwhelmingly powerful modern sentiment of nationality and nationalism tends to be obscured by the very intensity with which the feeling is held. And therefore many people come to think that nationalism and nationality constitute a much more important and final part of human beings and of human society than is necessarily true.

First, it should be clear that nationalism is not rooted in human nature, for human nature is most malleable and has expressed itself in many other political ways—such as loyalty to families, tribes, cities, empires, and religions. Nor is it rooted in geography, though without question geography has played an important part in uniting people.

A person who loves his farm loves but a very small part of the country which makes up the political unit to which he owes allegiance. If the form of government changed tomorrow, he could still love the trees and hills and plains which lie before him. Neither does a common language explain nationalism. Not merely do some countries have more than one language, but in some cases, as in Ireland, the nationalist spirit has led to a linguistic movement; and it is difficult to say which is the cause of the other. And as for religion, the attempt to make it a main source of nationalism also runs into difficulties. Many modern nations have a variety of religions within their borders, and the great religions have cast off the bonds of nationalism and empire and have become world-wide in their sympathy and membership.

Without question history has played a dominant role in inspiring nationalist feeling. National heroes, national institutions, and the struggle to win national independence, all these impress themselves upon the citizen and bring out the truth that the present owes much of what it is to the past. Historians have played a great part in promoting the sense of nationalism, and the public schools have been one of the most powerful instruments in using history to influence children's minds.

Nevertheless here too we must exercise care, for frequently it is not the process of history but the writing of history which has stimulated nationalism. Historical forces may be one thing, and historians' estimates of them another. Indeed one may argue that the economic developments of the last hundred years and the scientific developments too have led to the need for wider forms of government than the sovereign nation, and that it is by misreading history that national feeling has been heightened. The truth is that the history which has so largely created nationalism is a highly selective "history" picked out from the bewildering maze of inter-related events, a number of factors so arranged as to bring the national aspect into prominence. On the other hand, a history of religion, of art or literature, of invention, of everyday things such as sugar, tea, cotton, playing cards, plants and animals, might well lead to the conclusion that the source of human welfare increasingly is to be found outside of one's nation, or, more accurately, that the foundations of any one nation are far, far broader than those suggested by its boundaries.

Why, then, have people tended to emphasize nations as separate units? Partly because of the overemphasis upon the purely political, partly because the national state has been the modern administrative unit of much of the citizen's everyday life, partly because of the struggle for security which grows out of an imperfect international organization, partly because of the deep-seated tendency to take pride in the achievements of one's people (for it is easier to be impressed by spectacular national conquests, seeing the map of the world generously covered with one's own national color), and also because of the resultant opposition to these conquests felt by national groups which have come under the foreign imperial yoke.

However, neither the process of history nor the writing of history can serve as a final explanation of nationalism. On the contrary, the process of history—whatever that may be—may require changes in the units of governments and the loyalties of men. Already we have seen a marked change in the study and writing of history in the institutions of higher learning in many countries, although the rise of dictatorships has set back this desirable trend in a most distressing fashion. These dictatorships clearly illustrate the truth that "history" may be manufactured to serve national ends, that it may be as much the effect as the cause of nationalism. Every country has a most complicated set of relations, past and present, and from these one may select a great number of "histories" which may point to widely differing interpretations.

Nor can the economic explanation of nationalism suffice. Economic factors have undoubtedly stimulated nationalism in many countries, but economic factors also have promoted regional, international, and local movements in conflict with the national. And one may well argue that the economic nationalism of recent years was the effect of national sentiment rather than of exclusively economic forces. Nationalism tended to dominate economic policy rather than economics create nationalism.

The foregoing analysis should make it clear that while geography, history, economics, language, religion and institutions do contribute to national consciousness, they may also contribute to other forms of community self-consciousness and offer no adequate explanation of nationalism. We must make another approach. We suggest that *a nation is a group of people which thinks that it is a nation*. It will be bound together by a sense of purpose, by the remembrance of past deeds, by the way in which it lives at present; but since different countries will have different bonds of union, the elements outlined above will mix in varying proportions, and the groups within the nation will be bound by stronger or weaker ties. Thus, a nation is a *unit of changing content,* and we are mistaken to assume that it is a final entity. Individual, regional, and local differences persist. They are not obliterated. The Catalans, the Basques, and the Andalusians retain many of their historical differences in contemporary Spain. Regional differences are still to be noted in Italy. Flemish and Walloons still form contrasting groups in Belgium. One may note differences of accent in the various counties of England and in regions of the United States. Nor is this surprising. The character of the nation depends upon the compelling power of the uniting ideal. What holds people together is the consciousness of a common factor or factors which transcend their everyday economic and social life—loyalties which bind them into a wider fellowship without destroying the more intimate associations. National disintegration takes place because groups cease to feel themselves a part of a whole. (See José Ortega y Gasset, *Invertebrate Spain,* 1937, pp. 20–29.)

In 1934, one of the present writers ventured to predict that unless nationalism could be more restrained, unless it ceased over-reaching itself, unless it brought itself more in line with life itself in both the economic and moral spheres, unless it realized that the safety of nations and especially the freedom of nations in an age of increasing technological power must be safeguarded by an adequate international organization, then nations as we know them would probably have disappeared within fifty years. Looking back, he is surprised at his own conservative estimate. Today dozens of small, even medium-sized nations lie in ruins, owing to the emergence of a new factor—totalitarian nationalism. Here is a nationalism in Germany based upon a number of factors including a pseudo-philosophy of power, race, and leadership which came perilously near to enslaving a continent and perhaps even the world. This type of nationalism is incompatible with the existence of other nationalisms, and the other nations have at last joined in an organization as yet somewhat indefinite called the United Nations. They united indeed for the immediate task of overthrowing the enemy, but are they united in a sufficient recognition of the fact that nationalism must be considerably modified and purified if we are to win the peace? A curious mixture of fear, pride, and defiance amalgamates to produce an extreme sensitivity which brings the nation into over-sharp focus and causes people to lose sight of the significance of many other associations, such as churches, trade unions, employers' associations, service clubs, universities. Instead of being a balance of many loyalties life is being increasingly centered on the national state until all other values become subordinated to that of an excessive nationalism. And this at a time when even the greatest nation-state cannot by its own efforts maintain its independence and promote its welfare. Great problems confront nations which no longer can be solved by national governments acting as independent units.

The war may have redoubled national self-consciousness at the very time when nations are exhausted and have desperate need of one another and of a more adequate form of world society to keep the peace and to organize efficiently the thousands of international relations which have developed. The cruelties perpetrated upon millions of people and the unparalleled destruction of life and property will have awakened such wide-spread hate that national tempers will have become hardened, and in their blind hatred of neighbors they may look more to the past than to the future. Several years ago, Carleton J. Hayes said:

Nationalism as a religion inculcates neither charity nor justice; it is proud, not humble; and it signally fails to universalize human aims; it repudiates the revolutionary message of St. Paul and proclaims anew the primitive doctrine that there shall be Jew and Greek, only that now there shall be Jew and Greek more quintessentially than ever. Nationalism's kingdom is frankly of this world, and its attainment involves tribal selfishness and vainglory, a particularly ignorant and tyrannical intolerance and war. . . . Nationalism brings not peace but the sword.

The events of the last few years probably intensified this national self-consciousness and intolerance and pride, for the press and radio of the contending nations not only denounced enemies but constantly referred to military victories won by *their own* national forces, not by their forces *as members of the United Nations*. France, Holland, and Belgium animated by a sense of nationalism made even more pronounced may try to have their empires restored at a time when the peoples of Asia and Africa are stirring with a new national self-consciousness. And in Asia, the great danger exists that the Oriental peoples will have imitated the West in adopting nationalism as a way of life. If they do, and fall prey to militant, exclusive nationalism, they will run into contradictions even more quickly than did Europe in the nineteenth century; for the twentieth century should already have made clear the inadequacy of the national state in a world rendered intimately interdependent by long-range robots, atomic bombs, and the need of capital investments, markets, raw materials and cooperation to insure promotion of health and other forms of human welfare.

Nor must we overlook the danger that nationalism today can be further stimulated and inflamed by propaganda methods undreamed of a century ago. Radio, television, the press, and education constitute instruments which, in the hands of fanatical leaders, can transform people, particularly young people, within a generation—witness Germany and Italy.

The effort, however, must be made to enable mankind to see itself truly and to see nationalism in better perspective, if the United Nations are to succeed. For unless nationalism becomes more intelligent and capable of being a constructive force, we shall lose the peace. What must be done? First, history must be seen aright. We have had history written from the national point of view and taught in schools and even in universities to the exclusion of history of civilization as a whole. Delisle Burns, in 1924, wrote *A Short History of International Intercourse* primarily because he said there had been as yet no history which showed how far civilized life had arisen out of the peaceful cooperation between different peoples. Francis Delaisi also uttered an important note when he warned against the habit of writing national histories as if, for instance, the France of today bore any resemblance to the France of the tenth century or modern Britain had much in common with the England of Chaucer's time. There is an element of continuity in nations, but the historian tends to exaggerate it and assume an identity of national existence which has not existed in fact. We need, as Christopher Dawson and others have urged, a view of history in its wider sense; and while H. G. Wells may have made many blunders, the purpose behind his world history was a sound one.

We must cease looking at history through merely national eyes, but we must do more if nationalism is to develop into a constructive force and not become an obstinate sentimental attachment to a fixed idea; we must look about us and seek things as they are; we must face the realities of modern life. Of these realities surely one of the most obvious is that modern nationalist states can preserve their existence and civilization only by cooperating in the most intimate manner. Their sovereignty is no longer sufficient to prevent overwhelming destruction to their cities and villages, disastrous dislocation of their economic life and uprooting of their cultural institutions. Sober appraisal can lead to no other conclusion than that the democratic nations can only keep their freedom if they renounce their claims to prepare for their own armed defense independent of and perhaps in competition with one another, for war has made the modern nation as an instrument of self-defense as out of date as the feudal castle after the invention of gunpowder.

Intelligent nationalism must also face the stern reality that national independence thought of in terms of sovereignty can no longer even provide for the necessities and amenities of everyday national life. This statement may appear to be far too sweeping in view of the remarkable advances made by many nations in legislating higher standards of wages, labor conditions, unemployment relief, sickness and old-age insurance, housing, education, regulation of utilities, and conservation of resources. It would, indeed, be foolish to deny the national progress made in these matters but it would be equally foolish to ignore the international scope of many of the above problems. Space does not permit detailed treatment of the necessity for international cooperation in preventing the spread of disease, in eliminating traffic in women and children, in developing hydroelectric power, promoting soil conservation, developing a coordinated transportation system on land, sea, and in the air; nor is it necessary to do so at this point, for the other chapters of this volume will have demonstrated how much national welfare has come to depend upon international cooperation and the development of international institutions.

Thus the major problems of the world will demand effort along both national and international lines. Merely to erect international institutions for man's welfare will not be sufficient, for events within nations, especially the big nations, may well have disastrous international repercussions as the 1929 economic depression in the United States, Hitler's persecution of minorities and suppression of political parties, and the Fascist denial of freedom in Italy have so vividly showed. Just as the new social developments have made inadequate the old concept of American federalism, as that of states versus federal government, and have required the cooperation of state and federal governments, so in the international sphere the expanding area of the problems of health, prevention of crime, the promotion of economic welfare, and intellectual and spiritual advance requires the cooperation of national and international agencies. It is not a case of either/or; it is a case of both/and, a task of finding the most efficient division of powers between national and international agencies in order to promote the maximum welfare of human beings. The artificial separation in popular thought of national and international life must go if we are to plan the postwar world intelligently.

Thus we must recognize the necessity of an adequate degree of world government. Unless order can be achieved, the conditions for the development of civilized nationalism and love of country will be absent. Fear and the other meaner emotions will predominate, and the reserves of leisure, wealth, and reflective thought will have dried up. The conclusion to which the present chapter points is a simple yet perhaps profound one—that men must learn to distinguish between love of country and national sovereignty. Civilized living involves multiple loyalties, and these can only flourish in an atmosphere of creative peace. To the objection that patriotism requires national sovereignty, one may reply that the individual may still love the mountains and the plains, the rivers and lakes, and sunshine and the clouds, the fruits and the flowers of his own land even though new instruments of government are devised to take care of the relations of his own country with other countries. His language will still be the vehicle of the best literature which his fellow-countrymen have and will have written; its music will still be available to him as will its painting and sculptures; and above all, in an atmosphere of creative peace within a framework of adequate international world government, the exchange of the goods and treasures of mankind will be permitted—which are necessary, as Delisle Burns has pointed out, if nations are to fertilize one another and assist one another with their respective contributions. We may conclude then that nationalism is not necessarily inconsistent with world organization but that certain kinds of nationalism are, and that "the central question is not, as so many assert, nationalism versus internationalism. The fundamental issue is what kind of nationalism can best serve the interests of the people of the world and what kind of international organization can most efficiently minister to man's needs." The

highest patriotism today will consist in recognizing the limitations of
the national state and the nation; in so doing the patriot will not love
his country any the less, but he will see it in its true setting as part
of a world order set within a universe, man's servant and not the exclusive master which the mistaken prophets of recent years have preached.

The Pledge for Peace Committee, of which Justice Owen J. Roberts
is Honorary Chairman and many of the nation's leading citizens are
members, has set forth this truth in a remarkable document *A Pledge
for Peace,* the following quotation from which will serve as a fitting
conclusion of our argument:

Mindful that I am a citizen of a great country created one hundred
sixty years ago by the union of thirteen divided and quarreling colonies;
and convinced that the world of today holds as much wisdom as did
that of the Founding Fathers, I declare myself for these propositions.
[The eight propositions deal with the establishment and effective authority of a world organization.] Solemnly aware that the acceptance
of these propositions *involves the creation in myself of a loyalty to the
human race along with, but not conflicting with, my loyalty to my own
country,* I do hereby set my hand and pledge the allegiance of my
heart. [Italics ours.]

LINDEN A. MANDER<br>JOSEPH B. HARRISON

## CHAPTER XXIII

# *The Great Tradition and the Need for a World Order*

IN THE tradition of Western thought the dominant concepts are universalism and rationality, and then, following from these, liberty, human
equality, and the mutual interdependence of all beings. The necessary
implication of those ideas is the organization of all men everywhere
on earth under one set of institutions, based on consent and aiming
at the promotion of a general welfare not in any one country but in
the world as a whole. But it is obvious that we have not achieved this

goal and do not seem, particularly in view of recent happenings, to be far along the road to it. Why is this so?

First of all, while the ideal has existed from the very beginning of Western thought, the various ethical implications of the ideal have taken time to work themselves out. Second, it is surely clear that while men have in general shared this ideal and professed it, particularism and selfishness have always been characteristic of human behavior; and the history of civilization, whether it is put in Christian or in Pagan terms, has been the history of the continuously frustrated struggle to adopt the social behavior without which men cannot attain even individual welfare. Third, man's lack of control over nature, his lack of the means, therefore, to a good life, and until recently his inability to organize human affairs on a wide scale, had made it practically impossible to institutionalize his ethical insights effectively.

At the same time, the necessity to create controls within limited areas has militated against the achievement of the universal ideal. But in our own age the development of technology, intercommunication, scientific understanding and control over nature, as well as the basic ability to organize more widely, has removed major incentives to selfishness and broken many bonds of the local and the particular. Furthermore, these controls, as they already are and as they are clearly becoming, have made it possible not only to organize men to realize the lasting ideals of Western civilization (and, incidentally, those ideals are not fundamentally different from or opposed to the ones arising independently out of Eastern thought), but also necessary to do so— witness the atomic bomb.

In short, the selfishness and particularism that were practical until only yesterday are impractical today and will be more so tomorrow, with the result that it is imperative to human welfare that we hereafter embody in our institutions the ideals we have professed. To demonstrate this general thesis I want briefly to sketch the history of the dominant ideas in Western thought and the history of their frustration.

Perhaps the chief mark of Greek thought was its rationalism. Socrates, Plato, Aristotle, developed their ideas of man, of the state, of ethics and metaphysics in protest against particular appearances, against prejudice. They insisted that reality was rational, universal, monistic. Plato's attack on the family and property, however extreme, was an attack on prejudice; on the selfishness, ultimately, of individual beings, on their failure to see that the good was *one,* that man was essentially a social animal, and that only by reasoned institutions, by knowledge, by fearlessness, could he hope to live the good life. And while Aristotle condoned and even supported certain institutions which Plato attacked, his insistence on the social nature of man, on the complementary character of man and society, revealed the same insight. That these thinkers idealized the city-state was due both to the contemporary lack of technical skill in controlling nature and to a perversion of the thinkers' own best insights. Their ideal of rational universalism could not be realized in a particular, limited, and exclusive society; nor did they have the material means—the instruments of communication, the techniques of public administration and organization—to make possible a wide community in which the benefits of mutual interdependence and culture could be obtained. Their world was, in fact, defeated, and gave way to the first wide empire—Alexander's—which collapsed almost immediately, again through lack of organizational ability; and then to the Roman Empire which collapsed ultimately, in the main for the same reason.

The dominant philosophy of the Roman world, stoicism, supplemented the earlier Greek insights. In particular, it stressed the common personality and the common equality of man in society. Its ideal was by implication a world order. Rome, in its law and its empire, developed the idea of rational justice based on humanity, of a universal rule, with peace and order as its ideals, and of a uniform citizenship. Stoicism failed, through prejudice, through particular claims of already existing institutions fully to realize these values. It failed, too, to maintain even the imperfect organization of its own world, partly because the scale of organization was limited, partly because it, also, lacked the technical ability, the effective communication between center and circumference, the economic productiveness, to maintain its institutions. Its theory of empire and of imperial administration therefore proved incapable of a democratizing that would allow a genuine sharing in the life of a large community.

Before Rome fell, Christianity had arrived. What was the essential teaching of Christ Himself? It was, I think, a doctrine compatible with and reinforcing Stoicism by developing and universalizing the ethical ideas of Hebraism—goodness and duty. It gave to them an other-worldly sanction, and insisted that beyond reason itself, and illuminating and supporting reason, there must be an emotional drive such as derives from the Christian concept of charity and love. It superimposed on Greek theory the idea of God as the sanction and source of a reasoned law of nature and of man, and the idea of man's sharing in the godly perfection. It stressed brotherhood, peace, equality, sharing; but because it was especially concerned with the ultimate fate of man, it gave a stronger sanction than there ever had been in Stoicism to the non-political ideal of other-worldliness, an ideal which could too readily result in a purely personal pursuit of salvation.

The translation of these insights into institutions, or at least the provision of principles which would allow them so to be translated, was largely the work of Saint Augustine, who rejected the proposition that Christian love and humility, with their emphasis on ethical behavior and their protest against pomp, circumstance, and power of an earthly kind, were the causes of the failure of the great adventure toward universalism that was Rome. He argued that all earlier history was a preparation for Christianity and that all subsequent history would exhibit its inevitable realization. But, in propounding that thesis he developed the great idea of Christian liberty and responsibility, the idea of men as being responsible for their fate and having a duty to institutionalize their world in such fashion as practically to realize the ethical ideal of Christianity. He insisted, too, on the ambivalent character of men, who although tainted with evil and selfishness were capable of developing virtue. From his doctrine of human nature came necessarily the denial of human omniscience and the tremendous support for the opposition to tyranny that had been characteristic of the Greek world. Power was a trust, never a naked property. No earthly authority was right merely because it was authority, but only because it promoted the good life by giving men the means thereto.

Essentially the great work of the medieval church was to preserve and spread as a spiritual principle, not simply as an administrative expedient, the peace contained in the practice of the Roman Empire. It argued that man was ruled and must be ruled by law, and that law finally rested upon revelation. Law for man arose from natural law, which was universal ethics; authority on earth existed to realize that law and institutionalize it under particular circumstances, being judged by its performance of that duty. Moreover, while medieval organization was not egalitarian, it stressed always that men had rights wherever they found themselves, and that the complement of those rights was obligation. While medieval society was not democratic, the twin concepts of mutual rights and obligation and of power as a trust had in them, for moral purposes, potentially the idea of democracy, of consent as the basis of just law.

But the other side of medieval life was the breakdown of any practice of administrative or political universalism, even in its imperfect Roman form; the development of localism; and the failure of the remnants of Roman law and the Latin tongue and feudalism to create any common, uniform, and inclusive secular organization. The failure of communications plus, perhaps, the tribalism that had come from German thought sealed the fate of the Empire supposed to parallel the church and to be its secular arm. In a world of famine and pestilence and excessive localism, the church emphasized minimal standards and uniformities and combated an egoistic individualism which the material conditions aided and which might otherwise have prevented the very survival of the Western world.

The medieval undertaking failed chiefly because a purely spiritual organization, without a corresponding secular organization, proved practically incompetent to order or control a world which was gradually gaining both in wealth and in the potentialities for wealth. Indeed, as that world changed, its ideas and ambitions came to corrupt the church itself by destroying its purely spiritual character; spiritual sanctions proved inadequate in the face of material opportunities.

Though the medieval ideal was an ideal of peace, under feudalism the practical limitations on strife were imposed by economics and communication. The possibilities of the growth of communications, of cultural contacts, of productivity, and of an emergent science as against other-worldliness became clear, and men gradually refused to accept the ideals of humility and of fixed status, even though such status was complemented by mutual rights and duties. Freedom of movement became one of the ideals of liberty and, with it, freedom of acquisition. It is somewhat of a paradox that the church, which had stressed the importance of organizing the secular order to provide the material means to a good life, failed when those means were becoming more genuinely available. Increasing wealth meant possibilities for increasing selfishness, increasing conflict, increasing destructiveness, arising from that conflict.

Fortunately, it also gave possibilities for wider political organization and wider units of control, and thence emerged the monarchical nation-state. While that state was particularistic and while the ethics of its rulers were not always of the highest, nevertheless the ideal was to create a wider unit of organization for the pursuit of human welfare. Particularly the state sought to overcome internal strife which frustrated that welfare, and which the ideal of Christendom could not combat, especially when the church itself became a vested economic interest and a political power.

Thus Western civilization, following the Reformation and the Renaissance, became organized into nation-states, generally under monarchical rule and generally pursuing mercantilist policies to gain the blessings of greater material welfare on behalf of the nation. While the ideal of peace did not disappear, the attempts to attain it were made through dynastic alliances and the balance of power system. In practice, states were competing and conflicting, and the idea of gain for all through a common development was largely lost sight of. Subsequent political developments were within the nation-state. They consisted of attempts to restrain power, to remove arbitrariness, and to achieve liberty, equality, and justice by means of consent within the individual nation.

While society and politics throughout most of the Western world remained aristocratic, at least until well into the nineteenth century, the basic movement was toward democracy. On the economic side, the attack on arbitrariness became an attack on mercantilism in the name of freedom of enterprise, the opportunity for all to share in the potential wealth now available. This doctrine gained success after the coming of industrialism. Its dogmas were free trade and *laissez faire,* its institutions those of competitive capitalism.

On the political side, the slow movement toward democracy did not until very recently involve any concept of a world order, despite the libertarian and egalitarian ideas implicit in it and the theory of the rights of man which it professed. As men came to control their governments, particularly where they belonged to powerful and wealthy nations, they took a new and greater pride in their national heritage and their national citizenship; and this pride unfortunately expressed itself in opposition to outsiders and resulted in international anarchy, despite the ethics of common humanity which is the basis of democracy. This tendency was strengthened by the fact that nations which reached nationhood late, and often had to throw off foreign oppression to do so, tied up the ideas of nationalism with the idea of liberty from foreign oppression.

On the economic side, the ideas of *laissez faire* and of free trade did imply mutual interdependence and a collaborating world. Those doctrines involved an attack on national economy of the mercantilist type and a theory of mutual gain among nations through free exchange. The ideal was peace, from which would come prosperity. Unfortunately, however, nations were not in fact free and equal, and the practice of this doctrine meant particular advantage to certain among them, especially England. As a result, there rapidly developed the idea of protectionism to equalize competition; and this idea was later expanded and perverted to include the duty of the nation-state, supported by the pride of democratic citizenship, to aid trade adventure, to gain spheres of influence, and to seek for markets in competitive rivalry. Imperialism worked with nationalism against the concept of a rational and cooperating world.

Moreover, both the attack on arbitrary government and the theory of free enterprise had tended toward the idea of minimizing government in order to get rid of the abuses of particular governments. Hence the very idea of freedom to some extent militated against the development of any supernational regulatory order.

Men, in short, had created the nation-state as the widest practicable means of controlling their environment, and in doing so had overcome localism. But in working out its problems and in developing a wealth economy they had increased their attachment to it in the very course of gradually civilizing and democratizing it. And one may say that by and large the more they improved the national institutions and democratized them within the nation, the more their attachment to them became inimical to a world order. Only in those spheres where interests did not, even in the short run, conflict were men willing to create international administrative institutions.

But the very development of material well-being under industrialism and the growth of scientific knowledge which brought control of nature and the conquest of distance itself contradicted the whole practice of nationalism and made possible the realization of a world order and world community which had been implicit in the whole teaching of

Western thought. In short, at the same time men had narrowed their minds by limiting principles, supposedly of universal import, to the service of nationalism, they had created a technology and a science which at last made possible the harmony of material means and spiritual ends.

The concept of time-space is one of the most challenging scientific concepts of our age. Distance in space no longer means either long separation in time or the impossibility of transmitting knowledge and cultural gains rapidly and readily. At the same time, this conquest of distance, itself produced by the dynamics of trade and technology, makes interdependence inescapable.

The broad ideal of peace and international order has long been with us and, even in the days of extreme nationalism, has received continuous expression. Yet the first attempts seriously to institutionalize it were made only in the period following the First World War. They failed partly because the very idea of national freedom was itself not yet fully understood, partly because the search for the social-welfare order was still being made within the nation-state and insofar as it was successful had increased rather than decreased nationalist strength, and partly because internationalists, imbued with the idea of freedom, looked on that freedom as something to be realized merely by the prevention of conflict and by the removal of restraints. On the one hand, disarmament in the political sphere in combination with quite limited sanctions but without the organization of power to apply them, and, on the other, a return to free trade with the removal of national tariff barriers were the dominant ideas of the League of Nations. Even those men whose ethical sense of human interdependence was most profound and who were most far-sighted in seeing the actual fact had not come to realize that, because of diversities to be overcome, interdependence could be made fruitful only by positive and continuous governmental action and by the creation of a federal government for the world; meanwhile the majority of mankind, attached to the idea of national citizenship, found abhorrent the whole concept of a world citizenship to which particular national citizenship would be subordinated.

Though the recent struggle has shown, as clearly as it could be shown, the issue of common-sharing versus the issue of closed economy and the politics of naked power, and has demonstrated by bitter experience that we cannot in a world of conflicting nation-states enjoy and develop the prosperity open to us through our control of nature, prospects for a change of attitude do not thus far seem to be very bright. The provisions of the United Nations Charter somewhat timidly offer a slight advance over the League of Nations, but continue to accept the idea of national sovereignty in a world where that sovereignty can only mean the right of states to insist that in vital matters they may not be required to subordinate selfish interests to world needs. Further, while acceptance of the claims of great nations may appear to be immediately realistic, the practical implications are wider and more disruptively conflict. While nationalism may seem to mean decentralization, it is obvious that the great nation-states of today are, in fact, continental in scope and that spheres of influence promote an order consisting of a few powers organized on this scale, if not always on this specific geographical pattern. But a new international order so created retains the doctrine of sovereignty and offers no guarantee of world peace; it creates no sense of world citizenship and world responsibility, but rather lays the foundation for more gigantic conflict.

The Charter, it is true, promises a world police force. It does not, however, offer a basis that can make such a force effective. It proposes a national world of three empires; that this will create a positive world order and insure the social and economic good of mankind, historical experience would seem to deny.

A positive supernational order may indeed require sacrifices. As we have discovered in trying to work out the national social welfare state, there is in the economic field itself a kind of Gresham's law by which low and inadequate social conditions tend to make it hard to realize the highest. We have to enforce minimum standards, and in a world order it will be necessary to coerce those who would otherwise not observe them. At the same time it is clear that an international economic development, directed at the promotion of the highest possible standards of well-being everywhere, would involve temporary sacrifices on the part of the wealthiest nations. Even if they did not have to accept an actual decline in their standard of living they would see an immediate decrease in their relative advantage. But since the relative disadvantage would ultimately mean a higher standard for all, it seems not unreasonable to ask such sacrifice of those for whom the alternative is tremendous sacrifice in lives on the battlefield and in standards of living at home. War in defense of the ideals of Western civilization and the salvage from starvation and death of the peoples of suffering countries seem both a more expensive and a less rational way of dealing with the situation.

Clearly, too, the supernational order would necessitate interference with individual nations in their monetary policies, in their immigration policies, and even in their investment of capital and their development of industries. But here again, granted a democratic world order, and given a federal system in which administration is decentralized and where there is a considerable sphere of states' rights, the sacrifice of complete freedom of action would be more than counterbalanced by the common gains, especially since the consequence of freedom of national action would seem to be the need periodically for extreme national control and extreme sacrifice.

Moreover, our new technology with its diverse raw materials and their utilization for previously unimagined purposes through the chemical revolution has to a considerable extent destroyed or undermined the significance of control of certain raw materials, and will do so increasingly. As a result the nations with the most advanced technology temporarily have a differential advantage even greater than they enjoyed previously through the ownership of particular resources. But in the long run by its very nature this kind of advantage is harder to retain, while effective exploitation stimulates similar technological developments all over the world.

Meanwhile, modern techniques of attack, with the latest weapons, make distance no protection against destructive enemies, at the same time that modern communication makes sharing and mutual interchange obviously beneficial. The recent failure to gain an effective agreement between the major powers as to the use and development of airways shows that without a supernational government with power and without acceptance of planning on a world scale there will be unnecessary waste, bitter competition, and once more conflict. Those in authority today seem concerned with the preservation of the old disorder, and those under them, the vast majority of citizens, even in the most democratic nations and even though frightened by the present prospects and trends, give passive support to the old and outworn pattern. They retain their superstition that national loyalty is incompatible with world citizenship. The true ethics of nationalism, however, should increase attachment to the particular unit through a sense of its peculiar cultural contribution to mankind as a whole.

When the national state itself developed, and, even more clearly, when our own federal union developed, men had attachments to various particular institutions and local units. Yet the acceptance of a wider loyalty neither destroyed these attachments nor impaired any functionally useful institution. Rather, within the common citizenship of the nation, groups proliferated, more diverse voluntary loyalties were begotten, and life was enriched. It seems not unreasonable to believe that a like development would occur were citizenship broadened to a world citizenship, and were loyalty given to the common purposes of men as a whole, embodied in a constitutional world government with defined powers. Much of the opposition to such an undertaking, especially in these United States, is due to short-sighted fear of immediate and specific loss of differential advantage and of damage to the pride or superiority based upon it. Men's narrower loyalties may indeed be necessary for the development of the wider, since men without local roots and ties are at best uncertain lovers. Yet the value of the narrower loyalty is never fully realized when it is exclusive. It becomes perverted into jealousy and selfishness. It is most adequately realized when it most expands, the narrower devotion deepening and strengthening the wider. The essence of the Christian doctrine of charity is, after all, that it may be infinitely expanded.

Boundaries as an administrative device aid in the effective functioning of the units within them. Beyond this, however, they themselves create a psychology of difference and exclusion to the mutual loss of those on both sides of them, as in the postwar tariff rates after World War I, and in the diminishing of general freedom throughout the world.

We are aware that germs and plant diseases are no respecters of boundaries. We even know that successful quarantine requires collaboration. Slowly we accept the duty, let us say, not to import plants subject to disease or to transport them from one area to another within a nation. And we similarly accept, though very reluctantly, a new technological ethics. We no longer admit the right of employers to ignore safety devices in their factories; we take it for granted that they have an ethical as well as a legal obligation to observe certain standards of safety. On the highways, we acknowledge the duty to drive cautiously and on the right side of the road. Such behavior was not always an ethical compulsion. In many such situations no ethics was involved, because each person could follow his own whim without harm to others. Today we recognize that in more and more spheres of action some restraint of personal liberty is necessary for our own ultimate freedom to develop as social beings. It is generally accepted that in many fields government restraints are demanded if we are to enjoy the blessings of our own scientific knowledge; and such restraints have both a technical and a moral aspect. For example, no radio station would today demand as part of its liberty the right to broadcast on any wave length; and, in times of peace, international regulation of the air waves is obviously to the advantage of all concerned.

Yet though the facts of international interdependence are clear and though in more and more fields we are unable to use our knowledge to our own good without international regulation, we have not yet accepted the idea of supernational enforcement as an ethical imperative.

The whole course of modern events nevertheless superbly demonstrates that the effective pursuit of the moral ideals of our tradition, so long frustrated by man's weakness and ignorance and by man's inhumanity to man, has now been made ethically obligatory by the triumphant progress of human knowledge.

It can no doubt be argued that a supernational federal order must await the development of a popular conviction that it is in fact useful and necessary. But our own experience in making a federal union showed that a minority by speaking boldly and decisively could initiate the transformation which was to group individual colonies first into a loose federation of states and then into the first great continent-wide democratic nation. Though that minority made their cautious concessions to particularism, they nevertheless boldly recognized the necessity for minimal common institutions and for the surrendering of many local but temporary advantages. They were able to do this, true, because they confronted great potential enemies whose presence impelled them, however hesitantly, to abandon mere confederation.

A world order with a comparable government would not be drawn up against any outer power—attacks from Mars are still in the realm of fantasy rather than practical politics. Yet our experience surely shows that our continued quarrels, leading to increasingly destructive wars and to the abandonment of normal ethical behavior, are dangers greater than any the colonists faced. And the history of the League of Nations, which corresponded somewhat to American government under the Articles of Confederation, surely demonstrated not simply the particular chance defects but also the basic inadequacies of such a system. Moreover, though the Great Powers in the United Nations continue to profess a common cause, their time for giving it an implementation that will survive in peace is short. The signs of disharmony that have appeared are enough to warn us that any arrangement involving mere confederation after the battle will offer but slight hopes for peace, even "in our time." Man's conquest of his environment makes possible, indeed demands, what man has always professed to desire as the good. Refusal to take the necessary steps can no longer be excused on grounds of practical inability and expedient wisdom; on the contrary, it will amount to a confession that ideals which have dominated Western civilization for two thousand years have been abandoned, and to an acknowledgment of the moral triumph of those we have defeated on the field of battle.

THOMAS I. COOK

CHAPTER XXIV

*The Moral Basis of Peace*

IF THERE is any fact that has been clearly demonstrated by the modern world crisis, it is the necessity of right ideals to guarantee the effective use of the instrumentalities of peace and justice. There has been no lack of agencies and agreements for the maintenance of peace, such as the League of Nations, the World Court, the Kellogg-Briand Pact, and the decisions of the Washington Disarmament Conference; but there has been no sufficient conviction among men and nations that these are the right and necessary means. The League of Nations was doomed not only by American isolation but also by insufficient faith among the members. We can supply far better machinery for the maintenance of peace than has been created in the past, but any such machinery is condemned to sterility unless there is a spiritual substance to direct and enforce its use.

If we look at world events in this light, we can see that the Axis bears the blackest guilt but that responsibility for world catastrophe rests upon all nations. The forces that dictated the long, shameful policy of "appeasement" and "self-interest"—that connived in giving Mussolini a free hand in Ethiopia, that embargoed oil and military supplies to Republican Spain, that supplied Japan with scrap iron to ravage China and to prepare for Pearl Harbor, that withheld or withdrew support from the League of Nations and refused to create any new system of collective security, that deserted Czechoslovakia because she is "a far away country of which we know nothing"—the forces in the democracies mainly responsible for these and similar "realistic" policies, sacrificed principles for what appeared to be expediency but which was, in sober fact, the most tragic folly.

Because there have been so many who mocked at "visionary ideals" and "ideological crusades," millions of people have suffered and died, and the whole of civilization has been in extreme peril. Many of these same "realists" are prepared to carry on under the familiar slogans: "business is business," "politics as usual," "back to normalcy," "America first." They are prepared to undermine the peace, to return to the old, old game of profit, imperialism, power politics, and selfish nationalism, as they did after the war of 1914–1918. Here in milder form is the same disease that has afflicted the fascist countries: the same contempt for ideals, the same headlong scramble for power and gain, the same indifference to the enduring values of civilization.

In our healthy reaction against this sort of "realism," we must not make the mistake of underestimating the value of power when rightly employed. The famous maxim of Lord Acton, that "all power corrupts and absolute power corrupts absolutely," if interpreted literally, is the counsel of despair. The only alternative to power is no power; and that means anarchy, the war of each against all. It means "the state of nature" described by Hobbes: "no arts; no letters; no society; and, which is worse, continual fear, and danger of violent death; and the life of man, solitary, poor, nasty, brutish, and short." This, in sober fact, is the condition to which irresolute government and international anarchy reduced millions of human beings in our generation. The one escape from the Hobbesian "state of nature," from war and social chaos, is power exercised for the common good by responsible national and international authorities.

Let us admit or rather insist that irresponsible power corrupts and irresponsible absolute power corrupts absolutely. Government by private pressure, by "the boys in the back room," by fascist demagogues, by domineering imperialists, is corrupt; but not government of, by, and for the people. Power in itself is neutral: it may be put to vicious or beneficent uses; but if it is democratized and humanized, if it is united with good will, it is the only alternative to Chaos and Old Night.

The combination of power and good will is the fundamental requirement of a realistic international policy. Pious expressions of international friendship may be worse than futile if they do not rest upon the power to implement them. In the presence of sinister forces such as the Axis, they merely invite wars and more wars, for which men of good will, substituting wishes for deeds, are tragically unprepared. The sensible alternative is to utilize the strength of the United Nations, the greatest coalition ever achieved in the world's history. It would be folly to dissipate this nucleus of power: we should extend, institutionalize, and democratize it. Since strength cannot be suddenly created by fiat, since the future must develop organically out of the past, the power to win the victory must grow into the power to preserve the peace. China, Britain, Russia, and America, joined by the other United Nations, must remain united; they must consolidate their power into a decisive international force to prevent aggression. It is useless and Utopian to envisage a peace without reference to these vast forces actually at work in the world. In utilizing power as a basis of peace and justice, therefore, we must be no less mindful of strength than the Axis has been, but we must conceive it more subtly and broadly, as a complex of traditions, interests, ideals, and responsible military forces. We must realize, as Thucydides pointed out and Walter Lippmann has reminded us, that restraint is the most impressive manifestation of power.

We cannot insist too strongly, also, that right human relations within nations are the indispensable guarantee of the right use of power among nations. There is a direct causal relation between an inequitable power-structure in the domestic affairs of a nation and the immoral use of power in the foreign affairs of that nation. If a privileged class exercises its power to fetter the productive system and if unprivileged classes in consequence suffer extreme deprivation, the nation will necessarily be plunged into an internal crisis that will endanger the structure of peace. For example, it is highly significant that, in the years immediately before Hitler's advent to power, the working classes in Germany were receiving an extremely low proportion of the total national income, and that the privileged classes stubbornly refused to check the ever-intensifying concentration of wealth, with its accompanying maladjustment between the capacity of the nation to produce and its capacity to consume. This situation gave Hitler his golden opportunity slyly to promise the wealthy protection against the increasing "red menace" and simultaneously to promise the masses food, employment, and *"Lebensraum."*

No peace can stand that is based upon injustice, and any economic system is unjust that perpetuates scarcity when it is possible to have relative abundance. During four thousand years of civilization, the useful arts stagnated because the arts of invention were not sufficiently advanced. Extreme poverty and semi-starvation were the inevitable consequences for the masses of mankind. Since the beginning of the nineteenth century, however, the technological revolution has been very rapidly altering this condition. As a result, in the technologically advanced nations, it is now for the first time possible for man to achieve an economy of happiness and life-fulfillment. The need of such a transition is the more obvious when we consider the problem of attaining total use of our resources. In time of war, we have full employment and complete utilization of plant capacity, a system of total use; and the quantity of goods and services that we then create is truly prodigious. In peacetime, however, when the productive system is no longer linked to the arts of death, we have partial and restricted use, a system of scarcity. The greatest problem of our civilization is to achieve a peacetime system of total use to supply genuine human needs. So long as we fail to solve this problem, we shall continue to be plagued by the twin evils, poverty and war.

There is no simple and easy solution. Much of the present book is concerned with steps which may be taken to release productive capacities of the world and to guarantee their right use in benefiting common people everywhere. The problem, however, is not only economic and political but also moral. If technically we have the means to eliminate a vast deal of poverty and to organize a world community, the main reason we do not do so is that, because of fear or "vested interest" or some other reason, we lack the moral conviction. In wartime, as we have said, we simply do not permit the nonsense of mass-unemployment of men and machines: we insist upon whatever steps are necessary to utilize our human and physical resources, and, in consequence, the level of production rises to amazing heights. If we felt as keenly about the struggle to eliminate poverty and injustice, we would require a similar measure of production in peacetime. We would determine upon whatever steps are necessary to keep plants in efficient operation; and if private industry were unable to maintain full production, we the people would insist as we do in wartime, upon the necessary measure of social control. Our willingness in normal times to tolerate such a prodigious volume of unnecessary suffering is a moral disgrace.

We can no longer be satisfied with an economy of plus and minus or a politics of power and privilege. The only economics we can afford is the economics of welfare; the only politics we can tolerate is the politics of justice. Since the old order of things exacts the price of depression and total war, it is too costly.

If we, the people of the world, are to have the faith and iron determination to create a new order, we must regain the sense of the preciousness and intrinsic dignity of the human personality. The state of mind which has prevailed in recent years is a far cry from the attitudes that once were common. How strange it now seems that, prior to the First World War, civilized people everywhere became incensed when a German officer in Zabern attacked a single lame cobbler who had refused obsequiously to yield the sidewalk to him; and that the German Reichstag, because of this military arrogance, censured the government by a vote of 293 to 54. How remarkable it now seems that in France a crisis which churned the nation to its depths could have resulted from the mistreatment of a single Jew, Alfred Dreyfus. In recent years, in contrast, we have witnessed horror piled upon horror until we have almost ceased to react to the incredible sadism and beastiality of the world's criminals. As Erich Kahler has remarked in his *Man the Measure* (1944, p. 601), "It has been reserved for our era to witness such spectacles as steamers crowded with helpless people roaming the ocean because they are not permitted to land anywhere" as a refuge from fascist terrorism. All of this must be changed: we must once more set ourselves the task of protecting and nourishing personality: we must revive our numbed sympathy and conscience. The measure of our success in this endeavor will be the extent to which we bring justice and happiness to the common man, whether he be white, black, or yellow.

Our ultimate ideal, therefore, must be the creation of a world-wide community, without invidious distinction of race, nation, or class. This is the old, old ideal of human brotherhood, upon the basis of which so many great religions and moral systems have converged. As James Henry Breasted has proved, it is an ideal as old as the religions of ancient Egypt and Babylon. What gives it new urgency, however, is the creation of the material and technological conditions which make its realization possible. So long as poverty was the inevitable lot of the masses of mankind and so long as communication among the peoples of the world was scant or non-existent, such universal human fellowship was at best a hope or ideal to be cherished rather than an objective to be pursued. In the present age of air travel and wireless communication and potential abundance, the dream of the ancient seers has become the imperative of practical politics. Unless somehow the world community becomes a fact, we shall have war and more war, and the whole of civilization may be leveled in a vast chaos. All our material resources and marvelous techniques can be used either for good or for ill, and the time is not far distant when any gang of moral degenerates, if they gain control of the most advanced scientific information and "secret weapons," can put the whole world in mortal peril. When the very survival of civilization depends upon our faith in the world community, we dare not be complacent and shirk our duty.

Faith must be justified by works. Ideals are condemned to vacuity unless there is force and agency to give them expression. So long as there is no world government, the nations will continue to exist in a state of anarchy in their relations with one another; and as Professor Adler has clearly demonstrated in his *How to Think About War and Peace* (1944) this means continuous war, actual or potential. Thomas Hobbes, that hard-headed realist, has in his *Leviathan* likewise described the "state of nature" which prevails among nations in the absence of world government: "It may be perceived what manner of life there would be, where there were no common power to fear; by the manner of life which men that have formerly lived under a peaceful government, use to degenerate into a civil war. But though there had never been any time wherein particular men were in a condition of war one against another; yet in all times, kings, and persons of sovereign authority, because of their independency, are in continual jealousies, and in the state and posture of gladiators; having their weapons pointing, and their eyes fixed on one another; that is, their forts, garrisons, and guns upon the frontiers of their kingdoms; and continual spies upon their neighbors; which is a posture of war."

The remedy for such anarchy, as Hobbes perceived, is the creation of government with power to enforce its decisions. He saw that "covenants, without the sword, are but words," and that the covenant must be a surrender of sovereignty whether of individuals or of nations, to some central authority. He did not see, as did Rousseau, that the covenant may be a democratic instrument, resting upon the will of the governed. In the present book, it is maintained that national sovereignty must be at least severely modified, and that adequate power, under democratic auspices, must be conferred upon the international authority, if we are to have peace.

Professor Adler, in restating the argument of Hobbes with reference to the international field, has insisted that "anarchy is the only cause of war." His contention, in brief, is that "war results from anarchy and anarchy from the sovereignty of nations." He admits that there are positive forces, such as racial hatred and economic injustice, which lead to war unless restrained by government; but he paradoxically argues that anarchy, "the single negative factor which permits the positive causes to operate," may for all practical purposes be regarded as "the only cause of war," since *it is the only cause we can control.*" (*Op. cit.,* pp. 74–75. Adler's italics.)

Professor Adler's argument at this point is misleading and partly false. International anarchy is not the only controllable cause of war: we can do a vast deal to mitigate poverty and imperialism and racial antagonism even before we possess a full-fledged world government, although doubtless we can do much more in these respects once we achieve a working international authority with power to enforce its decrees. If we merely try to establish a world government without attacking the positive causes of war, we shall find that the new Government of the United Nations, like the League of Nations, will be sabotaged from within and destroyed from without because it will be inconsistent with the primary forces that govern the world. Once more we must insist that there is no simple and easy solution: that we require action in many fields at once. There is no single cause of war and no single remedy: there is no practicable course open to us except integrated action in many fields at once: economic, political, scientific, and moral; diplomatic, educational and if need be, military; ideological and institutional; both inner and outer, matching thought with deed and external force with spiritual conviction. Although we may agree with Professor Adler that the establishment of a world government is the most essential condition of peace, this government must deal with many economic and cultural factors, and must be supported by the determination of the member nations, both separately and in concert, to deal realistically with those causes of war which Mr. Adler wrongly classifies as uncontrollable.

Now, as Churchill promised, fascism has been ground down into "blood, dust, and ashes." Yet we face a danger more subtle but not less great than in the darkest hours of the war. We face that danger even now the war is over and military victory both in Europe and in Asia is complete. It is so easy and natural, after the weariness and strain of combat, to sink back into "normalcy," as we did in the wake of the First World War, and to forget that fascism, as a revolt against civilization, cannot be finally defeated until civilization is revitalized. This revitalization demands, as Herbert Agar has said in his *A Time for Greatness* (1942, p. 117), "that we work out a faith which all men can understand and which most men accept. Only with that final weapon in our hands can the powers of darkness be beaten." Ultimate victory can be won only in the months and years after the fighting has ceased: it can be won only in the councils of peace: it can be won only by a supreme and sustained effort.

The lineaments of a new world faith begin to be clear: we require power united with good will; total use of resources to supply genuine human needs; the sense of human worth and dignity, without restriction of race, nation, or class; the creation of a world community, given institutional expression in a forceful world government and given moral substance by the integral devotion of mankind. If faith without works is vacuous, works without faith are sterile. The one imperative is that we unite right ideals with material forces.

MELVIN M. RADER

# CHAPTER XXV

# *Concluding Statement on The United Nations*

THE preceding chapters have attempted to set forth the magnitude of the problems which confront the world and to indicate the broader policies and methods by which peace may be sought. But policies and methods require political institutions, require what is commonly called government, to attain continuity and effectiveness.

Within the United States we have a most intricate and far-flung system of police, legislative, executive, and judicial agencies which maintain order, make rules to meet changing needs, enforce those rules and interpret them. We cannot escape the conclusion that a growingly complex international system will require the same four major types of institutions: those which can prevent violence; those which can effect peaceful change by the systematic formulations of "laws" much as legislatures do within nations; international executive agencies which like national and state civil services apply the "laws"; and finally, international judicial agencies which must serve the same purpose for the world as national judiciaries do for their respective nations.

The United Nations Charter adopted at San Francisco in June 1945 and now ratified by a sufficient number of nations to bring it officially into existence must be examined with reference to its adequacy to perform these four tasks. We need not here repeat what has been given so often elsewhere, a detailed description of the Security Council, the Assembly, the Economic and Social Council, the Trustee Council, the International Court of Justice, and the Secretariat which comprise the institutional side of the United Nations. We confine ourselves to estimating the effectiveness of this structure as a whole by considering the relation of these institutions to the four problems of order, legislation or rule-making, rule enforcing, and rule interpreting.

Chapter II has stated the reasons for believing that already the

288

United Nations Charter is an inadequate instrument on which to rely for the preservation of world peace, and that unless this basic need is more effectively met each of the specific institutions for which it provides will be doomed to stultification.

The problems attendant upon the advent of the atomic bomb illustrate the necessity of the steps still to be taken. Some have advocated the immediate handing over of the secret of the bomb—if it is a secret —to the United Nations; others urge that the United Nations as it exists is too weak a body to ensure the necessary exclusive control which must be effected if the weapon is not to become the common property of contending big powers; a third group wants the adoption of an international convention outlawing the manufacture and use of the atomic bomb. Detailed analysis of these alternatives lies beyond the scope of this concluding chapter. We may, however, suggest that to outlaw the manufacture and use of the bomb will require a highly effective international inspection agency which must be provided for financially and have sufficient authority to enforce decisions. Moreover, to outlaw the atomic bomb only would leave the way open to robot bombs, poison gas, bacteriological warfare, and the many other deadly instruments which modern science has invented and will invent. Clearly it will be insufficient to outlaw one, though presently by far the most terrible, of the weapons of aggression. It seems impossible to avoid the conclusion that there must be either an overall drastic limitation of armaments and a concentration of power in the world community or an accelerating and catastrophic competition between the three or four great powers who have just won the victory.

The second problem, that of giving international rules a status equivalent to that of national laws, will largely confront the Assembly of the United Nations and especially the Economic and Social Council. Here we must expect a number of developments if we are to have satisfactory progress. First, the annual meetings of the Assembly and the adoption of a few or even of several general conventions will not suffice for the bewildering complexity of new problems which will demand systematic rule-making. The conferences must delegate a great deal of authority to special agencies. This process has existed for many years in a number of international bodies and we can expect it to develop on a much more impressive scale. There will also undoubtedly proceed more and more special conferences dealing with individual questions such as wheat, coffee, tin, rubber, and textiles. The findings of these conferences will be carried out by special agencies. The Economic and Social Council will have the responsibility of coordinating the activities of these specialized bodies into some degree of unity.

If international "legislation" is to play an adequate role, several improvements in the treaty and agreement process must be made. The United Nations will have to help eliminate faulty draftsmanship of treaties which has thus far constituted a serious difficulty; it should give earnest consideration to such proposals as that made by C. Wilfred Jenks to establish an International Parliamentary Counsels Office to do for the United Nations what the parliamentary draftsmen do for national parliaments, assisting in preparing drafts of multipartite instruments and proposing improvements in legislative techniques.

A general international authority should be given competence to deal with questions of uniform interpretation where multilateral conventions are signed. And above all, if international government is to keep pace with growing needs, the United Nations must speed up the process of treaty adoption and ratification. World complexity will necessarily mean some delay, but one views with alarm the fact that the Bretton Woods Agreement may take more than two years to result in a working Financial Organization for the United Nations. The world desperately needs rapidity of action on the policy level and the present cumbersome methods of treaty ratification are not suited to the needs of the new age.

Technical questions of treaty ratification cannot be dealt with here. We confine ourselves to suggesting that the United Nations must agree to a time limit on the ratification process, must limit the conditional ratification method which has often stymied effective international action, and perhaps should consider the possibility of dispensing with ratification altogether. That these steps will involve far-reaching changes in the balance of relations between nations and international organization is obvious. We believe that a clear choice must be made.

The third problem, that of applying the rules drawn up and adopted in what might be called a quasi-legislative process, must be solved through agencies of an administrative character. Many international arrangements provided for in the conventions or treaties may well be carried out by national administrative agencies, but without question effective world order will necessitate the recruiting of a large number of persons who will in effect be international civil servants. Two major factors will emerge in this connection, the preparation and training of such civil servants, and their status.

Just as within nations we have come to realize the importance of sound training of public servants, so we must realize its necessity in the international field where the technical and psychological demands will require the highest type of trained personnel. Recent criticisms of certain officials in the armies of occupation give point to the claim that universities and other institutions must develop courses and methods designed to train people in varying degrees of specialization for international service.

The League of Nations and the International Labor Organization had a civil service of approximately a thousand persons. If the United Nations is to be effective it will need many more than that. And above all, an international secretariat capable of fulfilling its exacting tasks must comprise officials who are not primarily citizens of a member state but who rather owe their first loyalty to the international organization itself.

The history of the last twenty years has shown the tremendous pressures to which public servants are subjected by local, regional, and group interests. We must expect the same frequently distorting pressures to be brought to bear upon the agencies of the United Nations. If the appointment of the national board to control atomic energy will place six or seven scientists in the United States in a position of importance transcending that even of the judges of the Supreme Court, what shall be said of the caliber of persons required to make decisions on the international policy level in this atomic age?

Finally, the liberties of men are not secure without the active and extensive operation of courts of justice. Chapter IV has set forth the lines upon which international law must develop if it is to keep pace with the requirements of the present. It is sufficient here to underline the conclusions there stated and to suggest the need for strengthening the legal order by relating national constitutions to the new international obligations. In the judgment of the editors, peace will remain on a precarious basis if the treaty obligations of nations do not become constitutional obligations of the respective member states so that a violation of an international obligation becomes at the same time a violation of the national constitution. The international obligation should be clearly written into national constitutions; even the provision in the United States Constitution that treaties are the supreme law of the land leaves a no-man's-land of vagueness which we can no longer afford.

It will be necessary also to gear national administrative systems to international requirements so as to avoid the many heartbreaking confusions, overlappings, delays, and omissions which occur under present arrangements. It may well be, too, that the old doctrine by which international law applies primarily if not exclusively to states must be recast to give some degree of status to the individual in his capacity as world citizen.

In this final statement we have been able to indicate only in the briefest manner some of the institutional questions that will arise and that must be decided promptly if an intelligent world order is to emerge. Some of the answers will come from specialists; many will come from experience gained in the multifarious activities of governments themselves; and above all, we have reason to hope that the determination for peace in the hearts of the citizens of all nations will promote the conditions for a transition at the minimum cost in suffering and disorder from the age of the independent national state to the age of interdependent national states within the framework of a strong and adequate United Nations. The will of the peoples is overwhelmingly for peace; the leaders of the peoples will be guilty of tragic irresponsibility if, following the political strategies of the moment, they stultify that will by warping it into traditional separatisms rather than guide it toward the creation of that world culture in a world society which is now for the first time in human history both possible and necessary to survival.

THE EDITORS